Contents

Acknowledgements   v

Introduction   vi

Part I The Well-Stocked Briefcase   **1**
1 All things to all people   5
2 The executive briefing   18
3 The inside track   21
4 The hidden job market   24

Part II Getting to Square One   **61**
5 Paint the perfect picture on the phone   63
6 Responding to buy signals   70
7 Responding to objections   77
8 Getting live leads from dead ends   82
9 The telephone interview   85
10 Dressing for interview success   90
11 Body language   105
12 The curtain goes up   119

Part III Great Answers to Tough Interview Questions   **125**
13 The five secrets of securing a job offer   129
14 Welcome to the real world   136
15 How to knock 'em dead   145
16 'What kind of person are you really, Mr Jones?'   170
17 The other side of the desk   184
18 The stress interview   197
19 Strange venues   227
20 The graceful exit   233

Part IV Finishing Touches   **237**
21 Out of sight, out of mind?   239

Contents

22 Snatching victory from the jaws of defeat   243
23 Negotiating the offer   248
24 Multiple interviews, multiple offers   271
25 Conclusion: the glittering prizes   273

Index to the questions   274

GREAT ANSWERS TO TOUGH INTERVIEW QUESTIONS

NEW 5th edition

MARTIN JOHN YATE

KOGAN
PAGE

First published as *Knock 'Em Dead* in the United States of America in 1985 by Bob Adams Inc, Boston, Massachusetts

First published as *Great Answers to Tough Interview Questions* in Great Britain in 1986 by Kogan Page Limited
Second edition 1988
Third edition 1992
Reprinted 1992, 1993 (twice), 1994, 1995 (twice), 1996 (twice), 1997
Fourth edition 1998
Reprinted 1998
Fifth edition 2001
Reprinted 2001, 2002

Kogan Page Limited
120 Pentonville Road
London
N1 9JN

British Library Cataloguing in Publication Data

A CIP record for this book is available from the British Library.

ISBN 0 7494 3552 6

Typeset by Saxon Graphics Ltd, Derby
Printed and bound in Great Britain by Clays Ltd, St Ives plc

Acknowledgements

Great Answers to Tough Interview Questions is now in its fifteenth year of publication and has become a staple for job hunters around the world. This is due to the ongoing support of my publisher Bob Adams and the tireless encouragement of the Adams Media sales team, headed by Wayne Jackson. This, and my other books, are kept fresh and vibrant thanks to the ministrations of my editor Ed Walters, the Associate Publisher of Adams Media. Finally, this year I am indebted to Jennifer Lantagne for her indefatigable work on three simultaneous sets of galleys.

Introduction

In 1985, when this book was first published, we began by answering the question 'Why another book about interviewing?' The answer was 'Because the others stop at that critical point when the tough questions start flying.' Sadly, that criticism of the many other books out there is still valid. With over four million *Great Answers to Tough Interview Questions* books in print worldwide, there seems ample evidence that readers agree with my 1985 assessment.

Still, *Great Answers to Tough Interview Questions* has not stood still. In the years since that first edition, this book has grown in size and scope every year. It has doubled in length and now covers the entire job search process. I am confident that it covers more ground, and with more depth and originality, than any other book in the field.

I wrote this book because too much of the job search advice I could find on the shelves of my bookshop was infantile at best and detrimental to my professional health at worst. The vast majority of job-hunting books lack the practical advice about what to do in the heat of battle. *Great Answers to Tough Interview Questions* will take you through the whole process – from putting the paperwork together to negotiating salary to your best advantage. Of course, the core of the book still helps you resolve the job seeker's most dreaded question: 'How on earth do I answer that one?'

Here, you'll get hundreds of the tough, sneaky, mean and low questions that interviewers love to throw at you. With each question, I will show you what the interviewer wants to find out about you and explain how you should reply. After each explanation, you'll get a sample answer and suggestions on how to customize it to your individual circumstances. The examples themselves come from real life, things people like you have done on the job that got them noticed. I'll show you how they packaged those experiences, how they used their practical experience to turn a job interview into a job offer.

Perhaps you are trying to land your first job or are returning to the workplace. Maybe you are a seasoned executive taking another step up the ladder of success. Whoever you are, this book will help you, because it shows you how to master any interview and succeed with any interviewer. You will learn that every interviewer tries to evaluate each candidate by the same three criteria, discovered by answering the following questions.

▌ Is the candidate able to do the job?

▌ Is he or she willing to put in the effort to make the job a success?

▌ Is he or she manageable?

You will learn how to demonstrate your superiority in each of these areas under all interview conditions.

The job interview is a measured and ritualistic mating dance in which the best partners whirl away with the glittering prizes. The steps of this dance are the give-and-take, question-and-response exchanges that make meaningful business conversations. Learn the steps and you, too, can dance the dance.

Your partner in the dance, obviously, is the interviewer, who will lead with tough questions that carry subtleties hidden from the untrained ear. You will learn how to recognize those questions-within-questions and, with this knowledge, be cool, calm and collected, while other candidates are falling apart with attacks of interview nerves.

How do you discover hidden meanings in questions? I recently heard a story about a young woman who was doing very well in an interview for a high-pressure job in a television studio. The interviewer wanted to know how she would react in the sudden, stressful situations common in TV and got his answer when he said, 'You know, I don't really think you're suitable for the job. Wouldn't you be better off in another company?' With wounded pride, the job hunter stormed out in a huff. She never knew how close she was, how easy it would have been to land the job. The interviewer smiled: he had caught her out with a tough question. Did the interviewer mean what he said? What was really behind the question? How could she have handled it and landed the job? The great answers to tough questions like that and many others are waiting for you in the following pages.

The job interview has many similarities to good social conversations. Job offers always go to the interviewee who can turn a one-sided examination of skills into a dynamic exchange between two professionals. In this book, you will learn the techniques for exciting and holding your interviewer's attention and, at the same time, promoting yourself as the best candidate for the job.

This book will carry you successfully through the worst interviews and job hunting scenarios you will ever face. It is written in four interconnected parts. Part I: The Well-Stocked Briefcase gets you ready for the fray. You will quickly learn to build a CV with broad appeal and use a unique customizing technique guaranteed to make your application stand out as something special. You will also learn how to tap into thousands of job openings at all levels that never reach the newspapers.

Once you are ready for action, Part II: Getting to Square One examines all the approaches to getting job interviews and teaches you simple and effective ways to set up multiple interviews. This section ends with techniques to steer you successfully through those increasingly common telephone screening interviews.

Part III: Great Answers to Tough Interview Questions gives you just that and teaches you some valuable business lessons that will contribute to your future success. All successful companies look for the same things in their employees and everything they're looking for you either have or can develop. Sounds impossible? I will show you the 20 key personality traits that can convey your potential for success to any interviewer.

Part IV: Finishing Touches assures that 'out of sight, out of mind' will not apply to you after you leave the interviewer's office. You will even discover how to get a job offer after you have been turned down for the position and how to negotiate the best salary and package for yourself when a job offer is made. Most important, the sum of these techniques will give you tremendous self-confidence when you go to an interview: no more jitters, no more sweaty palms.

If you want to know how business works and what savvy businesspeople look for in an employee, if you want to discover how to land the interview and conquer the interviewer, then this book is for you. *Great Answers to Tough Interview Questions* delivers everything you need to win the job of your dreams. Now get to it, step ahead in your career and knock 'em dead.

Part I

The Well-Stocked Briefcase

This section will show you how to discover, define, and package your skills and strong points, and to do the necessary legwork that will prepare you to sell them.

Have you heard the one about the poor man who wanted to become a famous bear-slayer? Once upon a time, in a town plagued by bears, lived a man. The man had always wanted to travel but had neither the right job nor the money to do so. If he could kill a bear, then he could travel to other places plagued with bears and make his living as a bear-slayer. Every day he sat on the porch and waited for a bear to come by. After many weeks of waiting, he thought he might go looking for bears. He didn't know much about them, except that they were out there.

Full of hope, he rose before dawn, loaded his single-shot musket and headed for the forest. On reaching the edge of the forest, he raised the musket and fired into the dense undergrowth.

Do you think he hit a bear or, for that matter, anything else? Why was he hunting for bears with a single-shot musket and why did he shoot before seeing a bear? What was his problem?

Our hero couldn't tell dreams from reality. He went hunting unprepared and earned what he deserved. The moral of the tale is this: when you look for a job, keep a grip on reality, go loaded for bears and don't go off half-cocked.

Out there in the forest of your profession hide many companies and countless opportunities. These are major organizations, small family affairs and some in between. They all have something in common – problems. To solve those problems, companies need people. Think about your present job function: what problems would occur if you weren't there? You were taken on to take care of those problems.

Being a problem solver is good, but companies prefer to employ and promote someone who also understands what business is all about. There are three lessons you should remember on this score.

- **Lesson 1** Companies are in business to make money. People have loyalty to companies; companies have loyalty only to the bottom line. They make money by being economical and saving money. They make money by being efficient and saving time. If they save time, they save money, so have more time to make more money.

- **Lesson 2** Companies and you are exactly alike. You both want to make as much money as possible in as short a time as possible. That allows you to do the things you really want with the rest of your time.

▌**Lesson 3** There are buyer's markets (advantage: prospective employer) and there are seller's markets (advantage: prospective employee). Job offers put you in a seller's market and give you the whip hand.

Lesson 1 tells you the three things every company is interested in. Lesson 2 is to recognize that you really have the same goals as the company. Lesson 3 is that anyone with any sense wants to be in a seller's market.

If you look for jobs one at a time, you put yourself in a buyer's market. If you implement my advice in this book, you will have multiple job offers. These, however good or bad they are, will put you in a seller's market, regardless of the economic climate.

Operating in a seller's market requires knowing who, where and what your buyers are in the market for, then being ready with the properly packaged product.

In this section, you will find out how to identify *every* company that could be in need of your services. You will learn how to discover the names of the CEO or MD, those on the Board and in management; the company sales volume; complete lines of company services or products; and the size of the outfit. You will evaluate and package your professional skills in a way that is guaranteed to have appeal to every employer. You will discover highly desirable professional skills you never knew you had.

It will take a couple of days' preparation. You are going to need to update your CV (or create a new one), generate some covering letters, research potential employers and create a comprehensive marketing plan.

While I cover each of these areas in sequence, I recommend that, in the execution, you mix and match the activities. In other words, when the direct research begins to addle the grey matter, switch to CV enhancement and so on. An hour of one activity followed by an hour of another will keep your mind fresh and your development balanced.

1 *All things to all people*

The goal of a CV is to show that you are a problem solver. Here are the five exercises that will help you identify the important aspects of your work history, the three types of CV you can use and the seven rules for making it broad and powerful.

HR and other managers today are continually asking for detailed examples of your past performance. They safely assume that you will do at least as well (or as poorly) in the new job as you did in the old one, so the examples you give will seal your fate. Therefore, you need to examine your past performance in a way that will empower you to handle these questions in a professional and competent manner.

This chapter will show you how to identify examples of problems solved, projects completed and contributions made that will impress any interviewer. As you complete the exercises in this chapter and concurrently proceed with your research, your added self-knowledge and confidence could well open your eyes to as yet unimagined professional opportunities. You will also get the correctly packaged information for a workmanlike CV. Two birds hit with one stone.

CVs, of course, are important and there are two facts you must know about them. First, you are going to need one. Second, no one will want to read it. The average interviewer has never been trained to interview effectively, probably finds the interview as uncomfortable as you do and will do everything possible to avoid discomfort. CVs, therefore, are used more to screen people *out* than screen them *in*. So, your CV must be all things to all people.

Another hurdle to clear is avoiding too much of your professional jargon in the CV. It is a cold, hard fact that the first person to see your CV is often in the HR department. This office screens for many different jobs and cannot be expected to have an in-depth knowledge of every specialism within the company – or their special languages.

For these reasons, your CV must be short, easy to read and understand and use words that are familiar to the reader and have universal appeal. Most important, it should portray you as a problem solver.

While this chapter covers ways to build an effective CV, its main goal is to help you perform better at the interview. You will achieve this as you evaluate your professional skills according to the exercises. In fact, you are likely to discover skills and achievements you didn't even know you had. A few you will use in your CV (merely a preview of coming attractions); the others you will use to knock 'em dead at the interview.

A good starting point is your current or last job title. Write it down. Then, jot down all the other different titles you have heard that describe that job. When you are finished, follow it with a three- or four-sentence description of your job functions. Don't think too hard about it, just do it. The titles and descriptions are not carved in stone – this written description is just the beginning of the CV-building exercises. You'll be surprised at what you've written; it will read better than you had thought.

All attributes that you discover and develop in the following exercises are valuable to an employer. You possess many desirable traits and these exercises help to reveal and package them.

Exercise 1

Reread your written job description, then write down your most important duty/function. Follow that with a list of the skills or special training necessary to perform that duty. Next, list the achievements of which you are most proud in that area. It could look something like this.

▌ **Duty** Train and motivate sales staff of six.

▌ **Skills** Formal training skills. Knowledge of market and ability to make untrained sales staff productive. Ability to keep successful salespeople motivated and tied to the company.

■ **Achievements** Reduced turnover 7 per cent; increased sales 14 per cent.

The potential employer is most interested in your achievements – those things that make you stand out from the crowd. Try to appeal to a company's interests by conservatively estimating what your achievements meant to your employer. If your achievements saved time, estimate how much. If you saved money, how much? If your achievements made money for the company, how much? Beware of exaggeration – if you were part of a team, identify your achievements as such. It will make your claims more believable and will demonstrate your ability to work with others.

Achievements, of course, differ according to your profession. Most of life's jobs fall into one of these broad categories, though:

■ sales and service;

■ management and administration;

■ technical and production.

While it is usual to cite the differences between those major job functions, at this point it is far more valuable to recognize the commonalities. In sales, the volume of money generated is important. In management or administration, the parallel is time saved, which is money saved; saving money is just the same as making money for your company. In the technical and production areas, increasing production (doing more in less time) accrues exactly the same benefits to the company. Job titles may differ, yet all employees have the same opportunity to benefit their employers and, in turn, themselves.

Today, companies are doing more with less; they are leaner, have higher expectations of their employees and plan to keep it that way. The people who are employed and get ahead today are those with a basic understanding of business goals. Successful job candidates are those who have the best interests of the company and its profitability constantly in mind.

Exercise 2

This simple exercise helps you get a clear picture of your achievements.

If you were to meet with your supervisor to discuss a pay rise, what achievements would you want to discuss? List all you can think of, quickly. Then come back and flesh out the details.

Exercise 3

This exercise is particularly valuable if you feel you can't see the forest for the trees.

▌ **Problem** Think of a job-related problem you have had to face in the last couple of years. Come on, everyone can remember one.

▌ **Solution** Describe your solution to the problem, step by step. List everything you did.

▌ **Results** Finally, consider the results of your solution in terms that would have value to an employer – money earned or saved, time saved.

Exercise 4

Now for a valuable exercise that turns the absence of a negative into a positive. This one helps you look at your job in a different light and accents important but often overlooked areas that help make you special. Begin discovering for yourself some of the key personal traits that all companies look for.

First, consider actions that, if not done properly, would affect the goal of your job. If that is difficult, remember an incompetent colleague. What did he or she do wrong? What did he or she do differently from competent employees?

Now, turn the absence of those negatives into positive attributes. For example, think of the employee who never managed to get to work on time. You could honestly say that someone who did come to work on time every day was punctual and reliable, believed in systems and procedures was efficiency minded, and cost- and profit-conscious.

If you witnessed the reprimands and ultimate firing of that tardy employee, you will see the value of the positive traits to your employer. The absence of negative traits makes you a desirable employee, but no one will know unless you say. On completion of the exercise, you will be able to make points about your background in a positive fashion. You will set yourself apart from others, if only because others do not understand the benefit of projecting all their positive attributes.

Exercise 5

Potential employers and interviewers are always interested in people who:

▌ are efficiency minded;

▌ have an eye for economy;

▌ follow procedures;

▌ are profit-oriented.

Proceed through your work history and identify the aspects of your background that exemplify those traits. These newly discovered personal pluses will not only be woven into your CV, but will be reflected in the framing of your answers when you get to the interview and in your performance when you land the right job.

Now you need to take some of that knowledge and package it in a CV. There are three standard types of CVs.

▌ **Chronological** The most frequently used format. Use it when your work history is stable and your professional growth is consistent. The chronological format is exactly what it sounds like: it follows your work history backwards from the current job, listing companies, dates and responsibilities. Avoid it if you have experienced performance problems, not grown professionally (but want to) or made frequent job changes. All these problems will show up in a glaring fashion if you use a chronological CV.

▌ **Functional** Use this type if you have been unemployed for long periods of time or have jumped jobs too frequently or if your career has been stagnant and you want to jump-start it. A functional CV is created without employment dates or company names and concentrates on skills and responsibilities. It can be useful if you have changed careers or when current responsibilities don't relate specifically to the job you want. It is written with the most relevant experience to the job you're seeking placed first and de-emphasizes jobs, employment dates and job titles by placing them inconspicuously at the end. It allows you to promote specific job skills without emphasizing where or when you developed those skills.

▌ **Combination** Use this format if you have a steady work history with demonstrated growth and if you have nothing you wish to de-emphasize. A combination CV is a combination of chronological and functional formats. It starts with a brief personal summary, then lists job-specific skills relevant to the objective, followed by a chronological format that lists the how, where and when for the acquiring of these skills.

Notice that each style is designed to emphasize strengths and minimize certain undesirable traits. In today's world, all of us need a powerful CV. It is not only a door opener, it is also there long after we are gone and will almost certainly be reviewed just before the choice of the successful candidate is made by the interviewer.

If you already have a CV and just want to make sure it measures up, check it against the six basic rules of CV writing below.

▌ **Rule 1** Use the most general of job titles. You are, after all, a hunter of interviews, not of specific titles. Cast your net wide. Use a title that is specific enough to put you in the field, yet vague enough to elicit further questions. One way you can make a job title specifically vague is to add the term _specialist_ (for example, computer specialist, administration specialist, production specialist).

▌ **Rule 2** If you must state a specific job objective, couch it in terms of contributions you can make in that position. Do not state what you expect of the employer.

▌ **Rule 3** Do not state your current salary. If you are earning too little or too much, you could rule yourself out before getting your foot in the door. For the same reason, do not mention your desired salary.

▌ **Rule 4** Remember that people get great joy from pleasant surprises. Show a little gold now, but let the interviewer discover the mother lode at the interview.

▌ **Rule 5** Try to keep your CV to one page. If you can't, take whatever steps are necessary to keep the CV no more than two pages long. No one reads long CVs – they are boring and every company is frightened that if it lets in a windbag, it will never get him or her out again.

▌ **Rule 6** Finally, emphasize your achievements and problem-solving skills. Keep the CV general.

A CV only a computer could love

The majority of medium to large companies now have automated CV-tracking systems in place. If you're applying to a large company or suspect that a potential employer is using computers instead of human beings to scan CVs, then you should prepare a computer-friendly one as well as a more traditional version.

To prepare a CV especially for a computerized recruiter:

▌ always send an original CV, never a photocopy;

▌ put your name on the first line of your CV and put nothing else before it;

▌ use common typefaces, such as Times, Palatino, Optima and Courier, avoid elaborate serif (letters with curlicues on them) or script typefaces that the computer might not recognize;

▌ keep the point size to between 10 and 14;

▌ if you want to use bold, save it for headings – never use it to type your name, address or telephone number;

▌ use few horizontal lines and no vertical lines, if you can help it.

Also:

▌ never use double columns or other complicated layouts;

▌ never use any paper except white, off white, cream or beige A4;

▌ never incorporate graphics, shading, ellipses, brackets, parentheses, italics, script, underlining or compressed type;

▌ never staple, fold or fax your CV.

Keying in to buzzwords

Begin and end your computer-friendly CV with a short section of 80 words or under called keywords, or talents. Talents encompass technical jargon and other nouns that can be used to label the job or yourself.

To compile a list of talents, check the classifieds for positions similar to the one you're looking for and cull any recurring nouns. Make sure to put the most important words first, in case the computer is limited in the number of buzzwords it can remember.

No plain, no gain

Remember, when you're preparing a CV to be scanned and understood by a computer, you are not necessarily writing one that would appeal to a human being. Your goal is not to catch the recruiter's eye with fancy fonts, a jazzy layout and exciting language, but simply to make it through the scanner intact, with enough information – in the appropriate order – so that when the computer is looking for somebody with your qualifications, your CV will pop up.

What follows is a selection of standard, non-computer-specific CVs for you to adapt as you see fit.

CHRONOLOGICAL CV

John Smith, 123 Anystreet, London, NW1 020 8123 4567

SUMMARY: Ten years of increasing responsibilities in the employment services industry. Concentration in the high-technology markets.

EXPERIENCE: Howard Systems International, Inc.   1994–Present
Management Consulting Firm
Personnel Manager

Responsible for recruiting and managing consulting staff of five. Set up office and organized the recruitment, selection, and hiring of consultants. Recruited all levels of MIS staff from financial to manufacturing markets.

Additional responsibilities:
- coordinated with outside advertising agencies
- developed PR with industry periodicals – placement with over twenty magazines and newsletters
- developed effective referral programmes – referrals increased 32 per cent

EXPERIENCE: Technical Aid Corporation   1987–1994
National Consulting Firm. MICRO/TEMPS Division

Division Manager   1993–1994
Area Manager   1990–1993
Branch Manager   1988–1990

As Division Manager, opened additional offices, staffed and trained all offices with appropriate personnel. Created and implemented all divisional operational policies responsible for P & L. Sales increased to £20 million from £15 million in 1988.

- Achieved and maintained 30 per cent annual growth over seven-year period.
- Maintained sales staff turnover at 14 per cent.

As Area Manager, opened additional offices, hiring staff, setting up office policies and training sales and recruiting personnel.

Additional responsibilities:
- supervised offices in two counties
- developed business relationships with accounts – 75 per cent of clients were regular customers
- client base increased 28 per cent per year
- generated over £200,000 worth of free trade-journal publicity

As Branch Manager, hired to establish the new MICRO/TEMPS operation. Recruited and managed consultants. Hired internal staff. Sold service to clients.

EDUCATION: London University
BA (Hons) Public Relations, 1987

FUNCTIONAL CV

John Smith
123 Anystreet
London NW1
020 8123 4567

OBJECTIVE: A position in Employment Services where my management, sales, and recruiting talents can be effectively utilized to improve operations and contribute to company profits.

SUMMARY: Over ten years of Human Resources experience. Extensive responsibility for multiple branch offices and an internal staff of forty-plus employees and 250 consultants.

SALES: Sold high-technology consulting services with consistently profitable margins throughout the United Kingdom. Grew sales from £15 million to over £20 million a year.

Created training programmes and trained salespeople in six metropolitan markets.

RECRUITING: Developed recruiting sourcing methods for multiple branch offices.

Recruited over 25,000 internal and external consultants in the high-technology professions.

MANAGEMENT Managed up to 40 people in sales, customer service, recruiting, and administration. Turnover maintained below 14 per cent in a 'turnover business'.

FINANCIAL: Prepared quarterly and yearly forecasts. Presented, reviewed, and defended these forecasts to the Board of Directors. Responsible for P & L of £20 million sales operation.

PRODUCTION: Responsible for opening multiple offices and accountable for growth and profitability. One hundred per cent success and maintained 30 per cent growth over a seven-year period in ten offices.

WORK EXPERIENCE: HOWARD SYSTEMS INTERNATIONAL, London
1994–Present National Consulting Firm
Personnel Manager

1987–1994 TECHNICAL AID CORPORATION, London
National Consulting & Search Firm
Division Manager

EDUCATION: BA (Hons) 1987, London University

REFERENCES: Available upon request

COMBINATION CV

EMPLOYMENT SERVICES MANAGEMENT

John Smith
123 Anystreet
London NW1
020 8123 4567

OBJECTIVE:
Employment Services Management

SUMMARY: Ten years of increasing responsibilities in the employment services marketplace. Concentration in the high-technology markets.

SALES: Sold high-technology consulting services with consistently profitable margins throughout the United Kingdom. Grew sales from £15 million to over £20 million a year.

PRODUCTION: Responsible for opening multiple offices and accountable for growth and profitability. One hundred per cent success and maintained 30 per cent growth over a seven-year period in ten offices.

MANAGEMENT: Managed up to forty people in sales, customer service, recruiting, and administration. Turnover maintained below 14 per cent in a 'turnover business'. Hired branch managers, sales, and recruiting staff throughout United Kingdom.

FINANCIAL: Prepared quarterly and yearly forecasts. Presented, reviewed, and defended these forecasts to the Board of Directors. Responsible for P & L of £20 million sales operation.

MARKETING: Performed numerous market studies for multiple branch openings. Resolved feasibility of combining two different sales offices. Study resulted in savings of over £5,000 per month in operating expenses.

COMBINATION CV (page 2)

EXPERIENCE: Howard Systems International, Inc.   1994–Present
Management Consulting Firm
Personnel Manager

Responsible for recruiting and managing consulting staff of five. Set up office and organized the recruitment, selection, and hiring of consultants. Recruited all levels of MIS staff from financial to manufacturing markets.

Additional responsibilities:
- developed P.R. with industry periodicals – placement with over twenty magazines and newsletters
- developed effective referral programmes – referrals increased 320 per cent.

Technical Aid Corporation   1987–1994
National Consulting Firm. MICRO/TEMPS Division
Division Manager   1993–1994
Area Manager   1990–1993
Branch Manager   1987–1990

As Division Manager, opened additional offices, staffed and trained all offices with appropriate personnel. Created and implemented all divisional operational policies. Responsible for P & L. Sales increased to £20 million from £15 million in 1988.

- Achieved and maintained 30 per cent annual growth over seven-year period.
- Maintained sales staff turnover at 14 per cent.

As Area Manager, opened additional offices, hiring staff, setting up office policies, training sales and recruiting personnel.

Additional responsibilities:
- supervised offices in two counties
- developed business relationships with accounts – 75 per cent of clients were regular customers
- client base increased 28 per cent per year
- generated over £200,000 worth of free trade-journal publicity.

As Branch Manager, hired to establish the new MICRO/TEMPS operation. Recruited and managed consultants. Hired internal staff. Sold service to clients.

EDUCATION: BA (Hons), 1987, London University

2 *The executive briefing*

If you know the specific requirements of a particular opening, the executive briefing will quickly – and impressively – line them up with your skills and qualities.

A general CV does have drawbacks. First, it is too general to relate your qualifications to each specific job. Second, more than one person will probably be interviewing you and that is a major stumbling block. While you will ultimately report to one person, you may well be interviewed by other team members. When that happens, the problems begin.

A manager says to a subordinate, 'Spend a few minutes with this candidate and tell me what you think.' Your general CV may be impressive, but the manager rarely adequately outlines the job being filled or the specific qualifications for which he or she is looking. This means that other interviewers do not have any way to qualify you fairly and specifically. While the manager will be looking for specific skills relating to projects at hand, personnel will be trying to match your skills to the vagaries of the job description and the other interviewers will fumble in the dark because no one told them what to look for. Such problems can reduce your chances of landing a job offer.

A neat trick I helped develop for the executive search industry is the *executive briefing*. It enables you to customize your CV quickly to each specific job and acts as a focusing device for the person who interviews you.

While the executive briefing is only one form of cover letter, I am including it here for one very important reason – namely, that you are, in your research, going to come across 'dream opportunities' before your new CV is finished. The executive briefing allows you to update and customize that old CV with lightning speed without delaying the rest of your research.

Like many great ideas, the executive briefing is beautiful in its simplicity. It is a sheet of paper with the company's requirements for the job opening listed on the left side and your skills – matching point by point the company's needs – on the right. Here is an example.

Executive Briefing

Dear Sir/Madam:

While my attached CV will provide you with a general outline of my work history, my problem-solving abilities, and some achievements, I have taken the time to list your current specific requirements and my applicable skills in those areas. I hope this will enable you to use your time effectively today.

Your Requirements:	My Skills:
1. Management of public library service area (for circulation, reference, etc)	1. Experience as head reference librarian at University of Smithtown
2. Supervision of 14 full-time support employees	2. Supervised support staff of 17
3. Ability to work with larger supervisory team in planning, budgeting, and policy formulating	3. Responsible for budget and reformation of circulation rules during my last year
4. ALA	4. I have this qualification
5. Three years' experience	5. One year with public library; two with University of Smithtown

---

This briefing assures that each CV you send out addresses the job's specific needs and that every interviewer at that company will be interviewing you for the same job.

Send an executive briefing with every CV – it will substantially increase your chances of obtaining an interview with the company. An executive briefing sent with a CV provides a comprehensive picture of a thorough professional, plus a personalized, fast and easy-to-read synopsis that details exactly how you can help with the company's current needs.

The use of an executive briefing is naturally restricted to jobs that you have discovered through your own efforts or seen advertised. It is obviously not appropriate for sending when the requirements of a specific job are unavailable. Finally, using the executive briefing as a covering letter for your CV will greatly increase the chances of your enquiry being picked out of the pile in the HR department and passed straight to the appropriate manager.

3 *The inside track*

Why some people stay on a plateau longer, while others get more offers at better companies.

There used to be a stigma about changing jobs or looking for a new one. Today, we live in a different climate. Everyone you speak with in your job hunt has been through your experience. Career moves and unemployment are an integral part of our working lives, but how long this phase lasts is entirely up to you.

I recently met an unemployed executive who was looking for a job for the first time in 20 years. He had been looking for seven months and wasn't the least bit concerned. He seemed to have this mistaken idea that someone would magically appear with another top management job for him.

His method of job hunting was networking 'because that is what I've been told is the best way to find jobs.' It is if it works, but, all too often, a single-shot approach misfires.

The employment market varies from year to year. Sometimes it's a buyer's market and sometimes a seller's, but the fact remains that, regardless of the state of the economy, there are good jobs out there for the job hunter who employs a systematic and comprehensive approach.

Too many job hunters rely solely on applications to the well-known companies, the IBMs of this world. They forget that the majority of growth in industry is with small companies with fewer than 50 employees. Your goal is to land the best possible job for you and your needs. The problem is, you won't have the chance to pick the best opportunity unless you check them all out.

What you have to do is make sure that you are aware of the opportunity and the company and, in turn, the company is aware of you when that opportunity arises.

There is a multipronged approach that combines active and

passive job hunting strategies that every job hunter can use to cover all the bases and tap the very best opportunities.

▮ **Direct research** Search company profiles on-line.

▮ **Online job sites** Literally millions of jobs at your fingertips.

▮ **CV databases** Post your CV on-line and let employers find you.

▮ **Newspapers** There are thousands of overlooked opportunities here.

▮ **Employment agencies** Whoever you allow to represent you will decide who you get to meet and how seriously your initial candidacy will be considered.

▮ **References** The references you supply to potential employers in the later stages of the job hunt can be utilized effectively at the beginning, too.

▮ **School and university and careers offices and alumni/ae organizations** Even if you have long since left school or graduated, these organizations can be a big help.

▮ **Professional associations** It is sometimes said that it is not what you know, but who you know.

▮ **Job fairs** Home of employers in a feeding frenzy for today and tomorrow.

▮ **Business and trade publications** These are a much underrated resource for telling you what is happening on your profession's main street and who is making it happen.

▮ **Networking** It is more than an empty phrase – there are numerous networks we can all tap into effectively.

▮ **Job hunters' networks** If one doesn't exist, create your own.

Tapping the hidden job market need not be scary if you follow a sound plan. In the following pages, you'll examine insider tricks to get you up to speed and ensure you maintain momentum in each of these areas.

4 *The hidden job market*

A plethora of innovative interview-generating techniques to get you up to speed and ensure you maintain momentum.

On a radio talk show earlier this year I listened to a problem from a listener. She said, 'I'm in the academic field, I've been unemployed for two years, and I don't know what to do.' I asked her how many organizations she had contacted and she said 250. I asked her how many possible employers there were and she said about 3,000. I said, 'Next caller please.' The world owes no one a living. You have to go out and find a job.

While I was revising this chapter, I heard from the producer of a national talk show on which I had recently appeared. She told me she used the techniques described in this part of the book to get 30 interviews in 3 weeks!

Electronic job hunting

The Internet is now the most comprehensive job-hunting resource. You can search through thousands of job openings and send your CV to hundreds of employers and headhunters in just a few hours. You can also use salary calculators to help you compare earnings and the cost of living in different parts of the country. You can ask questions of career experts, live, and there are special-interest forums for virtually all professional areas. Job hunting on the Internet can make your job hunt faster, more efficient and more comprehensive. Use this tool to stack the odds in your favour.

My advice is to spend a couple of days at the start of your job hunt kick-starting your search with Internet tools. Visit the incredible job banks to look for suitable openings and sign up for the e-mail alerts that will automatically update you when jobs matching your needs appear. Post your CV on the CV banks – employers and headhunters are scanning them daily.

Do all these things and whatever else the Internet offers your unique job hunting needs, focusing on it for three or four full days to get the best out of the medium and the stars out of your eyes. Then, focus on the traditional job-hunting techniques explained in the rest of this chapter that will help you focus on your home geography. Then, take an hour at the end of the day to maintain your online momentum. If you continue ad nauseum to potter around the Internet, surfing from this site to the next, you will feel busy but you won't be maximally productive.

Direct research

No job search is going to be truly comprehensive without research. The Internet is a great place to conduct a search of potential employers. Many Web sites provide access to employer descriptions and will often lead you to other tools, such as CV banks and more specialized job directories.

Visiting your local library's reference section can be helpful, too. There are several reference books you can consult. I won't use up precious space here teaching you how to use them – the librarian will be happy to do that.

Wherever you conduct your search, your goal is to identify and build personalized dossiers on the companies in your chosen geographic area. Do not be judgmental about what and who they might appear to be: you are fishing for possible job openings, so cast your net wide and list them all. Copy all the relevant information for each company. So that we agree on 'relevant', take a look at the example overleaf.

In the example, you see the names of the MD and chairman of the Board, a description of the company's services and products, the size of the company and any other interesting information – in this case, its acquisition of a company in Germany. You might come across other interesting information on growth or shrinkage in a particular area of a company – write it all down.

Company Ltd
Head Office: 231 Piccadilly
London W1V 97Y
Phone: 020 7246 8031
Personnel (George Wanstead, dir) 020 7246 8093

MD: Gordon Blair
Chairman: Sir Geoffrey Jones
Export Sales director: David Macdonald

Company produces high-performance sports cars at
its Northampton plant, supplies tooling and key
components for local assembly overseas. Exports
expanding to markets in Germany, USA and Middle
East.

Turnover £4.5m
Profits + 11.5%

Recently acquired machine tool company in
Dusseldorf.

This information will help you shine at the interview in three
ways. Your knowledge creates a favourable impression at your
first meeting; that you made an effort is noticed. No one else
bothers, so that is a second benefit; you have set yourself apart
from the others. Third, you are showing that you respect the company and, therefore, by inference, the interviewer; this sets a
favourable tone.

All your effort has an obvious short-term value: it helps you
win job offers. It also has long-term value because you are building a personalized reference work of your industry/specialism/
profession that will help you throughout your career whenever
you wish to make a job change.

Unfortunately, no single reference work you will find is complete. As you don't know which company has the very best job for you, you need to research as many businesses in your area as possible, so you will have to look through several resources. Be sure to check out any specialist guides mentioned in the bibliographies of your reference books.

Your local _Yellow Pages_ is also worth a look. Information found here will range from a company name and telephone number to a full-page advertisement providing considerable information.

Even if you can get only names and telephone numbers, these directories can still be a valuable resource. While most directories are updated infrequently and tend only to list major players in the field, _Yellow Pages_ are updated annually. They are used extensively by growth companies as a marketing tool. Most of the economic growth (and therefore most of the promising new job opportunities) is with the small, growing companies.

Making the battle map

At the end of the day, remember to buy a large-scale map of your local area, drawing pins and small stick-on labels for implementing the next step of your plan.

Put the map on a wall. Attach some string to a drawing pin, stick the pin on the spot where you live and draw concentric circles at intervals of one mile.

Next, take out the company biographies you prepared at the library or gleaned from the Internet and write 'No. 1' on the first. Find the firm's location on the map and mark it with a pin. Then, mark an adhesive label 'No. 1' and attach it to the head of a drawing pin. As you progress, a dramatic picture of your day's work appears. Each pin-filled circle is a territory that needs to be covered and each of those pins represents a potential job. In short, you will have defaced a perfectly good map, but you'll have a physical outline of your job hunting efforts.

It is likely you will return to the Internet and the resource books at the library to continue your research work and preparing your CV. The initial research might take a few days. Your goal during this stage is to generate a couple of hundred sources, enough to get you started. Then, once your campaign is up to speed, you can visit sites and the library again as prudence dictates. It is the person who is best prepared who wins every time. Job hunters who succeed at interview are those who do their homework.

State and private employment agencies

There are essentially five categories:

- state employment agencies;

- private employment agencies;

- executive recruiters;

- temporary help organizations;

- career counsellors.

Let us look at each of these in turn.

State employment agencies

Jobcentres are funded by the state. They will make efforts to line you up with appropriate jobs and post CVs out on your behalf to interested employers who have jobs listed with them. It is not mandatory for employers to list jobs with state agencies, but more and more are taking advantage of these free services. The types of jobs available are getting wider.

If you are moving to another county or further, your local Jobcentre can see what jobs might be available there. The most effective way to use the service, though, is to visit your local office and ask for an introduction to the office in your destination area.

Other services available include Employment Service Direct (0845 6060234 – 9.00–6.00 weekdays, 9.00–1.00 Saturday) where you can discuss what jobs there are and be entered on the database to be notified when there is something suitable. You can also visit the Web site at www.employmentservice.gov.uk, which you can search to see if there are any jobs you are interested in.

Private employment agencies

Choose your agent, or 'headhunter' as they are commonly called, with the same care and attention with which you would choose a spouse or an accountant. The calibre of the individual and company you choose could well affect the calibre of the company you ultimately join. Further, if you choose prudently, an agent can become a lifetime counsellor who can guide you, step by step, up the ladder of success.

Understand that there are distinctly different types of employment services:

▌ permanent employment agencies where you pay the fee;

▌ permanent agencies where the employer pays the fee;

▌ contingency and retained search firms.

As this is the for-profit sector of the marketplace, the question arises: whose pocket is the profit coming from? To avoid misunderstanding, it is best to confirm which kind an agency is before entering into any relationship.

Only employment agencies and certain contingency search firms will actively market you to a large number of companies with whom they may or may not have an existing relationship. A true executive search firm will never market your services. It will only present your credentials on an existing assignment.

So, what type of company is best for you? Well, the answer is simple: the one that will get you the right job offer. The problem is there are thousands of companies in each of these broad categories, so how do you choose between the good, the bad and the ugly?

Fortunately, this is not as difficult as it sounds. Let's dispel one or two myths. A retained executive search firm is not necessarily any better or more professional than a contingency search firm, which, in turn, is not necessarily better or more professional than a regular employment agency. Each has its exemplary practitioners and its charlatans. Your goal is to avoid the charlatans and get representation by an exemplary outfit. Make the choice carefully and, having made the choice, stick with it and listen to the advice you are given.

Check on the date of the firm's establishment. If the company has been in business ever since you were in nappies, the chances are it's a good, reputable firm.

A company's involvement in professional associations is always a good sign. It demonstrates commitment and, through extensive professional training, an enhanced level of competence.

Involvement in independent or franchise networks of firms can also be a powerful plus. These networks also have extensive training that helps assure a high-calibre consultant. Franchise offices can be especially helpful if you are looking to change jobs and move across the country (or further) at the same time as they tend to have powerful symbiotic relationships with other network members; in fact this is often a primary reason for their being a member of that particular franchise or network.

Experienced consultants can also be relied on to have superior knowledge of the legalities and ethics of the recruitment process, along with the expertise and tricks of the trade that only come from years of hands-on experience. All of this can be put to work on your behalf.

It makes good sense to have a friend in the business with an ear to the ground on your behalf as you continue your upward climb. If you want my best advice, find an experienced consultant of good standing and listen to what he or she tells you.

Finally, don't be intimidated and, remember, you are not obliged to sign anything. Neither are you obliged to guarantee an agency that you will remain in any employment for any specific length of time. Don't get put in a trick bag by the occasional cowboy in an otherwise exemplary and honourable profession.

Executive recruiters

All the advice I have given you about employment agencies applies here (although you can take it for granted that the executive recruiter will not charge you a fee). They are going to be more interested in your CV for their files than in wanting to see you right then and there, unless you match a specific job they are trying to fill for a client. They are far more interested in the employed than the unemployed, because an employed person is less of a risk (they often guarantee their finds to the employer for up to a year) and a more desirable commodity. Executive recruiters are there to serve the client, not to find you a job. They neither want nor expect you to rely on them for employment counselling, unless they specifically request that you do – in which case you should listen closely.

Working with a headhunter

Few people realize it, but symbiotic relationships can be developed with headhunters in all these categories to help you professionally. Their livelihood depends on who and what they know. Perhaps you can exchange mutually beneficial information, but do be circumspect. An unethical headhunter can create further competition for you when you share information about companies you are talking to.

Select two or three firms that work in your field. Do not mass mail your CV to every agent in town. This can lead to multiple submissions of your CV to a single company and a resultant argument over which agency is due a fee. When such a situation arises, companies will sometimes choose to walk away from the candidate in question.

Determine who pays the fee and whether or not any contracts will need to be exchanged. Define titles and the employment levels they represent, along with geographical areas. Know what you want or ask for assistance in defining your parameters. This will include title, style of company, salary expectations, benefits and location.

If the professional is interested in representing you, expect a detailed analysis of your background and prepare to be honest. Do not overstate your job duties, accomplishments or education. If there are employment gaps, explain them.

Find out first what the professional expects of you in the relationship and then explain what you expect. Arrive at commitments you both can live with and stick with them. If you break those commitments, expect your representative to cease representation and withdraw your candidacy from potential employers. They are far more interested in long-term relationships than passing nuisances.

Keep the recruiter informed about any and all changes in your status, such as salary increases, promotions, layoffs or other offers of employment.

Don't consider yourself an employment expert. You get a job for yourself every three or four years; these people do it for a living every day of every week. Ask for their objective input and seek their advice on developing interviewing strategies with their clients.

Always tell the truth.

Temporary employment agencies

Such agencies provide corporate services to professionals at most levels, from unskilled and semi-skilled labour to administration, finance, technical, sales and marketing professionals, doctors, lawyers, teachers and even interim executives.

Temporary employment agencies can be a useful resource if you are unemployed. You can get temporary assignments, maintain continuity of employment and skills and perhaps enhance your marketability in the process.

If you are changing careers or returning to work after an absence, temporary assignments can help get new or rusty skills up to speed and provide you with a current work history in your chosen field. The temping life can help you break out of your rut as well. It is becoming increasingly common to hear of the career-motivated professional who has been categorized and pigeon-holed in the workplace, but who finds a highly reputable temp agency and subsequently completely overhauls his or her skills to such an extent that a new career is possible.

In both these situations, there are two other benefits:

▌ you will get exposure to employers in the community who, if you really shine, could ask you to join the staff full time;

▌ you will develop another group of networking contacts.

Working with a temporary employment agency

Investigate the turnover of the temporary staff. If other temps have stayed with the company long term, chances are it does a good job and has good clients.

Select a handful of firms that work in your field; this will increase the odds of suitable assignments appearing quickly.

Define the titles and the employment levels they represent, along with geographical areas they cover.

Do not overstate your job duties, accomplishments or education.

Find out first what the agency professional expects of you in the relationship, then explain what you expect. Reach commitments you both can live with and stick with them.

Judge the assignments not solely on the pay (although that can be important), but also on the long-term benefits that will accrue to your job search and ongoing career.

Keep your contact informed about any and all changes in your status, such as offers of employment or acquisition of new skills.

Remember that the agency is your employer. Its staff will appreciate extra effort when its clients really need it and will reciprocate.

Resolve key issues ahead of time. Should an employer want to take you on full time, will that employer have to pay a set amount or will you just stay on as a temp for a specific period and then go on the employer's payroll?

Careers counsellors

Careers counsellors charge for their services. For this you get assistance in your career realignment or job search skill development. What you don't get is a guarantee of employment.

If you consider this route, speak to a number of counsellors and check multiple references on all of them. As you are unlikely to be given poor references, you will want to check secondary and tertiary references. This is simple to do. Check the half dozen references you request, then ask each of the referees to refer someone else they know who used the service, then check that reference as well.

Find out how long the company has been in business and ascertain a complete work history of the individual counsellor who is likely to be assisting you. A number of people have been known to slip into this area of the employment services business for a quick buck with little expertise and commitment.

The person who can offer you the best advice in this area is the professional who has both corporate HR experience *and* employment agency or retained search experience. This exposure should be mandatory for anyone willing to charge you for career and employment assistance.

Newspapers

Almost everybody looking for a new job buys a newspaper and then carefully misuses it. A recent story tells of a job hunter who started by waiting for the Sunday paper to be published. He read the paper and circled six jobs. He called about the first, only to find it had already been filled and, in the process, was snubbed by someone whose voice had yet to break, requesting that, in the future, he write and send a CV rather than call. As anything is better than facing more telephone conversations like this, the job hunter didn't call the other five companies, but instead took a week to write a CV that no one would read, let alone understand. He sent it, then waited a week for someone to call. He waited another week, kicked the cat, felt bad about that, worse about himself and had a couple of drinks. The phone rang. Someone was interested in the CV, but, unfortunately, not in someone who slurred his words at lunchtime. He felt worse, stayed in bed late. The phone rang. An interview! He felt good and went to the interview. They said they'd contact him in a few days. They didn't and, when he called, everybody was mysteriously unavailable. The job hunter began to feel like a blot on God's landscape.

This is obviously an extreme example, but the story is a little too close to home for many and it illustrates the wrong way to use the newspaper when you're looking for a job. In today's changing economy, it is not unusual for an advertisement in a local paper to draw upwards of 150 responses. I know of ads that have drawn almost 2,000 responses. It is these odds of 1 in 150 or 1 in 2,000 that cause some to reject the 'wanted' ads as a hopeless method for finding employment. However, there are ways to answer 'wanted' ads correctly and narrow the odds to 1 in 10 or even 1 in 5. This is exactly what I am going to show you how to do now.

While reference books give you bags of hard information about a company, they tell you little about specific job openings. Newspapers tell you about specific jobs that need to be filled now, but give you few hard facts about the company. The Internet provides both hard information about a company and tells you about current job openings. The three types of information complement each other. Often you will find ads on the Internet and in the newspaper for companies you have already researched. What a powerful combination of information this gives you going in the door to the interview!

Use Internet job postings and newspaper ads to identify all companies in your field that are currently hiring, not just to identify specific openings. Write down pertinent details about each particular job opening on a separate sheet of paper, as you did earlier when using the reference books. Include the company's name, address, phone number and contacts.

In addition to finding openings that bear your particular title, look for all the companies that regularly hire in your field. Cross-check the categories. Don't rely solely on those ads advertising for your specific job title. For example, let's say you are a graphic artist looking for a job in advertising. You should flag any advertising or public relations agency with any kind of need. The fact that your job is not being advertised does not mean a company is not looking for you; if a company is in a hiring mode, a position for you might be available. In the instances when a company is active but has not been advertising specifically for your skills, write down all relevant company contact data. Then, contact the company. You could be the solution to a problem that has only just arisen or even one they have despaired of ever solving.

Virtually every newspaper has an employment edition each week (in addition to Sunday), when they have their largest selections of wanted ads. Make sure you always get this edition of the paper.

It is always a good idea to examine back issues of the newspapers. These can provide a rich source of job opportunities that remain unfilled from previous advertising efforts. I suggest working systematically through the want ads, going back 12 to 18 months. React to ads as if they were fresh: answer the ones with your job title and contact companies in your field even if they appear to be seeking people with different skills.

When you contact a company by phone or letter, your opening gambit is not to say, 'Hello Ms Jones, I'm answering your ad from last July's *Guardian*.' No. You mention that you've 'heard through the grapevine that the company might be looking' or that you 'have been intrigued by their company and hope they might be looking for…'

Sounds crazy? That's what a reader said to me recently in a letter. He also said this trick landed him a really good job from a seven-month-old wanted ad. Sometimes a position will never have been filled and the employer has simply despaired of getting someone through advertising. Sometimes the person hired left or didn't work out or perhaps the employer is only now starting to look for another person like the one they had advertised for earlier. They might even just be coming off a hiring freeze. Whatever the case, every old ad you follow up won't result in an opening, but when one does, the odds can be short indeed. Smart money always goes on the short odds.

In addition to your local papers, there are regional, national and international papers that employers favour to meet their professional needs.

The reason you must use a combination of reference books and advertisements is that companies tend to hire in cycles. When you rely exclusively on newspapers, you miss those companies just about to start or just ending their hiring cycles. Comprehensive research is the way to tap what the business press refers to as the hidden job market. It is paramount that you have as broad a base as possible – people know people who have your special job to fill.

Adding all these companies to your map, you will have a glittering panorama of prospects, the beginnings of a dossier on each one and an efficient way of finding any company's exact location. This is useful for finding your way to an interview and in evaluating job offers coming your way.

Box number wanted ads

Employed professionals are understandably wary of answering ads that give only box numbers. Unemployed professionals wonder if it is worth the effort. There are many reasons not to answer blind ads, but the two reasons for action far outweigh the negatives:

▎ if you don't respond, you aren't in the game, and you have to play to win;

▎ you may not be suitable for the job advertised, but may be for another position.

If you are employed and sceptical about 'blowing your cover' or unemployed and eager to increase your chances, try this technique. Call the main post office in the area and ask for the local office that handles the postcode given in the advert. Call that post office and speak to the local post office manager, or P.O. box manager. Introduce yourself as an employed job hunter and ask for the name of the box holder so that you won't jeopardize your current job. If you make your request pleasant and personal enough, you might get the information you need. If not, try asking, 'Is it my employer, _____?'

Your own wanted ads

It's better to use the money to fire up your barbecue.

Consistency

Consistent research is the key to gathering speed and maintaining momentum. Without it, your job hunt will stall for lack of people and companies to approach.

A few years ago, a neighbour of mine, in the airline business, found himself looking for a job. At the time, a new prestigious airline was just beginning its operations. The neighbour had a friend already with the company who was going to get him a job. It took a year of not looking for work before this job hunter realized that things you want to happen often don't … unless you make them. Not only did he never work for that airline, he never worked in the airline industry again.

When you look like a penguin, act like a penguin and hide among penguins, don't be surprised if you get lost in the flock.

Today's business marketplace demands a different approach. Your career does not take care of itself – you must go out and grab the opportunities.

Your references as a resource

As a rule, we have faith in ourselves and are confident that our referees will speak well of us. The fact is that some will speak well of us, some will speak excellently and some, we might be surprised to hear, bear us no good will.

The wrong references at a critical juncture could spell disaster. At the very start of your job hunt you need to identify as many potential references as possible. The more options you have, the better your likelihood of coming up with excellent references. When you are currently employed, however, unless you want your employer to know you are actively engaged in making a career move, you will want to avoid using current managers and colleagues as references.

Yet, at this point of the job search, excellent references, though important, are simply an added bonus. Your hidden agenda is to use these contacts as job search leads.

The process is simplicity itself. Simply say, 'John, this is _____. We worked together at Acme between 1998 and 2000. How's it going?' It is appropriate here to catch up on gossip and the like. Then, broach the subject of your call.

'John, I wanted to ask your advice.' (Everyone loves to be asked for an expert opinion.) 'We've had some cutbacks at Fly-By-Night Finance, as you've probably heard', or 'The last five years at Bank of Crooks and Criminals International have been great and the _____ project we are just winding down has been a fascinating job. Nevertheless, I have decided that this would be a perfect time for a career move to capitalize on my experience.'

Then, 'John, I realize how important references can be and I was wondering if you would have any reservations about my using you as a reference?' It's better to find out now rather than down the line when it could blow a job offer.

The response will usually be positive, so then you can move to the next step. 'Thanks, John, I hoped you would feel able to. Let me update you about what I have been doing recently and tell you about the type of opportunity I'm looking for.' Then proceed, in less than two minutes, to give a capsule of what has passed since you worked together and what you are looking for. With colleagues or past managers, be sure to restate why you left your last job as the referee is likely to be asked.

You can then, if appropriate and time allows, tell the referee some of the questions he might be asked. These might include the time he has known you, your relationship to each other, the title you worked under (be sure to remind your reference of promotions and title changes), your five or six most important duties, the key projects you worked on, your greatest strengths, your greatest weaknesses, your attitude towards your job, your attitude towards your peers, your attitude towards management, the timeliness, quality and quantity of your work, your willingness to achieve above and beyond the call of duty (remind him of all those weekends you worked), whether or not he would re-employ you (if company policy forbids re-employing, make sure your referee will mention this), your earnings and any additional comments the referee would like to make.

When references are about to be checked for a specific job, get back to your chosen referees, reacquaint them with any relevant areas the employer might wish to discuss and tell them to expect a call. I have even known professionals who, with the approval of the potential employer, have their referees call in with recommendations.

School, college and university careers services and alumni/ae associations

School, college and university careers services

If you are leaving school or college, take advantage of this resource. Remember that the careers service is not a substitute for your mother; it is not there to provide for you or hand you job offers. Rather, you will find there a wealth of experience that will accelerate the process and aid you in finding your own job.

Careers services and their staff are horrendously overworked and merely keeping pace with the Herculean task of providing assistance to the student body as a whole is more than a full-time job. Take the time to make yourself known here and stress your sincerity and willingness to listen to good advice. Act on it; then, when you come back for more, you will have earned the adviser's respect and, as such, will begin to earn yourself that extra bit of attention and guidance that winners always manage for themselves.

Don't wait until the last minute, especially if you are hoping to gain your foothold on the ladder of success from careers fair and milk round recruiters who represent the big companies. These recruiters visit schools, colleges and universities during the year, so, take an active part in such events and you may well find them coming after you.

Alumni/ae associations

Even when your student days are in the misty distant past, this isn't the time to forget the people of the old school tie. People employ people like themselves, people with whom they share something in common. Your school, college or university alumni/ae association is a complete and valuable network just waiting for you.

As a member of the association you are likely to have access to a membership listing. Additionally, many of the larger schools or universities have alumni/ae placement networks, so you may want to check with the alma mater and tap into the old boy and girl network.

Professional associations

Professional associations provide excellent networks for your benefit. Almost all committed professionals are members of at least one or two professional associations. Their membership is based on:

▮ commitment to the profession;

■ the knowledge that people who know people know where the opportunities are hidden.

If you never got around to joining or your membership has lapsed, it is time to think again.

There are two ways to make memberships of professional organizations work. The first is the membership directory, which provides you with a direct networking resource for direct verbal contact and mail campaigns. All associations supply their members with a directory of contact information for all other members. Additionally, all associations schedule regular meetings, which provide further opportunities to mingle with your professional peers on an informal basis, as well as chances to get involved on a volunteer basis with organizing such meetings or speaking at a meeting. Networking at the meetings and using an association's directory for contacts are wise and accepted uses of membership.

Professional associations all have newsletters. In addition to using the 'wanted' section, you will be able to utilize them in other ways by following the advice on trade and business publications later in this chapter.

It is often one's active membership of professional associations that leads other disgruntled job hunters to mutter, 'It's not what you know, it's who you know.' Membership of professional associations is also an excellent way to maintain long-term career stability.

Job fairs

Job fairs and career days are occasions where local or regional companies that are actively looking for people get together, usually under the auspices of a job fair promoter or local employment agency, to attract large numbers of potential employees.

There aren't many of these occasions, so they won't be taking much of your time, but you shouldn't miss them when they do occur. They are always advertised in the local newspapers and frequently on local radio.

When the job fair is organized by a promoter, entrance is either free or there is a nominal charge. When it is organized by a local employment agency or service, it helps to be on its mailing list.

In addition to the exhibition hall, there are likely to be formal group presentations by employers. As all speakers love to get feedback, move in when the crush of presenter groupies has died down; you'll get more time and closer attention. You will also gain additional knowledge about the company and the chance to spend a few minutes customizing the emphasis of your skills to meet the stated needs and interests of the employer in question.

When you attend job fairs, go prepared. Take:

▌ business cards – if you are employed, remember to request the courtesy of confidentiality when calls are made to your place of work;

▌ CVs – the number of exhibitors times two, as you'll need one to leave at the exhibition stand and an additional copy for anyone you have a meaningful conversation with;

▌ notepad and pen, preferably in a folder.

Go with specific objectives in mind:

▌ visit every stand, not just the ones with the flashing lights and professional models stopping traffic;

▌ talk to someone at every stand – as they are the ones who are selling, you have a slight advantage because you can walk up and ask questions about the company – who they are and what they are doing – before you talk about yourself, allowing you to present yourself in the most relevant light;

▌ collect business cards from everyone you speak to so that you can follow up with a letter and a call when they are not so harried – very few people actually get job offers at these fairs as, for most companies, the exercise is usually one of collecting CVs so that meaningful meetings can take place in the ensuing week, but be 'on' in case someone wants to sit down and give you a serious interview on the spot (this is most likely to happen when you least expect it, so be prepared);

▌ collect company brochures and other relevant materials;

▌ arrange times and dates to follow up with each employer – for example, 'Ms Jones, I realize you are very busy today, but I would like to speak to you further. Your company sounds very exciting. I should like to set up a time when we could meet to talk further or perhaps to call you in the next few days';

▌ dress for business – you may be meeting your new boss and you don't want the first impression you make to be less than professional.

Job fairs provide opportunities for administrative, professional and technical people up to the middle management ranks. However, this doesn't mean that senior executives should feel such an event is beneath them. The opportunity still exists to have meaningful conversations with tens or hundreds of employers in a single day, from which may come further fruitful conversations.

On leaving each stand, and at the end of the day, go through your notes while everything is still fresh in your mind. Review each company and what possibilities it holds for you. Then, review all the companies as a whole to see what you might glean about needs in your chosen industry or marketplace shifts and long-term staffing needs. Make notes.

Trade and business magazines

This resource includes professional association periodicals, trade magazines and the general business press. They can all be utilized in a similar fashion by contacting the individuals and companies mentioned and using the article to begin a discussion.

In these publications, you may find the following:

▌ focus articles about interesting companies, which can alert you to specific growth opportunities;

▌ industry overviews and market development pieces, which can tip you off to subtle shifts in your professional market-place and thereby alert you to opportunities and provide you with the chance to customize your letters, calls and CV for specific targets;

▌ quotations – 'The art of press writing demands frequent quotes and, by necessity, attributions', says Peregrine McCoy, senior partner of Connem, Covertrax and Splitt – contacting the person quoted is flattering and shows that you have your finger on the pulse of your profession;

▌ articles by industry professionals – when contacting the author of an article, you might include how much you agree with what was said, a little additional information on the sub-ject or words to the effect that 'It's about time someone told it like it is' – never say anything in the vein of, 'Hey, the article is great but you missed...';

▌ opportunities to write to the editors – they are always on the lookout for quotable letters, so a flattering note about an arti-cle with a line or two about your background in the field may get you some valuable free publicity down the line;

▌ columns on promotions, executive moves and obituaries – if someone has just received a promotion, there are reasonable odds that somewhere in the chain is an opening – that is, if executive A has moved to company B, it could mean com-pany A is looking for someone; the same applies to obituaries;

▌ 'wanted' sections – many employers will give the general newspapers only token attention when it comes to filling hard-to-find professional and trade positions, concentrating their advertising budgets instead on the trade press;

▌ advertisements for new products that can tell you about com-panies that are making things happen, and so need people who can make things happen.

In all of the above instances, it is advisable to clip and keep, in retrievable fashion, all the items that generate leads. There are two reasons for this: you can send a copy to the person you intend to approach and you will have a copy on file to refresh your memory before any direct communication.

In short, just about every page of your average trade journal holds a valuable job lead. You just need to know how and where to look. Then, having found something, you need to take action.

Networking

People frequently think networking means annoying the hell out of your friends until they stop taking your calls. What it should mean is using others to assist in your job search. You will find it surprising how willing friends, colleagues and even strangers are to help you.

The bad news is that networks need nurturing and development. Networking is more than calling your relatives and waiting for them to call back with job offers. People know people, not just in your home town but all over the country and sometimes the world.

I used the word *networks*, not *network*. We all have a number of networks, any of which may produce that all-important job offer. Here are the typical networks we can all tap into:

▮ **family and relatives** including your spouse's family and relatives;

▮ **friends** including neighbours and casual acquaintances;

▮ **colleagues** not forgetting past colleagues, especially to ask about headhunters they know or might hear from and professional affiliations they have found valuable;

▮ **managers, past and present** whose success depends on tapping good talent, so, even if a particular manager can't use you, a judicious referral to a colleague can gain goodwill for the future;

■ **service industry acquaintances** your banker, lawyer, insurance agent, estate agent, doctor, dentist;

■ **other job hunters;**

■ **other professionals in your field**.

Over a period of a few days, you need to develop the most extensive lists you can in each of these categories. Start lists and add to them every day. The experienced professional should be able to come up with a minimum of 20 names for, say, the service industry network list and upwards of 200 professional colleagues.

Here are some tips for writing networking letters and e-mails or making calls asking for assistance.

■ Establish connectivity – recall the last memorable contact you had or mention someone you both knew who you have spoken to recently.

■ Say why you are writing or calling: 'It's time for me to make a move. I just got laid off with one thousand others and I'm taking a couple of days to catch up with old friends.'

■ Ask for advice and guidance about your tactics, which are the happening companies and if the person can take a look at your CV, because you really need an objective opinion and have always respected his or her viewpoint. Don't ask specifically, 'Can you or your company give me a job?' as, if there is something available, he or she will let you know.

■ Don't rely on a contact with a particular company to get you into that company. Mount and execute your own plan of attack as no one is as interested as you are in putting bread on your table;

■ Let contacts know what you are open to. They will usually want to help, but you have to give them a framework within which to target their efforts.

▌ Discuss the profession, industry, areas of opportunity and people worthwhile contacting. If you comport yourself in a professional manner, most fellow professionals will come up with a lead. If they can't think of a person, back off and ask them about companies. Everyone can think of a company. If they come up with a company, respond, 'Hey, that's a great idea. I never thought of those people', even if you have just spoken to that outfit. Then, after a suitable pause, ask for another company. When people see that their advice is appreciated, they will often come up with more. When you have gathered two or three company names, backtrack with, 'Do you know of anyone I could speak to at _____ [company A, B, C]?' Every time you get a referral, be sure to ask whether or not you can use your contact's name as an introduction. The answer will invariably be yes, but asking demonstrates professionalism and will encourage your contact to come up with more leads. Remember to ask for information about, and specific leads from, your targeted companies.

▌ At the end of the call, make sure the contact knows how to get in touch with you. I find the nicest and most effective way of doing this is to say something like, 'David, I really appreciate your help. I'd like to leave you my name and number in the hope that one day in the future I can return the favour.' Not only is this a supremely professional gesture, it ensures that your contact information is available to that individual should openings arise within his sphere of influence. Say that you hope you'll get to see each other again soon and that you look forward to doing something together. Invite the contact over for drinks, dinner or a barbecue.

▌ When you do get help, say thank you. If you get it verbally, follow it up in writing. The impression is indelible and just might get you another lead. Include a copy of your CV with the thank-you letter.

▌ Keep an open mind. You never know who your friends are. You will be surprised at how someone you always regarded as a real pal won't give you the time of day and how someone you never thought of as a friend will go above and beyond the call of duty for you.

▌ Whether your contacts help you or not, let them know when you get a job and maintain contact at least once a year. A career is a long time. It might be next week or a decade from now when a group of managers (including one from your personal network) are talking about filling a new position and the first thing they'll do is ask, 'Who do we know?' That could be you.

Networking is more than one call or letter to each person on your list. Once the first conversation is in the bag, another call in a couple of months won't be taken amiss.

When you get referrals as a result of your networking, use your source as an introduction: 'Jane, my name is Martin Yate. Our mutual friend George Smith suggested I call, so, before I go any further, I must pass on George's regards.'

The job hunter's network

In your job hunt, you will invariably find that companies are looking for everyone but you. The recent graduate is told to come back when he or she has experience, the experienced professional is told that only entry-level people are being taken on. That's the luck of the draw, but one person's problem is another's opportunity.

The solution is to join or create a support group and job hunting network of your own with people in the same situation.

Existing support groups

In many communities these are sponsored by church or other social organizations. They meet, usually on a weekly basis, to discuss ideas, exchange tips and job leads and provide encouragement and the opportunity to support and be supported by others in the same situation.

Creating your own support group

All this takes is finding someone in the same situation as yourself. Among your neighbours and friends someone probably knows someone who has the same needs as you do; all it takes is two. Your goals are quite simple – to meet on a regular basis to exchange ideas and tips; review each other's CVs, letters and verbal presentations; and check on each other's progress. This means that if I tell you that in the last five days I've sent out only three CVs and made only two follow-up calls, you are obliged to get on my case. The purpose of such a group is to provide the pressure to perform that you experience at work.

You can advertise for members in your local paper. It might even be talked into running the ad for free as a community service.

Once you are involved in a group, you will meet others with different skill levels and areas of expertise. Then, when an employer tells you they are only taking on accountants this month, you can offer a referral to the employer or give the lead to your accountant friend. In turn, the accountant will be turning up leads in your field. If these openings don't make themselves known during your conversations, you can tag on a question of your own when the conversation is winding down: 'John, I'm a member of an informal job hunting network. If you don't have a need for someone with my background right now, perhaps one of my colleagues could be just what you are looking for. What needs do you have at present and in the foreseeable future?'

Becoming an active member in an existing group or creating one of your own can get you leads and provide a forum for you to discuss your fears and hopes with others who understand your concerns.

With all of these networks working for you, you will have maximum coverage and minimized the chances of your exhausting any one member or network through overworking their good will and patience. Do it. You have nothing to lose and everything to gain.

Getting the word out

So we now know those paths most likely to lead you to the hidden job market. Remember, there is no single approach to landing your dream job. Friends may tell you that the only effective way is the way that worked for them. Of course, we are all different people and some things will be harder for you than others.

Although each of these techniques has proved effective, no single one is guaranteed for any one individual. Your plan of attack must be balanced and comprehensive. It should include elements of every technique discussed so far. A man who goes fishing and puts one hook in the water has but one chance of catching any one of the millions of fish in the sea; a man with two hooks in the water has double the chances of getting a bite. At this stage of the game you are looking for bites. The more hooks you have in the water, the better your chances.

In the end, of course, you will want to know how to contact the companies you learn about through your various types of research. You have two basic approaches to choose from: the verbal approach, usually by telephone, and the written approach, by letter and CV, sent either as an e-mail or by post.

One of these is likely to appeal to you more than the other. However, in doing both you will see that they simply become different steps in the same process. When you send out letters and CVs, you will invariably find yourself following up with phone calls. When you make phone contact, you will inevitably be following up with letters and CVs. Your activities need to maintain a delicate balance between the two, so that your calls force you to follow up in writing and your CVs and letters force you to follow up with phone calls.

The trick is not to overemphasize the approach that is easiest for you (say, networking with friends and colleagues) at the expense of other approaches (say, direct research calls). Now, while ultimately it is the conversations, not the letters, that get you interviews, I recommend that you begin your campaign by researching contacts in every single category I have discussed; then begin with a combination of mailings and direct calls, because every letter and every CV and every call is another hook in the water. We will examine the written part of the campaign now; initial phone calls will be the topic of the next few chapters.

E-mail and letters

Must you send out hundreds or even thousands of e-mails and letters in the coming weeks? Yes and no. The goal is to communicate as much as you need in your field and no more. One thing is sure, two employer contacts a week will not get you accelerating along that career path again. Only if you approach and establish communication with every possible employer will you create the maximum opportunity for yourself. *Two contacts a week is the behaviour of the long-term unemployed.*

On the other hand, I am not recommending that you immediately make up a list of 700 companies and contact them all today. That isn't the answer either. Your campaign needs strategy. While every job hunting campaign is unique, you will want to maintain a balance between the *number* of contacts you send out on a daily and weekly basis and the *types* of letters you send out. Start off with balanced mailings and your phone contacts will maintain equilibrium, too.

The key is to send out a balanced mailing representing all the different types of leads, and to send them out regularly and in a volume that will allow you to make follow-up calls. Many headhunters manage their time so well that they average over 50 calls per day, year in and year out. While you may aim at building your call volume up to this number, I recommend that you start out with more modest goals. Make 5 to 10 contacts per day in each of the following areas:

- Internet job postings;

- responses to newspaper advertisements;

- friends;

- professional colleagues;

- research contacts from the Internet, reference works, newspapers and so on;

- headhunters.

With adequate research and the resources I have mentioned, there are literally thousands of contacts waiting to be made, so this breakdown of contacts is a daily quota. If it seems a bit steep to begin with, scale down the numbers until they are achievable and gradually build up the volume. Remember, though, the lower the volume, the longer the job search.

Do you need to write more than one letter? Almost certainly. There is a case to be made for having letters and CVs in more than one format. There is no need to waste precious time crafting your written communication entirely from scratch when templates exist. The key is to do each variation once and do it right, so make sure you save copies of your letters and CVs. This way you'll be ready when opportunity comes knocking on your door.

Multiple submissions

You may sometimes find it valuable to send half a dozen contact letters to a given company, to assure that all the important players know of your existence. Let's say you are a young engineer who wants to work for Last Chance Electronics. It is well within the bounds of reason to post or e-mail speculative letters to any or all of the following people (each addressed by name so the letter doesn't end up in the bin): the managing director, director of engineering, chief engineer, engineering manager, director of HR, technical engineering recruitment manager and technical recruiter.

A professionally organized and conducted campaign will proceed on two fronts.

Front 1

A carefully targeted rifle approach to a select group of companies. You will have first identified these super-desirable places to work when you researched your long list of potential employers. You will continue to add to this primary target list as you unearth fresh opportunities in your day-to-day research efforts.

In this instance you have two choices:

▌ write to everyone at once, remembering that the letters have to be personalized and followed up;

▮ start off by contacting a line manager and someone in HR, following this up in a few days by repeating the process to other names on your list.

Front 2

A carpet bombing approach to every possible employer in the area. After all, you won't know what opportunities exist unless you go and find out.

Here you will begin by writing to one or two contacts within a company and then repeating this process with other contacts when your initial follow-up calls result in referrals or dead ends. Remember, just because Harry in engineering says there are no openings in the company doesn't necessarily make it so. Besides, any one of the additional contacts you make could well be the person who knows the person who is just dying to meet you.

Once your campaign is in motion and you have received some responses to your letters and scheduled some interviews from your calls (how to make the calls is covered in the next chapter), your emphasis will change. Those contacts and interviews will require follow-up letters and conversations. You will be spending time preparing for the interviews.

This is exactly the point at which most job hunts stall. We get so excited about the interview activity that we convince ourselves that 'This will be the offer.' Experienced headhunters know that the offer that can't fail always will. The offer doesn't materialize, and we are left sitting with absolutely no interview activity. We let the interview funnel empty itself.

The more contacts you make, the more follow-up calls you can make to schedule interviews. The more direct calls you make, the more interviews you will schedule and the more leads you will generate. The more interviews you get, the better you feel and the better you get at interviewing. The better you get at interviewing, the better the offers you get – and the more offers you get.

So, no matter how good things look, you must continue the campaign. While you have to maintain activity with those companies you are negotiating with, you must also make yourself maintain your daily marketing schedule. Write contact letters or e-mails in each of the following areas:

- Internet job postings;

- newspaper ads;

- associations, alumni/ae, colleagues;

- direct research contacts;

- headhunters;

- follow-up letters.

Small but consistent mailings have many benefits. The balance you maintain is important because most job hunters are tempted to send the easy letters and make the easy calls (networking with old friends), but this will knock you out of balance and kick you into a tailspin.

Don't stop searching even when an offer is pending and your potential boss says, 'Robin, you've got the job and we're glad you can start on Monday. The offer letter is in the post.' Never accept any 'yes' until you have it in writing, you have started work and the first payslip has cleared at the bank! Until then, keep your momentum building: it is the professional and circumspect thing to do.

It is no use sending tens or even hundreds of CVs without following up on your efforts. If you are not getting a response with one CV format, you might want to redo it; try changing from a chronological to a functional or combination format, just as you would change the bait if the fish weren't taking what you had on the hook.

Keep things in perspective. Although your 224th contact may not have an opening for you, with a few polite and judicious questions she may well have a good lead. You will learn how to do this in Chapter 8, Getting live leads from dead ends.

In the job hunt there are only two types of 'yes' – their 'yes, I want you to work for us' and your 'yes, I can start on Monday.' Every 'no' brings you closer to the big 'yes'. Never take rejections of your CV or your phone call as rejections of yourself; just as every job is not for you, you aren't right for every job.

Stacking the odds in your favour

We all have 168 hours a week to become bag people or billionaires and to make our lives as fulfilling as they can be. For some of us this means a better job, for others it means getting back to work to keep a roof over our heads.

How we manage these hours will determine our success. The following job-hunting commandments will see you successfully through the job-change process or career transition.

▌ Those in the professional employment field reckon an average of 700 fresh contacts is required per job placement. You should anticipate at least this number. In a 40-hour week these professionals average approximately 35 to 50 contacts per day. Build to this momentum.

▌ Work at getting a new job. Work at least 40 hours per week at it. Divide your time between contacting potential employers and generating new leads. Never stop the research and job-hunting process until you have a written job offer in hand and you have accepted that job in writing with an agreed-on start date.

▌ Research the companies you contact. In a tightly run job race the candidate who is most knowledgeable about the employer has a distinct advantage.

▌ Contact and recontact your job leads. Follow up on the CVs you send out. Resubmit your CV after six weeks. Change the format of your CV and resubmit yet again.

▌ Stay in regular telephone contact with your job leads on a monthly basis to maintain top-of-the-mind awareness.

▌ Take off the blinkers. We all have two specific skills: our professional/technical skills – say, computer programming – and our industry skills – say, banking. Professional/technical skills can be transferable to other industries, such as manufacturing, and industry skills can open up other opportunities in

55

your industry – as a technical trainer for programmers and/or technophobes, for example.

▋ Develop examples of the personality traits that make you special, such as determination. Rehearse building these examples into your interview responses. (See Chapter 15.)

▋ Send follow-up notes with relevant news clippings, cartoons and so on to those in your networks.

▋ Work on your self-image. Use this time to get physically fit. Studies show that unfit, overweight people take longer to find suitable work. The more you do today, the better you will feel about yourself.

▋ Maintain a professional demeanour during the work week (clothing, posture, personal hygiene).

▋ Use normal business hours for making contacts. Use the early morning, lunchtime, after 5 pm and Saturday for doing the ongoing research to maintain momentum.

▋ Don't feel guilty about taking time off from your job-hunting job. Just do it conscientiously. If you regularly spend Saturday morning in the library doing research, take Wednesday afternoon off.

▋ Maintain records of your contacts. They will benefit not only this job search, but maybe those in the future, too.

▋ Remember, it's all up to you. There are many excuses not to make calls or send CVs on any given day. There are many excuses to get up later or knock off earlier. There are many excuses to back off because this one's in the bag. There are no real reasons. There are no jobs out there for those who won't look. There are countless opportunities for those who assiduously turn over the stones.

Contact trackers

Job hunting requires multiple contacts with employers and others. You should call an employer and schedule a follow-up conversation for a specific time and date next week or you should send a CV today and schedule a follow-up call four to eight days later. When you get up to speed, important opportunities will fall through the cracks unless you maintain a contact tracker.

How to use the contact tracker

I recommend you make your own contact tracker using a spreadsheet program. Create columns for the company name, telephone number, contact name, e-mail address, the date you should send your follow-up letter and the date you sent your CV. In addition to your contact tracker, it may be helpful to use your computer address book to keep track of the companies you contact.

Before posting a day's letters and e-mails, fill out your contact tracker. This will help you structure your job-hunting days. A mailing today will allow you to have a follow-up plan set and ready to go at the appropriate time. As a rule of thumb, a mailing today is ripe for follow-up four to eight days later. Much sooner and you can't guarantee the post has arrived; much later, and it will already be lost in an in-tray or passed on.

You will know that you are on track when you are adding more contacts every day as a result of a mailing and creating new spreadsheets as a result of your follow-up calls.

Every month, I hear from people who use these techniques effectively. Just last week I had a gentleman speak to me on a radio show who explained that he had been out of work for six months. He said he had bought the book just five weeks earlier, had followed my advice to the letter and had since generated four job offers. Follow my advice in letter and spirit and the same good fortune can be yours.

Follow-up: the key ingredient

In theory, the perfect letters or e-mails you send cold or as a result of phone calls will receive a response rate of 100 per cent. Unfortunately, there is no perfect letter, e-mail or call in this less-than-perfect world. If you sit there like some fat Buddha waiting for the world to beat a path to your door, you may wait a long time.

While I was writing this chapter, a pal of mine advertised for a programmer analyst, a two-line ad in the local paper. By Wednesday of the following week, he had over 100 responses. Ten days later, he was still ploughing through them when he received a follow-up call (the only one he received) from one of the respondents. The job hunter was in the office within two hours, returned the following morning and was offered the job before lunchtime.

The story? The candidate's paperwork was simply languishing there in the pile, waiting to be discovered. The follow-up phone call got it discovered. The call made the interviewer sort through the enormous pile of paper, pull out the letter and CV and act on it. Follow-up calls, and follow-up calls on the follow-up calls, do work.

The best managers maintain a private file of great professionals they can't use today but want to keep available. I know of someone who got a top job as a result of being in these files. She got an interview and job offer from a speculative letter she had sent *three years earlier.*

Grant yourself, with this approach, the right to pick and choose among many job offers. Because you are in control, it is possible to set your multiple interviews close together. This way your interviewing skills improve from one meeting to the next. And soon, instead of scheduling multiple interviews, you can be weighing up multiple job offers.

Date
CONTACT TRACKER

	Company	Tel no.	Contact Name	Result	F/U Date	Sent CV
1.						
2.						
3.						
4.						
5.						
6.						
7.						
8.						
9.						
10.						
11.						
12.						
13.						
14.						
15.						
16.						
17.						
18.						
19.						
20.						

NETWORK INDEX SHEET

Name: _____

Relationship: _____

How known: _____

Time known: _____

People in common: _____

_____

Telephone: (H) _____ , (O) _____

Home address: _____

_____

Office address: _____

_____

Secretary: _____

Leads given: _____

_____

_____

BIOGRAPHICAL INFORMATION

Spouse: _____

Children: _____

Interests: _____

_____

Affiliations: _____

_____

Professional experience: _____

_____

_____

Date last contacted: _____

Result: _____

_____

_____

_____

Part II

Getting to Square One

With the grunt work completed, you are prepared to set up multiple interviews with just a few phone calls. Ready?

It bears repeating that you must take the initiative when it comes to finding a job. You must do so in a distinctive way. What is your first instinct when you must 'go looking for a job'? Read online job postings? Everybody else does. Send CVs to companies on the off-chance that they have a job that fits your CV? Everybody else does. Alternatively, of course, you can wait for someone to call you. Employ those tactics as your main thrust for hunting down the best jobs in town and you will fail, as do millions of others who fall into the trap of using such outdated job hunting techniques.

Today's business marketplace demands a different approach. Your career does not take care of itself – you must go out and grab the opportunities.

'Hello, Mr Smith? My name is Martin Yate. I am an experienced training specialist...'

It's as easy as that.

Guide your destiny by speaking directly to the professionals who make their living in the same way you do. A few minutes spent calling different companies from your research dossier and you will have an interview. When you get one interview from making a few calls, how many do you think could be arranged with a day's concerted effort?

5 *Paint the perfect picture on the phone*

When you call the company, you must have four goals: get attention, generate interest, create a desire to know more about you and make the person you speak to take action. Here are three easy steps that will get you closer to landing the interview. Also, invaluable tips on how to deal with pesky receptionists.

Before making that first nerve-wracking telephone call, you must be prepared to achieve one of three goals. They are listed below in order of priority:

1. I will arrange a meeting;

2. I will arrange a time to talk further on the phone;

3. I will ask for a lead on a promising job opening elsewhere.

Always keep these goals in mind. By the time you finish the next four chapters, you'll be able to achieve any one of these goals quickly and easily.

To make the initial phone call a success, all you need to do is paint a convincing word picture of yourself. To start, remember the old saying: 'No one really listens; we are all just waiting for our turn to speak.' With this in mind, you shouldn't expect to hold anyone's attention for an extended period, so the picture you create needs to be brief yet thorough. Most of all, it should be specifically vague – specific enough to arouse interest, to make the person you are talking to prick up his or her ears, yet vague enough to encourage questions, to make him or her pursue you. The aim is to paint a representation of your skills in broad brush-strokes with examples of the money-making, money-saving or time-saving accomplishments all companies like to hear about.

A presentation made over the telephone must possess four characteristics to be successful. These can best be remembered by an old acronym from the advertising world: AIDA.

■ *A* – You must get the person's **A**ttention.

■ *I* –You must get the person's **I**nterest.

■ *D* – You must create a **D**esire to know more about you.

■ *A* – You must encourage the person to take **A**ction.

With AIDA you get noticed. The interest you generate will be evident by the questions that are being asked: 'How much are you making?', 'Do you have a degree?', 'How much experience do you have?' By giving the appropriate answers to these and other questions (which I will discuss in detail), you will change interest into a desire to know more and then turn that desire into an interview.

The types of questions you are asked also enable you to identify the company's specific needs and, once they are identified, you can gear the ongoing conversation towards those needs.

Here are the steps to take to build your AIDA presentation.

Step 1

This covers who you are and what you do. It is planned to get the attention of the person you are talking to, to give that person a reason to stay on the phone. This introduction will include your job title and a brief generalized description of your duties and responsibilities. Use a non-specific job title, as you did for your CV. Remember, getting a foot in the door with a generalized title can provide the occasion to sell your superior skills.

Tell just enough about yourself to whet the company's appetite and cause the person to start asking questions. Again, keep your description a little vague. For example, if you describe yourself simply as experienced, the person must try to qualify your statement with a question: 'How much experience do you have?' – you have established a level of interest. However, if you describe yourself as having four years' experience, while the company is looking for seven, you are likely to be ruled out before you are even aware a job exists. Never specify exact experience or list all your accomplishments during the initial presentation. Your aim is just to open a dialogue.

EXAMPLE
'Good morning, Mr Smith. My name is Joan Jones. I am an experienced office equipment salesperson with an in-depth knowledge of the office products industry. Have I caught you at a good time?'

Never ever ask if you have caught someone at a bad time. You are offering your contact an excuse to say 'yes'. By the same token, asking if you have caught someone at a good time will usually get you a 'yes'. Then you can go directly into the rest of your presentation.

Step 2

Now you are ready to generate interest and, from that, desire; it's time to sell one or two of your accomplishments. You already should have identified these during earlier CV-building exercises. Pull out no more than two items and follow your introductory sentence with them. Keep them brief and to the point, without embellishments.

EXAMPLE
'As the number three salesperson in my company, I increased sales in my territory 15 per cent to over £1 million. In the last six months, I won three major accounts from my competitors.'

Step 3

You have made the person want to know more about you, so now you can make him or her take action. Include the reason for your call and a request to meet. It should be carefully constructed to finish with a question that will bring a positive response, which will launch the two of you into a nuts-and-bolts discussion.

> EXAMPLE
> **'The reason I'm calling, Mr Smith, is that I'm looking for a new challenge and, having researched your company, I felt we might have some areas for discussion. Are these the types of skills and accomplishments you look for in your staff?'**

Your presentation ends with a question that guarantees a positive response and the conversation gets moving.

Your task before calling is to write out a presentation using these guidelines and your work experience. Knowing exactly what you are going to say and what you wish to achieve is the only way to generate multiple interviews and multiple job offers. When your presentation is prepared and written, read it loud to yourself and imagine the faceless person on the other end of the line. Practise with a friend or spouse or use a tape recorder to appraise yourself.

After you make the actual presentation on the phone, you'll really begin to work on arranging a meeting, another phone conversation or establishing a referral. There will likely be a silence on the other end after your initial pitch. Be patient. The person needs time to digest your words. If you feel tempted to break the silence, resist – you do not want to break the person's train of thought, nor do you want the ball back in your court.

This contemplative silence may last as long as 20 seconds, but when the person responds, only three things can happen. The person on the phone can:

▌ agree with you and arrange a meeting;

▌ ask questions that show interest – 'Do you have a degree?', 'How much are you earning?' (any question, because it denotes interest, is considered a buy signal, so, handled properly, it will enable you to arrange a meeting);

▌ raise an objection – 'I don't need anyone like that now', 'Send me a CV'.

These objections, when handled properly, will also result in an interview with the company or at least a referral to someone else who has job openings. In fact, you will frequently find that objections prove to be terrific opportunities.

I hope you can handle the first option – 'I'd like to meet with you' – with little assistance. For obvious reasons, it doesn't get its own chapter.

It will sometimes happen that an overly officious receptionist or secretary will try to thwart you in your efforts to present your credentials directly to a potential employer. At least it appears that way to you.

In fact, it is very rare that these 'corporate gatekeepers' are specifically directed to screen calls from professionals seeking employment, as to do so can only increase employment costs to the company. What they are there to do is screen the nuisance calls from salespeople and the like.

However, to arm you for the occasional objectionable gatekeeper standing between you and making a living, you might try the following techniques used by investigative reporters, private eyes and headhunters.

Go up the ladder

If you can't get through to the person you want to speak to – say the accounting manager – go up the ladder to the controller or deputy manager of finance. Interestingly enough, the higher you go, the more accessible people are. In this instance, the senior manager may well not schedule an interview with you but, instead, refer you back down to the appropriate level. Which means that to the pesky gatekeeper you can now say, 'Mr Bigshot, your divisional deputy manager of finance, asked me to call Mr Jones. Is he there?' Alternatively, if you didn't get through and Bigshot's secretary referred you down the ladder, you say, 'Mr Bigshot's office recommended...' Then the conversation with your target can begin with your standard introduction, but be sure to mention first that so-and-so suggested you call.

Pre-empt

Most gatekeepers are trained, at most, to find out your name and the nature of your business, but when they are asking the questions, they control the conversation. You can remain in control by pre-empting their standard script. 'Hi, I'm Mr Yate [always use your surname for the intimidation value]. I need to speak to Ms Jones about an accounting matter. Is she there?' Should a truly obnoxious gatekeeper ask snidely, 'Perhaps I can help you?' you can effectively utilize any of the following options: 'Thank you, but I'd rather discuss it with Ms Jones', 'It's personal' (well, it's your livelihood isn't it) or you can blind them with science, saying 'Yes, if you can talk to me about the finer points of X, Y and Z', which invariably they can't, so you're in like Flynn.

When you are clear about who you want to speak to and can predict possible screening devices, you are usually assured of getting through. When you don't have the name, try these techniques.

Explain to gatekeepers that you 'need to send a letter to…' then say whatever the title is and ask for the correct spelling of the name. There is usually more than one person worth speaking to at any company, so ask for more than one name and title. In the finance area, and depending on the title, any or all of the following could provide useful contacts: the accounting supervisor, accounting manager, assistant controller, controller, deputy manager of finance, manager, finance director and the managing director.

Anyone who will give you one name will invariably give you more. Some years ago in Colorado I sat with a job hunter using this technique who gathered 142 names in an hour!

In companies where security is paramount, the gatekeepers are expressly forbidden to give out names and titles. In this case, use some of my blind-siding techniques. There are certain people in every company who, by the very nature of their jobs, have contacts with people at all levels of the company and who are not given the responsibility to screen calls. These include people in the post room and in the gatehouse, security, import and export employees, second-, third-, and fourth-shift employees, new or temporary employees, people in advertising and public relations, sales and marketing or customer service.

Voice mail

Voice mail is on the increase. If the techniques I've mentioned don't do the trick for you, these will. When the recorded voice tells you to enter the extension key, keep keying until you hit one that is on the money. It doesn't matter who answers as long as someone does. The conversation goes like this:

'Jack speaking.'

'Jack, this is Martin Yate. I'm calling from outside and I'm lost on this damn telephone system.' This usually gets a laugh. 'I'm trying to get hold of [say whatever the title is]. Could you check who that would be for me?'

or

'Jack, this is Martin Yate. I'm lost on this damn telephone system. I need some help. Can you spare me a minute?'

Whichever technique you use, be sensitive to the person in a rush and don't leave numerous messages. Try to get the extension number of the person you want rather than let yourself be transferred.

6

Responding to buy signals

When you are on the phone, certain questions will tell you that the person at the company is interested in you. Learn how to respond correctly to keep the interest alive.

With just a touch of nervous excitement you finish your presentation: 'Are these the types of skills and accomplishments you look for in your staff?' There is silence on the other end. It is broken by a question. You breathe a sigh of relief because you remember that any question denotes interest and is a buy signal.

Now, conversation is a two-way street and you are most likely to win an interview when you take responsibility for your half. Just as the employer's questions show interest in you, your questions should show your interest in the work done at the company. By asking questions of your own in the normal course of conversation – questions usually tagged on to the end of one of your answers – you will forward the conversation. Also, such questions help you find out what particular skills and qualities are important to the employer. Inquisitiveness will increase your knowledge of the opportunity at hand and that knowledge will give you the power to arrange a meeting.

The alternative is to leave all the interrogation to the employer. That will place you on the defensive and, at the end of the talk, you will be as ignorant of the real parameters of the job as you were at the start. Also, the employer will know less about you than you might want.

Applying the technique of giving a short answer and finishing that reply with a question will carry your call to its logical conclusion: the interviewer will tell you the job specifics and, as that happens, you will present the relevant skills or attributes. In any conversation, the person who asks the questions controls its outcome. You called the employer to get an interview as the first step in generating a job offer, so take control of your destiny by taking control of the conversation.

EXAMPLE

Joan Jones: 'Good morning, Mr Smith. My name is Joan Jones. I am an experienced office equipment salesperson with an in-depth knowledge of the office products industry. Have I caught you at a good time? ... As the number three salesperson in my company, I increased sales in my territory 15 per cent to over £1 million. In the last six months, I won three major accounts from my competitors. The reason I'm calling, Mr Smith, is that I'm looking for a new challenge and, having researched your company, I felt we might have areas for discussion. Are these the types of skills and accomplishments you look for in your staff?'
[Pause.]

Mr Smith: 'Yes, they are. What type of equipment have you been selling?' *[Buy signal!]*

J: 'My company carries a comprehensive range and I sell both the top and bottom of the line, according to my customers' needs. I have been noticing a considerable interest in the latest fax and scanning equipment.' *[You've made it a conversation; you further it with the following.]* 'Has that been your experience recently?'

S: 'Yes, especially in the colour and acetate capability machines.' *[Useful information for you.]* 'Do you have a degree?' *[Buy signal!]*

J: 'Yes, I do.' *[Just enough information to keep him chasing you.]* 'I understand your company prefers degreed salespeople to deal with its more sophisticated clients.' *[Your research is paying off.]*

S: 'Our customer base is very sophisticated and they expect a certain professionalism and competence from us.' *[An inkling of the kind of person they want to hire.]* 'How much experience do you have?' *[Buy signal!]*

J: 'Well, I've worked in both operations and sales, so I have a wide experience base.' *[General but thorough.]* 'How many years of experience are you looking for?' *[Turning it around, but furthering the conversation.]*

> *S:* 'Ideally, four or five for the position I have in mind.' *[More good information.]* 'How many do you have?' *[Buy signal!]*
>
> *J:* 'I have two with this company and one and a half before that. I fit right in with your needs, don't you agree?' *[How can Mr Smith say 'no'?]*
>
> *S:* 'Uhmmm… What's your territory?' *[Buy signal!]*
>
> *J:* 'I cover the metropolitan area. Mr Smith, it really does sound as if we might have something to talk about.' *[Remember, your first goal is the face-to-face interview.]* 'I am planning to take Thursday and Friday off this week. Can we meet then?' *[Make Mr Smith decide what day he can see you, rather than if he will see you at all.]* 'Which would be best for you?'
>
> *S:* 'How about Friday morning? Can you bring a CV?'

Your conversation should proceed with that kind of give-and-take. Your questions show interest, carry the conversation forward and teach you more about the company's needs. By the end of the conversation you have an interview arranged and several key areas to promote when you arrive:

▌ the company sees growth in the latest fax and scanning equipment, especially those with colour and acetate capabilities;

▌ they want business and personal sophistication;

▌ they ideally want four or five years' experience;

▌ they are interested in your metropolitan contacts.

The above is a fairly simple scenario, but, even though it is constructive, it doesn't show you the tricky buy signals that can spell disaster in your job hunt. These are questions that appear to be simple buy signals, yet, in reality, are a part of every interviewer's arsenal called 'knock-out' questions – questions that can save the interviewer time by quickly ruling out certain types of candidates. Although these questions most frequently arise during the initial telephone conversation, they can crop up at the face-to-face interview; the answering techniques are applicable throughout the interview cycle.

Note: We all come from different backgrounds and geographical areas, so understand that while my answers cover correct approaches and responses, they do not attempt to capture the regional and personal flavours of conversation. You and I will never talk alike, so don't learn the example answers parrot fashion. Instead, you should take the essence of the responses and personalize them until the words fall easily from your lips.

Buy signals

'How much are you making/do you want?'

This is a direct question looking for a direct answer, yet it is a knock-out question. Earning either too little or too much could ruin your chances before you're given the opportunity to shine in person.

There are a number of options that could serve you better than a direct answer. First, you must understand that questions about money at this point in the conversation are being used to screen you in or screen you out of the 'ballpark' – the answers you give now should be geared specifically towards getting you in the door and into a face-to-face meeting. (Handling the serious salary negotiations that are attached to a job offer are covered extensively in Chapter 23, Negotiating the offer.) For now, your main options are as follows:

▌ put yourself above the money – 'I'm looking for a job and a company to call home. If I am the right person for you, I'm sure you'll make me a fair offer. What is the salary range for the position?'

▌ give a vague answer – 'The most important things to me are the job itself and the company. What is the salary range for the position?'

▌ you could answer a question with a question – 'How much does the job pay?'

When you are pressed a second time for an exact figure, be as honest and forthright as circumstances permit. Some people – often, unfortunately, women – are underpaid for their jobs when their work is compared with that of others in similar positions. It is not a question of perception; these women in fact make less money than they should. If you have the skills for the job and are concerned that your current low salary will eliminate you before you have the chance to show your worth, you might want to add into your base salary the value of your benefits. If it turns out to be too much, you can then simply explain that you were including the value of your benefits. Alternatively, you could say, 'Mr Smith, my previous employers felt I am well worth the money I earn due to my skills, dedication and honesty. Were we to meet, I'm sure I could demonstrate my value and my ability to contribute to your department. You'd like an opportunity to make that evaluation, wouldn't you?'

Notice the 'wouldn't you?' at the end of the reply. A reflexive question such as this is a great conversation-forwarding technique because it encourages a positive response. Conservative use of reflexive questions can really help you move things along. Watch the sound of your voice, though. A reflexive question can sound pleasantly conversational or pointed and accusatory; it's not really what you say, but how you say it.

Such questions are easy to create. Just conclude with 'wouldn't you?', 'didn't you?', 'won't you?', 'couldn't you?', 'shouldn't you?' or 'don't you?' as appropriate at the end of virtually any statement and the interviewer will almost always answer 'yes'. You have kept the conversation alive and moved it closer to your goal. Repeat the reflexive questions to yourself. They have a certain rhythm that will help you remember them.

'Do you have a degree?'

Always answer the exact question; beware of giving unrequested (and possibly excessive) information. For example, if you have a BA in fine arts from Anytown University, your answer is 'Yes', not 'Yes, I have a BA in fine arts from Anytown University.' Perhaps the company wants an architecture degree. Perhaps the company representative has bad feelings about Anytown University graduates. You don't want to be knocked out before you've been given the chance to prove yourself.

'Yes, I have a degree. What background are you looking for?' Alternatively, you can always answer a question with a question: 'I have a diverse educational background. Ideally, what are you looking for?'

When a degree is perceived as mandatory and you barely scraped through secondary school, don't be intimidated. As Calvin Coolidge used to say, 'The world is full of educated layabouts.' You may want to use the 'Life University' answer. For instance, 'My education was cut short by the necessity of earning a living at an early age. My past managers have found that my life experience and responsible attitude is a valuable asset to the department. Also, I intend to continue my education.'

A small proportion of the more sensitive employers are verifying educational credentials and if yours are checked, it means the employer takes such matters seriously, so an untruth or an exaggeration could cost you a job. Think hard and long before inflating your educational background.

'How much experience do you have?'

Too much or too little could easily rule you out. Be careful how you answer and try to gain time. It is a vague question and you have a right to ask for qualifications.

'Could you help me with that question?' or 'Are you looking for overall experience or in some specific areas?' or 'Which areas are most important to you?' Again, you answer a question with a question. The employer's response, while gaining you time, tells you what it takes to do the job and therefore what you have to say to get it, so take mental notes – you can even write them down if you have time. Then, give an appropriate response.

You might want to retain control of the conversation by asking another question – for example, 'The areas of expertise you require sound very interesting and it sounds as if you have some exciting projects at hand. Exactly what projects would I be involved with in the first few months?'

After one or two buy signal questions are asked, ask for a meeting. Apart from those just outlined, questions asked over the phone tend not to contain traps. If you simply ask, 'Would you like to meet me?' there are only two possible responses: 'yes' and 'no'. Your chances of success are greatly decreased. When you intimate, however, that you will be in the area on a particular date or dates – 'I'm going to be in town on Thursday and Friday, Mr Smith. Which would be better for you?' – you have asked a question that moves the conversation along dramatically. Your question gives the person the choice of meeting you on Thursday or Friday rather than meeting you or not meeting you. By presuming the 'yes', you reduce the chances of hearing a negative and increase the possibility of a face-to-face meeting.

7 *Responding to objections*

Being stonewalled? This chapter shows you how to turn flat statements of no interest into opportunity.

Even with the most convincing word picture, the silence may be broken not by a buy signal, but by an objection. An objection is usually a statement, not a question: 'Send me a CV' or 'I don't have time to see you' or 'You are earning too much' or 'You'll have to talk to HR' or 'I don't need anyone like you right now.'

Although these seem like brush-off lines, often they are really disguised opportunities to get yourself a job offer – handled properly, almost all objections can be converted into interviews. This section will teach you to seize hidden opportunities successfully; notice that all your responses have a commonality with buy signal responses. They all end with a question, one that will enable you to learn more about the reason for the objection, overcome it and, once again, lead the conversation towards a face-to-face interview.

In dealing with objections, as with differences of opinion, nothing is gained by confrontation, though much is to be gained by appreciation of the other's viewpoint. Most objections you hear are best handled by first demonstrating your understanding of the other's viewpoint. Always start your response with 'I understand' or 'I can appreciate your position' or 'I see your point' or 'Of course' followed by 'However' or 'Also consider' or a similar line that puts you back into consideration.

Remember, these responses should not be learnt merely to be repeated. You need to understand and implement their meaning, to understand their concept and put the answers in your own words. Personalize all the suggestions to your character and style of speech.

Objections

'Why don't you send me a CV?'

Danger here. The person you are talking to may be genuinely interested in seeing your CV as a first step in the interview cycle or this may be a polite way of getting you off the phone. You should identify what the real reason is without causing antagonism. At the same time, you want to open up the conversation. A good reply would be, 'Of course, Mr Smith. Would you give me your exact title and the full address?… Thank you. So that I can be sure my qualifications fit your needs, what skills are you looking for in this position?'

Notice the steps:

▌ apparent agreement to start;

▌ a show of consideration;

▌ a question to further the conversation.

Answering in that fashion will open up the conversation. Mr Smith will relay the aspects of the job that are important to him and, with this knowledge, you can sell Smith on your skills over the phone. Also, you will be able to use the information to draw attention to your skills in the future, in:

▌ following conversations;

▌ the covering letter for your CV;

▌ your executive briefing;

▌ your face-to-face meeting;

▌ the follow-up after the meeting.

The information you glean will give you power and increase your chances of receiving a job offer.

'I don't have time to see you'

If the employer is too busy to see you, he or she has a problem and, by recognizing that, perhaps you can show yourself as the one to solve it. You should avoid confrontation, however – it is important that you demonstrate empathy with the speaker. Agree, empathize and ask a question that moves the conversation forward.

'I understand how busy you must be; it sounds like a competent, dedicated and efficient professional [whatever your title is] could be of some assistance. Perhaps I could call you back at a better time, to discuss how I might make you some time. When are you least busy – in the morning or afternoon?'

The person will either make time to talk now or arrange a better time for the two of you to talk further.

Here are some other ideas you could use to phrase the same objection: 'As you are so busy, what is the best time of day for you? First thing in the morning or is the afternoon a quieter time?' or 'I will be in your area tomorrow, so why don't I come by and see you?'

Of course, you can combine the two: 'I'm going to be in your part of town tomorrow and I could drop by and see you. What is your quietest time, morning or afternoon?' By presuming the invitation for a meeting, you make it harder for the person to object. If he or she is truly busy, your consideration will be appreciated and will still make it hard to object.

'You are earning too much'

You should not have brought up salary in the first place. Go straight to jail. If the person you are talking to brought up the matter, that's a buy signal, which was discussed in the last chapter. If the job really doesn't pay enough, you got (as the carnival barker says) close, but no cigar! How to make a success of this seeming dead end is handled in the next chapter. You may also refer to helpful information covered in Chapter 23, Negotiating the offer.

'We only promote from within'

Your response could be, 'I realize that, Mr Smith. Your development of employees is a major reason I want to get in! I am bright, conscientious and motivated. When you do take on people from the outside, what assets are you looking for?'

This response finishes with a question designed to carry the conversation forward and give you a new opportunity to sell yourself. Notice that the response assumes that the company is employing people from outside even though Mr Smith has said otherwise. You have called his bluff, but in a professional, inoffensive manner.

'You'll have to talk to HR'

Your reply is, 'Of course, Mr Smith. Whom should I speak to in HR and what specific position should I mention?'

You cover a good deal of ground with that response. You establish whether or not there is a job there or if you are being fobbed off to HR to waste their time and your own. Also, you move the conversation forward again while changing the thrust of it to your advantage. Develop a specific job-related question to ask while Mr Smith is answering the first question. It can open a fruitful line for you to pursue. If you receive a non-specific reply, probe a little deeper. A simple phrase like, 'That's interesting, please tell me more' or 'Why's that?' will usually do the trick.

Alternatively, you can ask, 'When I speak to HR, will it be about a specific job you have or is it to see if I might fill a position elsewhere in the company?'

Armed with the resulting information, you can talk to HR about your conversation with Mr Smith. Remember to get the name of a specific person with whom to speak and to quote the person you've spoken to already.

EXAMPLE
'Good morning, Mr Johnson. Mr Smith, the Regional Sales Manager, suggested we should speak to arrange an interview.'

That way, you will show HR that you are not a waste of time. As you know someone in the company, you won't be regarded as one of the frequent cold calls they get every day. As the most overworked, understaffed department in a company, they will appreciate that. Most important, you will stand out and be noticed.

Don't look at the HR department as a roadblock; it may contain a host of opportunities for you. Because a large company may have many different departments that can use your talents, HR is likely to be the only department that knows all the openings. You might be able to arrange three or four interviews with the same company for three or four different positions!

'I really wanted someone with a degree'

You could respond to this by saying, 'Mr Smith, I appreciate your position. It was necessary that I start earning a living early in life. If we meet, I am certain you would recognize the value of my additional practical experience.'

You might then wish to ask what the company policy is for support and encouragement of employees taking night classes or other education courses and will naturally explain how you are hoping to find an employer who encourages employees to further their education. Your response will end with 'If we were to meet, I am certain you would recognize the value of my practical experience. I am going to be in your area next week. When would be the best time of day to get together?'

'I don't need anyone like you now'

Short of suggesting that the employer fire someone to make room for you (which, incidentally, has been done successfully on a few occasions), chances of getting an interview with this particular company are slim. With the right question, however, that person will give you a personal introduction to someone else who could use your talents. Asking the right question or series of questions is what networking, and the next chapter, are all about. So, on the occasions when the techniques for answering buy signals or rebutting objections do not get you a meeting, Chapter 8, Getting live leads from dead ends, will!

8 *Getting live leads from dead ends*

Not every company has an opening for you. It's up to you to create leads, though, and there are some excellent questions you can ask that will steer you to opportunities elsewhere.

There will be times when you have said all the right things on the phone, but hear, 'I can't use anyone like you right now.' Not every company has a job opening for you, nor are you right for every job. Sometimes you must accept a temporary setback and understand that the rejection is not one of you as a human being. By using the special interview development questions given in this chapter, though, you should be able to turn those setbacks into job interviews.

The person you are talking to is a professional and knows other professionals in his or her field, in other departments, subsidiaries and even other companies. If you approach the phone presentation in a professional manner, he or she, as a fellow professional, will be glad to advise you on who is looking for someone with your skills. Nearly everyone you call will be pleased to point you in the right direction, but only if you *ask*! And you'll be able to ask as many questions as you wish, because you will be recognized as a colleague intelligently using the professional network. The person also knows that his or her good turn in referring you to a colleague at another company will be returned in the future. As a general rule, companies prefer candidates to be referred this way over any other method.

Do not expect people to be clairvoyant, though. There are two sayings: 'You get what you ask for' and 'If you don't ask, you don't get.' Each is pertinent here.

When you are sure that no job openings exist within a particular department, ask one of the following questions.

▐ 'Who else in the company might need someone with my qualifications?'

▐ 'Does your company have any other divisions or subsidiaries that might need someone with my attributes?'

▐ 'Who do you know in the business community who might have a lead for me?'

▐ 'Which are the most rapidly growing companies in the area?'

▐ 'Whom should I speak to there?'

▐ 'Do you know anyone at the ABC Electronics Company?'

▐ 'When do you anticipate there being an opening in your company?'

▐ 'Are you planning any expansion or new projects that might create an opening?'

▐ 'When do you anticipate change in your manpower needs?'

Each one of these interview development questions can gain you an introduction or lead to a fresh opportunity. The questions have not been put in any order of importance – that is for you to do. Take a sheet of paper and, looking at the list, figure out what question you would ask if you had time to ask only one. Write it down. Do that with the remaining questions on the list. As you advance, you will develop a comfortable set of prioritized questions. Add questions of your own. For instance, the type of computer or word-processing equipment a company has might be important to some professions but not to others, and the person you speak to might be able to lead you to companies that have your machines. Be sure that any question you add to your list is specific and leads to a job opening. Avoid questions like, 'How's business these days?' Time is valuable and time is money to both of you. When you're satisfied with your list of interview development questions, put them on a fresh sheet of paper and store it safely with your telephone presentation and CV.

Those interview development questions will lead you to a substantial number of jobs in the hidden job market. You are getting referrals from the 'in' crowd who know who is hiring whom long before that news is generally circulated. By being in with the 'in' crowd, you establish a very effective referral network.

When you get leads on companies and specific individuals to talk to, be sure to thank your benefactor and ask to use his or her name as an introduction. The answer, you will find, will always be 'yes', but asking shows you to be someone with manners – in this day and age, that alone will set you apart.

You might also suggest to your contact that you leave your telephone number in case he or she runs into someone who can use you. You'll be surprised at how many people call back with a lead.

With personal permission to use someone's name on your next networking call, you have been given the greatest of job search gifts: a personal introduction. Your call will begin with something like, 'Hello, Ms White, my name is Jack Jones. Joseph McDonald recommended I give you a call. By the way, he sends his regards.' [Pause for any response to this.] 'He felt we might have something valuable to discuss.'

Follow up on every lead you get. Too many people become elated at securing an interview for themselves and then cease all effort to generate additional interviews, believing a job offer is definitely on its way. Your goal is to have a choice of the best jobs in town and without multiple interviews, there is no way you'll have that choice. Asking interview development questions ensures that you are tapping all the secret recesses of the hidden job market.

Networking is a continuous cycle. Make a commitment to sell yourself, make telephone calls, make a referral network and recognize buy signals and objections for what they really are – opportunities to shine. Make a commitment to ask interview development questions at every seeming dead end – they will lead you to all the jobs in town.

9 *The telephone interview*

In this electronic age, interviewers use the telephone to weed out applicants. Your goal is a face-to-face meeting, so use these methods to achieve it.

The first substantive contact with a potential employer is virtually always by telephone. Even in the age of e-mail, phone contact remains extremely important.

It happens in one of three ways:

▌ you are networking and the person you are talking to goes into a screening process immediately because you have aroused his or her interest;

▌ a company calls unexpectedly as a result of a CV you have sent and catches you off-guard;

▌ you or a headhunter who has agreed to take you on has set up a specific time for a telephone interview.

Whatever circumstance creates the telephone interview, you must be prepared to handle the questioning and use every means at your disposal to win the real thing you want – the face-to-face meeting. The telephone interview is the trial run for the face-to-face and is an opportunity you must not bumble; your happiness and prosperity may hinge on it.

This, the first contact with your future employer, will test your mental preparation. Remember: you can plant in your mind any thought, plan, desire, strategy or purpose and translate it into reality. Put your goal down on paper and read it aloud to yourself every day, because the constant reiteration will crystallize your aims, and clear goals provide the most solid base of preparation.

Being prepared for a telephone interview takes organization. You never know when a company is going to call once you have started networking and sending your CV out (the word gets around more quickly than you think if it's one that impresses). Usually the call comes at the worst of times, such as 8 am on a Monday when you are sleeping late or 4 pm, just as you return from walking the dog. You can avoid being caught completely off-guard by keeping your CV and alphabetized company dossiers by the telephone.

The most obvious (and often most neglected) point to remember is this: during the interview, the person from the company has only ears with which to judge you, and that is something you must overcome. Here are some tips.

▌ **Take a surprise call in your stride.** If you receive a call as a result of a CV you sent or a telephone message you left and you are unprepared, be calm. Sound positive, friendly and collected: 'Thank you for calling, Mr Smith. Would you wait just a moment while I close the door?' Put the phone down, take three deep breaths to slow your heart down, pull out the appropriate company dossier and your CV, put a smile on your face (it improves the timbre of your voice) and pick up the phone again. Now you are in control of yourself and the situation.

▌ **Beware of over-familiarity.** You should always refer to the interviewer by his or her surname until invited to do otherwise.

▌ **Allow the person on the phone to do most of the talking** – to ask most (but not all) of the questions. Keep up your end of the conversation – this is, after all, a sales presentation, so be sure to ask a few questions of your own that will reveal you as an intelligent person and provide you with the opportunity to promote your candidacy. For example, ask what immediate projects the interviewer's department is involved in or the biggest challenges that are being tackled. When the interviewer answers your question, you will either have a clear picture of how to sell yourself or you will ask a follow-up question for clarification. For example, 'What specific skills and personality traits do you think are necessary for a person to succeed with those challenges?' Everyone wants to employ a problem solver – find the problem and you are already halfway towards the offer.

■ **Beware of giving yes/no answers.** They give no real information about your abilities.

■ **Be factual in your answers.** You should be brief yet thorough.

■ **Speak directly into the telephone.** Keep the mouthpiece about one inch from your mouth. Do not smoke or eat while on the phone. Numbered among the mystical properties of our telephone system is its excellence at picking up and amplifying background music and voices, especially young ones. That is excelled only by its power to transmit the sounds of food or gum being chewed or smoke being inhaled or exhaled. Smokers, take note: there are no laws about discriminating against smokers and therefore, all non-smokers naturally discriminate. They will assume that even if you don't actually light up at the interview, you'll have been chain-smoking beforehand and will carry the smell with you as long as you are around. Taking no chances, they probably won't even give you a chance to get through the door once they hear you puffing away over the phone.

■ **Take notes.** They will be invaluable to you in preparing for the face-to-face meeting. Were it not for the recent furore over the clandestine use of tape recorders, I would have recommended that you buy a cheap tape recorder and a phone attachment from your local electronics shop and tape the whole conversation. If, for any reason, the person you are speaking is interrupted, jot down the topic under discussion. When he or she gets back on the line, you can helpfully recap, 'We were just discussing...' That will be appreciated and set you apart from the others.

The person from the company may talk about the business and, from the dossier in front of you, you will also know facts about the outfit. A little flattery goes a long way – admire the company's achievements and you are, in fact, admiring the interviewer. Likewise, if any areas of common interest arise, comment on them and agree with the interviewer when possible – people take on people like themselves.

If the interviewer does not give you the openings you need to sell yourself, be ready to salvage the situation and turn it to your advantage. Have a few work-related questions prepared – for example, 'What exactly will be the three major responsibilities in this job?' or 'What will be the first job I get my teeth into?' While you are getting the explanation, wait for a pause so that you can tell the interviewer your appropriate skills: 'Would it be of value if I described my experience in the area of office management?' or 'Then my experience in word processing should be a great help to you' or 'I recently completed an accounting project just like that.'

Under no circumstances, though, should you ask about the money you want or benefits and holidays; that comes later.

Remember that your single objective at this point is to sell yourself and your skills; if you don't do that, you may never get the face-to-face interview.

The telephone interview has come to an end when you are asked if you have any questions. Ask any more questions that will improve your understanding of the job requirements. If you haven't asked before, now is the time to establish what projects you would be working on in the first six months. By discovering them now, you will have time before the face-to-face meeting to package your skills to the needs at hand and create the appropriate executive briefing.

If you have not already asked or been invited to meet the interviewer, now is the time. Take the initiative: 'It sounds like a very interesting opportunity, Ms Smith, and a situation where I could definitely make a contribution. The most pressing question I have now is, when can we get together?' (*Note: Even though the emphasis throughout has been on putting things in your own words, do use the phrase 'make a contribution'. It shows that you take pride in your work – a key personal trait.*)

Once the details are confirmed, finish with this request: 'If I need any additional information before the interview, I would like to feel free to get back to you.' The person you've been speaking to will naturally agree. No matter how many questions you get answered in the initial conversation, there will always be something you forgot. This allows you to call again to satisfy any curiosity, which will also enable you to increase rapport. Don't take too much advantage of it, though: one well-placed phone call that contains two or three considered questions will be appreciated; four or five phone calls will not.

Taking care to ascertain the correct spelling and pronunciation of the interviewer's name shows your concern for the small but important things in life – it will be noticed. This is also a good time to establish who else will be interviewing you, their titles and how long the meeting is expected to last.

Follow with a casual enquiry as to what direction the meeting will take. You might ask, 'Would you tell me some of the critical areas we will discuss on Thursday?' The knowledge gained will help you to package and present yourself and allow you time to bone up on any weak or rusty areas.

It is difficult to evaluate an opportunity properly over the telephone. Even if the job doesn't sound right, go to the interview. It will give you practice and the job may look better when you have more facts. You might even discover a more suitable opening elsewhere within the company when you go to the face-to-face interview.

10 Dressing for interview success

If you don't look the part, don't expect an offer. Here are guidelines for men's and women's suits, shirts, shoes, neckwear, accessories, jewellery, overcoats, make-up and personal hygiene.

The moment we set eyes on someone, our minds make evaluations and judgments with lightning speed. The same is true for the potential employers who must assess us.

What you see is what you get!

'If a candidate can't put himself together in a professional manner, why should you assume he can put it all together on the job? Unless you look the part, don't expect an offer!' It may sound harsh, but that's an accurate summary of most employers' feelings on this issue. It's a fair estimate that 9 out of 10 of today's employers will reject an unsuitably dressed applicant without a second thought. Similarly dispiriting odds confront those who expect promotions but wear less than appropriate attire on the job. Like it or not, your outward image, attitude, confidence level and overall delivery are all affected by the clothes you wear.

The respect you receive at the interview is in direct proportion to the respect your visual image earns for you before you have the chance to say a word. If you wear clothes that are generally associated with leisure activities, you may be telling those who see you that you do not take your career seriously and therefore are not committed to your work. By the same token, if you report for work the first day on a new job wearing clothes that undercut your perceived effectiveness, personal skills and professionalism,

it will be hard for you to be seen as a major contributor – no matter what you do between nine and five.

Employers rarely make overt statements about acceptable dress
codes to their employees, much less to interviewees; more often
there is an unspoken dictum that those who wish to climb the
professional career ladder will dress appropriately and those who
don't, won't.

There are some areas of employment where on-the-job dress
(as opposed to interview dress) is somewhat less conservative
than in the mainstream – fashion, entertainment and advertising
are three examples. In these and a few other fields, there is a good
deal of leeway with regard to personal expression in workplace
attire, but for most of us, our jobs and our employers require a certain minimal level of professionalism in our dress. Interviewees
must exceed these standards. That is not to say that you must
dress like the Chairman of the Board (although that probably
won't hurt), but you should be aware that dressing for the Friday
night party (or even 'dress down Friday') on the day of your
interview is not in your best professional interests. For the interview, it is generally accepted that you should dress one or two
levels up from the job you are applying for, while remaining consistent with the type occupation it is within.

Dressing sharp: your interviewing advantage

Our appearance tells people how we feel about ourselves as
applicants, as well as how we feel about the interviewer(s), the
company and the process of interviewing itself. By dressing professionally, we tell people that we understand the niceties of corporate life and send a subtle 'reinforcing' message that we can, for
example, be relied on to deal one-to-one with members of a company's prized client base.

More to the point, the correct image at an interview will give
you a real edge over your competition. In fact, your overall
appearance and presentation may even leave a more tangible
impression than the words you say, as memory is rooted most
strongly in pictures and impressions. At the very least, you can
expect what you say to be strongly influenced in the mind of your

interviewer by the way you present yourself – if he or she likes the look of you, he or she will listen to what you have to say.

Of course, the act of taking time to present an attractive professional image before your interview will add to your own sense of self-esteem and confidence, too. That is perhaps the greatest advantage of all. Therefore, it is important that your professional dress code matches your own personal flavour. You must feel comfortable and 'yourself' in what you wear in order to present a confident image. As G Bruce Boyer, fashion editor for *GQ* and *Esquire* magazines in the United States so aptly puts it, 'The whole idea of individualized clothing is devoted to personal comfort. But what we have always been conscious of is that individuality and comfort are not the enemies of propriety and appropriateness. In the end the clothes that make sense are the ones that bring together the public and private person. Individuality, propriety and comfort can be nicely brought together in a good-fitting, well-made suit.'

The look

The safest look for both men and women at interviews is traditional and conservative. Look at investing in a 'good-fitting, well-made' suit as your first step to a successful new career. Up until recent years, this was fairly easy for men, as their professional fashions tended not to change much from year to year. These days, men's fashions are experiencing a metamorphosis, with high-fashion designers offering affordable lines of updated, yet professionally acceptable looks. However, a man can always interview with confidence and poise in his three-year-old good-quality suit, provided that it isn't worn to a shine.

For women, the matter is a little more complicated. Appropriate female attire for the interview should ideally reflect the current fashion if the applicant is to be taken seriously. Moreover, in selecting her current professional look the female applicant must walk a fine line, combining elements of both conformity (to show she belongs) and panache (to show a measure of individuality and style).

The key for both sexes is to dress for the position you want, not the one you have. This means that the upwardly mobile profes-sional might need to invest in the clothes that project the desired image. The employee who dresses like one of the corporate walk-ing wounded is unlikely to move upwards. Positions of responsi-bility are awarded to those who demonstrate that they are able to shoulder the burden. Looking capable will inspire others with the confidence to give you the most visible challenges.

The correct appearance alone probably won't get you a job offer, but it will go a long way towards winning attention and respect. When you know you look right, you can stop worrying about the impression your clothes are making and concentrate on communicating your message.

To be sure, every interview and every interviewer is different; because of this, it isn't possible to set down rigid guidelines for exactly what to wear in each situation. There is, however, relevant broadly based counsel that will help you make the right decision for your interview.

As we have seen, much of what we believe about others is based on our perception of their appearance. This chapter will help you ensure that you are perceived as practical, well-man-nered, competent, ethical and professional.

General guidelines

Appropriate attire, as we have noted, varies from industry to industry. The university professor can sport tweed jackets with elbow patches on the job, but is, nevertheless, likely to wear a suit to an interview. The advertising executive may wear wild ties as a badge of creativity (that is what he is being paid for), but he, too, is likely to dress more conservatively for an interview. In all instances, our clothes are sending a message about our image, and the image we want to convey is one of reliability, trustwor-thiness and attention to detail.

Most of us are far more adept at recognizing the dress mistakes of others than at spotting our own sartorial failings. When we do look for a second opinion, we often make the mistake of asking only a loved one. It's not that spouses, lovers and parents lack taste; these people are, however, more in tune with our positive qualities than the rest of the world and so, frequently, they do not recognize how essential it is to reflect those qualities in our dress. Better candidates for evaluation of your interview attire are trusted friends who have proved their objectivity in such matters or even a colleague at work.

Whenever possible, find out the dress code of the company you are visiting. For example, if you are an engineer applying for a job at a high-tech company, a blue three-piece suit might be overpowering. It is perfectly acceptable to ask someone in HR about the dress code (written or informal) of the company. You may even want to make an anonymous visit to get a sense of the corporate style of the company. In the above example, you might be perfectly comfortable showing up *for work* in a jacket or blazer; nevertheless, you are advised to wear a suit for at least the first interview.

You may simply decide to change your look somewhat after learning that there is a more informal atmosphere with regard to dress at the firm you visit. If you are told that everyone works in shirt-sleeves and that there is never a tie in sight, a prudent and completely acceptable approach is to opt for your less formal suit, rather than dark blues, greys or pinstripes. One final piece of advice: be wary of 100 per cent synthetic garments. Their sheen can make them unattractive and they often retain body odour despite many washings.

Men

Following are the best current dress guidelines for men preparing for a professional interview.

Men's suits

The most acceptable colours for men's suits are navy through to medium-dark blue and charcoal through to light grey, followed by brown and, at some distance, beige (except in summer when a lightweight beige suit is fine, especially at second or third interviews). Preferably, the fabric should be 100 per cent (or a high percentage) wool; wool looks and wears better than any other suit material. The darker the suit, the more authority it carries, but, beware, a man should *not* wear a black suit to an interview unless applying for an undertaker's job. Pinstripes are acceptable, so long as the stripes themselves are muted and very narrow. Of the plain colours, dark grey, navy or medium-dark blue are equally acceptable. In fact, many feel that a dark plain-coloured suit is the best option, because it gives authority to the wearer and is less intimidating than a pinstripe suit. Equally as important, the colour of your suit should complement your own colouring and should be one *you* feel comfortable wearing.

Above all, it's the quality and fit of your suit that matter. Fashions change, but the fit and cut must complement your own build. Whatever style you choose, it should be fairly classic. There should be no pull at the jacket shoulders, no gape at the back, the cuffs should break just at your wrists. Your trousers should fit comfortably at the waist and there should be only a slight break at the hemline. Trousers without turnups are a height enhancer!

Men's shirts

The principles here are simple:

▌ Rule 1: always wear a long-sleeved shirt.

▌ Rule 2: always wear a white, cream or pale-blue shirt.

▌ Rule 3: never violate rules 1 or 2.

By white, I do not mean to exclude, for instance, shirts with very thin red or blue pinstripes: these white shirts are acceptable, although not really first rate. There is something about a pure white shirt that conveys honesty, intelligence and stability; it should be your first choice. It is true that artists, writers, engineers and other creative types are sometimes known to object to white shirts; for them pale blue may be the best option. Remember that the paler and more subtle the shade, the better the impression you will make. Pale colours draw attention and your collar is right next to your face, which is where we want the interviewer to stay focused.

While monograms are common enough, those who don't like them usually feel strongly about the implied ostentation of stylized initials on clothing. If you can avoid it, don't take the chance of giving your interviewer the opportunity to find fault in this area. (On the other hand, if the choice facing you is between wearing your monogrammed shirt or pulling out the old Motley Crue tee-shirt, then what you should do is clear, and so should be your conscience.)

Cotton shirts look better and hold up to perspiration more impressively than their synthetic counterparts. Make sure yours is flawlessly ironed. A cotton and polyester blend can be an acceptable alternative, but keep in mind that the higher the cotton content, the better the shirt will look. While these blend shirts wrinkle less easily, you are advised to ignore the 'wash-and-wear-no-need-to-iron' claims you'll read on the front of the packaging when you purchase them. Experience has shown that any shirt you wear to an interview must be ironed.

Make sure your shirt fits properly; the collar should fit the neck properly, the sleeve cuff ends just at the wrist. Details such as frayed fabric and loose buttons will not go unnoticed when you are under professional scrutiny.

Men's neckwear: ties

While an expensive suit can be ruined by a cheap-looking tie, the right tie can do a lot to pull the less-than-perfect suit together for a professional look. When you can't afford a new suit for an interview, you can upgrade your whole look with the right tie.

A pure silk tie makes the most powerful professional impact, has the best finish and feel and is easiest to tie well. Linen or cotton ties are too informal, wrinkle too easily and may only be worn during warmer weather. (What's more, they can only be tied once between cleanings because they wrinkle so easily.) A wool tie is casual in appearance and has knot problems. Man-made fibres are shiny, make colours look harsh when you want them to look subtle and may undercut your professional image. A pure silk tie or a 50–50 wool and silk blend (which is almost wrinkle-proof) should be your choice for the interview.

The tie should complement your suit. This means that there should be a physical balance. The rule of thumb is that the width of your tie should approximate the width of your lapels. The prevailing standard, which has held good for many years now, is that ties can range in width between 7 and 9 cm (2.75 and 3.5 in). Wearing anything wider may mark you out as someone still trapped in the disco era.

Choose an appropriate tie that neither vanishes into nor does battle with your suit pattern. The most popular and safest styles are found within the categories of plain colours, smallish dots, stripes and paisleys.

Do not wear ties with large polka dots, pictures of animals such as leaping trout or soaring mallards or sporting symbols such as golf clubs. Avoid wearing any piece of apparel that has a manufacturer's symbol emblazoned on the front as part of the decoration.

Other considerations include the length of the tie (it should, when tied, extend to your trouser belt), the size of the knot (smaller is better) and if you should wear a bow tie to an interview (you shouldn't).

Men's shoes

Shoes should be either black or brown leather. Stay away from all other materials and colours – they are too risky.

Plain or brogue lace-ups are the most conservative choice and are almost universally acceptable. Slightly less conservative, but equally appropriate, are smart slip-on shoes – not deck shoes. The slip-on, even one with a tassel, is versatile enough to be used for both day and evening business wear. (Some lace-ups can look a bit cloddish at dinner.)

Men's socks

Socks should complement your suit. Accordingly, they should be blue, black, grey or brown. They should also be long enough for you to cross your legs without showing off lots of bare skin and should not fall in a bunch towards the ankle as you move.

Men's accessories

The right accessories can enhance the professional image of any applicant, male or female; the wrong accessories can destroy it.

The guiding principle here is to include nothing that could conceivably be misconstrued or leave a bad impression. Never, for instance, should you wear religious or political insignia in the form of rings, ties or pins. If you would not initiate a conversation about such topics at a job interview (and you shouldn't), why send smoke signals asking your interviewer to do so? The watch you wear should be simple and plain. This means Mickey Mouse is out, as are sports-oriented and Swatch-style watches. No one is impressed by digital watches these days; don't be afraid to wear a simple analogue model with a leather strap. (Besides, you don't want people wondering if you can really tell the time, do you?) Avoid cheap-looking pseudo-gold watchbands at all costs.

Your briefcase, if you carry one, can make a strong professional statement about you. Leather makes the best impression, while all other materials follow far behind. Black, brown and deep burgundy are the colours of choice. The case itself should be plain, although some very expensive models offer a host of embellishments that only detract from the effect you want.

Having a plain white cotton or linen handkerchief in your trouser pocket is a good idea. It can also be used to relieve the clammy hands syndrome so common before the interview – anything to avoid the infamous 'wet fish' handshake! However, avoid the matching tie and pocket handkerchief look at all costs. It's hideous and inappropriate for a professional interview.

Belts should match or complement the shoes you select. Accordingly, a blue, black or grey suit will require a black belt and black shoes, while brown or beige suits call for brown. With regard to materials, stick with plain leather. The most common mistake made with belts is the buckle: an interview is not the place for your favorite Harley-Davidson, Grateful Dead or Bart Simpson buckle. Select a small, simple buckle that doesn't overwhelm the rest of your look.

Men's jewellery

Men may wear a wedding ring, if applicable, and a small pair of subdued cufflinks (if wearing double cuffs, of course). Anything more is dangerous. Other kinds of rings – much less bracelets, neck chains, earrings or medallions – can send the wrong message. Tie tack and clips are passé.

Men's overcoats

The safest and most utilitarian colours for overcoats are taupe and navy; stick to these two exclusively. If you can avoid wearing an overcoat, do so (it's an encumbrance and adds to clutter).

Women

Following are the best current dress guidelines for women preparing for a professional interview.

Women's suits

You have more room for creativity in this area than men do, but also more room for mistakes. Until recent years, your professional fashion creativity had to remain within certain accepted guidelines created not by the fashion industry, but by the consensus of the business world, which, alas, tends to trail behind the rest of us. While there are still the limits of good taste and necessary conservatism for the interviewee, the fashion designers have worked hard to create workable professional alternatives for the ever-growing female workforce.

A woman's business wardrobe need no longer be simply a pseudo-male selection of drab grey skirts and blouses. (Recent advice that women should avoid pinstripes or ties is dated. With the right cuts, pinstripes and ties or scarves can look both stylish and professional.)

Wool and linen are both accepted as the right look for professional women's suits, but there is a problem. Linen wrinkles so quickly that you may feel as though you leave the house dressed for success and arrive at your destination destined for bag-lady-hood. Cotton and polyester blends are great for warm climates: they look like linen but lack the 'wrinklability' factor. Combinations of synthetics and natural fabrics do have their advantages: suits made of such materials will certainly retain their shape better. The eye trained to pay attention to detail, however (read: your interviewer's), may well detect the type of fabric – say, a cheap polyester blend – and draw unwarranted conclusions about your personality and taste. The choice is up to you; if you do opt for natural fabrics, you will probably want to stay with wool. It provides the smartest look of all and is most versatile and rugged. There are wonderful ultra-light wool fabrics available now that will take you through the toughest interview, even on the hottest summer day.

While men are usually limited to either plain or pinstripe suits, a woman can add to this list the varied category of tartans and checks. The Prince of Wales tartan, for instance, is attractive and utterly acceptable for businesswomen. A plain-coloured skirt with a coordinating subtle tartan or checked jacket is also acceptable, but make sure there is not too much contrast or it will detract from the focus of your meeting: the interview. Colours most suitable for interview suits include charcoal, medium grey, steel grey, black and navy blue. Of all these looks, the cleanest and most professional is the simple plain-coloured navy or grey suit with a white blouse.

Jackets should be simple, well-tailored and stylish, but not stylized. This is probably not the time to wear a peplum-style jacket; a standard length that falls just at the hips is preferable. The cut and style should flatter your build and reflect your personal style, without detracting from what you have to say. Attention to details, such as smooth seams, even hemlines, correctly hanging linings and well-sewn buttons, is essential.

How long a skirt should you wear? Any hard-and-fast rule I could offer here would be in danger of being outdated almost immediately, as the fashion industry demands dramatically different looks every season in order to fuel sales. (After all, keeping the same hemlines would mean that last season's clothes could last another season or two.) It should go without saying that you don't want to sport something that soars to the upper thigh if you want to be taken seriously as an applicant. Your best bet is to dress somewhat more conservatively than you would if you were simply showing up for work at the organization in question. Hemlines rise and fall and, while there is some leeway as to what is appropriate for everyday wear on the job, the safest bet is usually to select something that falls just at or no more than 5 cm (2 in) above the knee.

Increasingly popular is the shift dress with a matching jacket. This outfit is particularly useful for the business day into evening crowd, but can be perfectly suitable for interviews if it is impeccably styled and fitted. It is particularly important to stick with tasteful and not too loud plain colours for this look.

Blouses

With regard to blouses, long sleeves will project the authoritative, professional look you desire. Three-quarter-length sleeves are less desirable and they are followed in turn by short sleeves. Never wear a sleeveless blouse to an interview. (You may be confident that there is absolutely no chance that you will be required to remove your jacket, but why take the risk?)

Plain colours and natural fabrics (particularly cotton and silk) are the best selections for blouses. Combinations of natural and synthetic fabrics, while wrinkle-resistant, do not absorb moisture well.

The acceptable colour spectrum is wider for blouses than for men's shirts, but it is not limitless. The most prudent choices are still white or cream as these offer a universal professional appeal. Pale pink, soft yellow or light blue can also work, but should be worn only if they fully blend into your overall look. Light colours are friendly and draw attention to your face, yet will not distract the interviewer from what you have to say. The blouse with a front-tie bow has become dated; a classic, softened shirt collar works best with a suit. The button-down collar always looks great, particularly if you are interviewing with a conservative company or industry.

Women's neckwear: scarves

While a woman might choose to wear a string of pearls instead of a scarf to an interview, the scarf can still serve as a powerful status symbol. A good outfit can be ruined by a cheap-looking scarf. Opting to wear a scarf means that it will be saying something dramatic about you: make sure it's something dramatically positive. A pure silk scarf will offer a conservative look, a good finish and be easy to tie. Some of the better synthetic blends achieve an overall effect that is almost as good. While some books on women's clothing will recommend buying blouses that have matching scarves attached to the collar, there is an increasingly vocal lobby of stylish businesswomen who feel this is the equivalent of mandating that a man wear a clip-on bow tie. As with men's ties, the objective is to complement the outfit, not match it. Avoid overly flamboyant styles and stick with the basics: plain colours, fine silk, small polka dots or paisleys and always in subtle colours that will complement, not compete with, your outfit or your conversation.

Women's shoes

Female applicants have a greater colour selection for footwear than do their male counterparts. Shoes should preferably be leather, but, in addition to brown and black, a woman is safe wearing navy, burgundy, forest green or even, if circumstances warrant, red. The colour of your shoes should always be the same or a darker tone than your skirt.

It is safest to stay away from faddish or multicoloured shoes (even such classics as two-toned court shoes or slingbacks). There are two reasons for this. First, all fashion is transitory and, even if you are up to date, you cannot assume that your interviewer is. Second, many interviewers are male and thus likely to exhibit an inability to appreciate vivid colour combinations. As with the rest of your wardrobe, stay away from radical choices and opt for the easily comprehensible professional look.

Heel height is important, as well. Flat shoes are fine; a shoe with a heel of up to about 6 cm (2.5 in) is perfectly acceptable. Stay away from high heels: at best you will wobble slightly and at worst you will walk at an angle. The pump or court shoe, with its closed toe and heel, is perhaps the safest and most conservative look. A closed heel with a slightly open toe is acceptable, too, as is the slingback shoe with a closed toe. The toe on any style should not be overly pointed.

Stockings or tights

These should not make a statement of their own. Neutral skin tones are the safest, most conservative choice, though you are perfectly within the realms of professional etiquette wearing sheer white or cream if it complements your blouse or dress. You may be able to make an exception if you are interviewing for a job in the fashion industry, in which case you might coordinate the colour with your outfit, but be very sure of the company standard already in place. Even in such an instance, avoid loud or glitzy looks.

Tights and stockings are prone to developing ladders at the worst possible moment. Keep an extra pair in your bag or briefcase.

Women's accessories

Because a briefcase is a symbol of authority, it is an excellent choice for the female applicant. Do not, however, bring both your bag and a briefcase to the interview. (You'll look awkward juggling them around.) Instead, transfer essential items to a small clutch bag you can store in the case. In addition to black, brown and burgundy (recommended colours for the men), you may include navy and taupe as possible colours for your case. Whatever you choose, it should be free of expensive and distracting embellishments.

With regard to belts, the advice given for men holds for women as well. Belts should match or complement the shoes you select, so a black or grey suit will require a black belt and black shoes, while brown, tan or beige suits will call for brown, and navy looks best with navy or burgundy accessories. Remember that the belt is a functional item; if it is instantly noticeable, it is wrong.

Women's jewellery

As far as jewellery goes, less is more. A woman should restrict rings to engagement or wedding bands if these are applicable, but she can wear a necklace and earrings, as long as these are subdued and professional-looking. Keep them small, discreet and in good taste. Avoid fake or strangely coloured pearls, anything with your name or initials on it and earrings that are large or dangle a long way or jangle. In addition, a single bracelet on a woman's wrist is acceptable; anything around the ankle is not. Remember, too much of the wrong kind of jewellery can keep a woman from receiving an offer she might otherwise receive or inhibit her promotional opportunities once on the team, so, if you like this sort of thing, keep it for when you are going out.

Women's make-up

Take care never to appear overly made-up. Natural is the key word. Eye make-up should be subtle, so as not to overwhelm the rest of the face. As a general rule, I advise using very little lipstick at an interview as it can cause negative reactions in some interviewers and because it can smudge and wear off as the hours wear on. (Who can say, going in, how long the meeting will last?) However, you might feel you look pale and washed out without lipstick. So, if you feel 'undressed' without it, use some; but apply it sparingly and carefully, using a subdued colour.

For men and women: a note on personal hygiene

It should go without saying that bad breath, dandruff, body odour and dirty, unmanicured nails have the potential to undo all your efforts at putting across a good first impression. These and related problems denote an underlying professional slovenliness, which an interviewer will feel is likely to reflect itself in your work. You want to show yourself to be appealing, self-respecting and enjoyable to be around. You can't do that if the people you meet with have to call on exceptional powers of self-control in order to stay in the same room with you.

Don't ask yourself if any friend or colleague has actually come out and suggested that you pay more attention to these matters; ask yourself how you felt the last time you had to conduct business of any sort with a person who had a hygiene problem. Then resolve never to leave that kind of impression.

11 *Body language*

Learn to control negative body movements and employ positive ones. Discover the seven guidelines for good body language during an interview.

Given the choice of going blind or going deaf, which would you choose?

If you are like 9 out of 10 other people, you would choose to go deaf. The vast majority of us rely to a remarkable degree on our ability to gather information visually. This really is not all that surprising. While speech is a comparatively recent development, humans have been sending and receiving non-verbal signals from the dawn of the species.

In fact, body language is one of the earliest methods of communication we learn after birth. We master the spoken word later in life and, in so doing, forget the importance of non-verbal cues. However, the signals are still sent and received (usually at a subconscious level), even if most of us discount their importance.

It is common to hear people say of the body language they use, 'Take me or leave me as I am.' This is all very well if you have no concern for what others think of you. For those seeking professional employment, however, it is of paramount importance that the correct body language be utilized. If your mouth says 'Give me the job', but your body says something quite different, you are likely to leave the interviewer confused. 'Well,' he or she will think, 'the right answers all came out, but there was something about that candidate that just rubbed me the wrong way.' Such misgivings are generally sufficient to keep any candidate from making the shortlist.

When we are in stressful situations (and a job interview is certainly right there in Stress Hell), our bodies react accordingly. The way they react can send unintentional negative messages. The interviewer may or may not be aware of what causes the concern, but the messages will be sent and our cause will suffer.

Of course, interviewers can be expected to listen carefully to what we say, too. When our body language doesn't contradict our statements, we will generally be given credence. When our body language complements our verbal statements, our message will gain a great deal of impact. When our body language *contradicts* what we say, though, it is human nature for the interviewer to be sceptical. In short, learning to control negative body movements during an interview – and learning to use positive body signals – will greatly increase the chances of job interview success.

Under the microscope

What is the interviewer watching us for during the interview? The answer is: clues. The mystery for the interviewer is what kind of an employee we would make. It is incumbent on us to provide not just any old clues but the ones most likely to prompt a decision to offer us the job.

Let's begin at the beginning. When we are invited to an interview, we are probably safe in assuming that our interviewer believes we meet certain minimum standards and could conceivably be wanting to give the job to us. Otherwise, why take the time to interview? Once in the door, we can assume that we will be scrutinized in three main areas:

■ ability – whether or not we can do the job;

■ willingness – if we will do the job;

■ manageability – if we will be a pleasure or a pain to have around.

Appropriate control and use of our gestures can help us emphasize positive features of our personality in these key areas – and also project integrity, honesty, attention to detail and the like.

The adage that actions speak louder than words appears to be something we should take quite literally. Studies done at the

University of Chicago found that over 50 per cent of all effective communication relies on body language. As we can expect interviewers to respond to the body language we employ at the interview, it is up to us to decide what messages we want them to receive.

There are also studies that suggest that the impression we create in the first few minutes of the interview is the most lasting. As the first few minutes after we meet the interviewer is a time when he or she is doing the vast majority of the talking, we have very little control over the impression we create with our words – we can't say much of anything! It is up to our bodies, then, to do the job for us.

The greeting

Giving a 'dead fish' handshake will not advance your candidacy; neither will the opposite extreme, the iron-man bonecrusher grip.

The ideal handshake starts before the meeting actually occurs. Creating the right impression with the handshake is a three-step process. Be sure that:

1. your hands are clean and adequately manicured;

2. your hands are warm and reasonably free of perspiration – there are several ways to ensure the first, including washing your hands in warm water just before the interview or holding your hand close to your cheek for a few seconds, and in the second applying a little talcum powder;

3. the handshake itself is executed professionally and politely, with a firm but not too tight grip, and a warm smile.

Remember that if you initiate the handshake, you may send the message that you have a desire to dominate the interview; this is not a good impression to leave with a potential boss. Better to wait a moment and allow the interviewer to initiate it. (If for any reason you do find yourself initiating the handshake, do not pull back; if you do, you will appear indecisive. Instead, make the best of it, smile confidently and make good eye contact.)

The handshake should signal cooperation and friendliness. Match the pressure extended by the interviewer – never exceed it. Ideally, the handshake should last for between three and five seconds, and should 'pump' no more than six times. (The parting handshake may last a little longer. Smile and lean forward very slightly as you shake hands before departing.)

Certain cultural and professional differences should be considered with regard to handshakes, as well. Many doctors, artists and others who do delicate work with their hands can and do give less enthusiastic handshakes than other people. Similarly, the English handshake is considerably less firm than the American, while the German variety is more firm.

Use only one hand; always shake vertically. Do not extend your hand parallel to the floor, with the palm up, as this conveys submissiveness. By the same token, you may be seen as being too aggressive if you extend your flat hand outwards with the palm facing down.

Taking your seat

Some thirty inches from my nose
The frontier of my person goes.
Beware of rudely crossing it;
I have no gun, but I can spit.

With apologies to W H Auden

Encroaching on another's 'personal space' is a bad idea in any business situation, but it is particularly dangerous in an interview. The 76 cm (30 in) standard is a good one to follow. It is the distance that allows you to extend your hand comfortably for a handshake. Maintain this distance throughout the interview and be particularly watchful of intrusions during the early stages when you meet, greet and take a seat.

Applying this principle may seem simple enough, but how often have you found yourself dodging awkwardly in front of someone to take a seat before it has been offered? A person's office is an extension of sorts of his or her personal space. This is why it is not only polite but also sound business sense to wait until the interviewer offers you a seat.

It is not uncommon to meet with an interviewer in a conference room or other supposedly 'neutral' site. Again, wait for the interviewer to motion you to a spot or, if you feel uncomfortable doing this, tactfully ask the interviewer to take the initiative: 'Where would you like me to sit?'

Facial/head signals

Once you take your seat, you can expect the interviewer to do most of the talking. You can also probably expect your nervousness to be at its height. Accordingly, you must be particularly careful about the non-verbal messages you send at this stage.

Now, while all parts of the body are capable of sending positive and negative signals, the head (including the eyes and mouth) is under closest scrutiny. Most good interviewers will make an effort to establish and maintain eye contact, so you should expect that whatever messages you are sending from the facial region will be picked up, at least on a subliminal level.

Our language is full of expressions testifying to the powerful influence of facial signals. When we say that someone is tight-lipped, has a furrowed brow, flashes bedroom eyes, stares into space or grins like a Cheshire cat, we are speaking in a kind of shorthand and using a set of stereotypes that enables us to make judgements – consciously or unconsciously – about the person's abilities and qualities. Those judgements may not be accurate, but they are usually difficult to reverse.

Tight smiles and tension in the facial muscles often tell of an inability to handle stress; little eye contact can communicate a desire to hide something; pursed lips are often associated with a secretive nature; and frowning, looking sideways or peering over one's glasses can send signals of haughtiness and arrogance. Hardly the stuff of which winning interviews are made!

The eyes

Looking at someone means showing interest in that person, and showing interest is a giant step forward in making the right impression. (Remember, each of us is our own favourite subject!)

Your aim should be to stay with a calm, steady and non-threatening gaze. It is easy to mismanage this, so you may have to prac-tise a bit to overcome the common hurdles in this area. Looking away from the interviewer for long periods while he is talking, closing your eyes while being addressed and repeatedly shifting focus from the subject to some other point are likely to leave the wrong impression.

Of course, there is a big difference between looking and staring at someone! Rather than looking at the speaker straight-on at all times, create a mental triangle incorporating both eyes and the mouth; your eyes will follow a natural, continuous path along the three points. Maintain this approach for roughly three-quarters of the time. You can break your gaze to look at the interviewer's hands as points are emphasized or refer to your notepad. These techniques will allow you to leave the impression that you are attentive, sincere and committed. Staring will only send the mes-sage that you are aggressive or belligerent.

Be wary of breaking eye contact too abruptly and of shifting your focus in ways that will disrupt the atmosphere of profes-sionalism. Examining the interviewer below the head and shoul-ders, for instance, is a sign of overfamiliarity. (This is an especially important point for men to keep in mind when being interviewed by a woman.)

The eyebrows send messages as well. Under stress, our brows may wrinkle; as we have seen, this sends a negative signal about our ability to handle challenges in the business world. The best advice on this score is simply to take a deep breath and collect yourself. Most of the tension that people feel at interviews has to do with anxiety about how to respond to what the interviewer will ask. As a reader of this book, you will be prepared with cred-ible responses for even the toughest queries, so relax.

The head

Rapidly nodding your head can leave the impression that you are impatient and eager to add something to the conversation – if only the interviewer would let you. Slower nodding, on the other hand, emphasizes interest, shows that you are validating the comments of your interviewer and subtly encourages him or her to continue. Tilting the head slightly, when combined with eye contact and a natural smile, demonstrates friendliness and approachability. The tilt should be momentary and not exaggerated, almost like a bob of the head to one side. (Do not overuse this technique!)

The mouth

One guiding principle of good body language is to turn upwards rather than downwards. Look at two boxers after a fight. The loser is slumped forwards, brows knit and eyes downcast, while the winner's smiling face is thrust upwards and outwards. The victor's arms are raised high, his back is straight, his shoulders are square. In the first instance, the signals we receive are those of anger, frustration, belligerence and defeat; in the second, happiness, openness, warmth and confidence.

Your smile is one of the most powerful positive body signals in your arsenal; it best exemplifies the up-is-best principle, as well. Offer an unforced, confident smile as frequently as opportunity and circumstances dictate. _Avoid at all costs_ the technique some applicants use – grinning idiotically for the length of the interview, no matter what. This will only communicate that you are either insincere or not quite on the right track.

It's worth remembering that the mouth provides a seemingly limitless supply of opportunities to convey weakness. This may be done by touching the mouth frequently (and, typically, unconsciously); 'faking' a cough when confronted with a difficult question; and/or gnawing on one's lips absentmindedly. Employing any of these 'insincerity signs' when you are asked about, say, why you lost your last job, will confirm or instil suspicions about your honesty and effectiveness.

Glasses

Those who wear glasses sometimes leave them off when going to an interview in an attempt to project a more favourable image. There are difficulties with this approach. The first is that many of those who don't wear their glasses will (unwittingly) seem to stare long and hard at the people they converse with and this, as we have seen, is a negative signal. The second problem is that peering over the top of your glasses – even if you wear reading glasses and have been handed something to read and subsequently asked a question – carries professorial connotations that are frequently interpreted as critical. (If you wear glasses for reading, you should remove them when conversing, replacing them only when appropriate.)

Wearing dark glasses to an interview will paint you as secretive, cold and devious. Even if your prescription glasses are tinted, the effect will be the same. Try to obtain non-tinted glasses for your interview. Contact lenses, of course, solve all these problems – and could save you the possible embarrassment of remembering you've left your reading specs in the HR office as you are handed blueprints for comments in the Boardroom.

Body signal barricades

Folding or crossing your arms or holding things in front of the body is a wonderful way to send negative messages to the interviewer. The signal is, essentially, 'I know you're there, but you can't come in. I'm nervous and closed for business.'

It is bad enough to feel this way, but worse to express it with blatant signals. Don't fold your arms or 'protect' your chest with hands, clipboard, briefcase or anything else during the interview. (These positions, in fact, should be avoided in any and every business situation.)

Hands

As we have seen, a confident and positive handshake breaks the ice and gets the interview moving in the right direction. Proper use of the hands throughout the rest of the interview will help to convey an above board, 'nothing to hide' message.

Watch out for hands and fingers that take on a life of their own, fidgeting with themselves or other objects, such as pens, paper or your hair. Pen tapping is interpreted as the action of an impatient person; this is an example of an otherwise trivial habit that can take on immense significance in an interview situation. Rarely will an interviewer ask you to stop doing something annoying. Instead, he or she'll simply make a mental note that you are an annoying person and be glad this has been picked up before you have become an employee.

Negative hand messages are legion. Some of the most dangerous are listed below.

- You can demonstrate smugness and superiority by clasping your hands behind your head. You may also expose any perspiration marks that are under your arms.

- A man can show insecurity by simply adjusting his tie, but that's not the worst of it. When interviewing with a woman, this gesture will show he has something other than a businesslike interest in her.

- Slouching in your chair, with hands in pockets or thumbs in belt, can brand you as insolent and aggressive. When this error is made in the presence of an interviewer of the opposite sex, it carries sexually aggressive overtones as well. (Beware, too, of sending these signals while you are walking on a tour of the facility.)

- Pulling your collar away from your neck for a moment may seem like an innocent enough reaction to the heat of the day, but the interviewer might assume that you are tense and/or masking an untruth. The same goes for scratching the neck during, before or after your response to a question.

- Moving the hands towards a feature one perceives as deficient is a common unconscious reaction to stress. A man with thinning hair, for example, may thoughtlessly put his hand to his forehead when pondering how to respond to the query, 'Why aren't you earning more at your age?' This habit may be extremely difficult for you to detect in the first place, much less reverse, but make the effort. Such protective movements are likely to be perceived – if only on a subliminal level – as acknowledgments of low status.

- Picking at invisible bits of fluff on one's suit looks like what it is: a nervous tic. Keep your focus on the interviewer. If you do have some bit of lint somewhere on your clothing, the best advice is usually to ignore it rather than call attention to it by brushing it away.

By contrast, employing the hands in a positive way can further your candidacy. Here are a couple of the best techniques.

▌ Subtly exposing your palms now and then as you speak can help to demonstrate that you are open, friendly and have nothing to hide. The technique is used to great effect by many politicians and television talk show hosts. Watch for it.

▌ When considering a question, it can sometimes be beneficial to 'steeple' your fingers for a few seconds as you think and when you first start to talk. Unless you hold the gesture for long periods of time, it will be perceived as a neutral demonstration of your thoughtfulness. Of course, if you overuse this or hold the position for too long, you may be thought of as condescending. Steepling will also give you something constructive to do with your hands; it offers a change from holding your pad and pen.

Seating

The signals you send with your body during an interview can be affected by the type of chair you sit on. If you have a choice, go with an upright chair with arms. Deep armchairs can restrict your ability to send certain positive signals and encourage the likelihood of negative ones. They're best suited to watching television, not for projecting the image of a competent professional.

There is only one way to sit during an interview: bottom well back in the chair and back straight. Slouching, of course, is out, but leaning slightly forwards will show interest and friendliness towards the interviewer. Keep your hands on the sides of the chair. If there are no arms on the chair, keep your hands in your lap or on your pad of paper.

Crossed legs, in all their many forms, send a mixture of signals; most of them are negative:

▌ Resting one ankle on the other knee can show a certain stubborn and recalcitrant outlook (as well as the bottom of your shoe, which is not always a pretty sight). The negative signal is intensified when you grasp the horizontally crossed leg or, worst of all, cross your arms across your chest.

▌ Crossed ankles have often been assumed to indicate that the person doing the crossing is withholding information. However, some dress fashions encourage decorous ankle crossing. Of course, as the majority of interviews take place across a desk, crossed ankles will often be virtually unnoticeable. The best advice on this body signal is that it is probably the most permissible barrier you can erect; if you must allow yourself one body language vice, this is the one to choose.

▌ When sitting in armchairs or on sofas, crossing the legs may be necessary to create some stability amid all the plush upholstery. In this instance, the signals you send by crossing your legs will be neutral, as long as your crossed legs point towards, rather than away from, the interviewer.

Feet

Some foot signals can have negative connotations. Women and men wearing slip-on shoes should beware dangling the loose shoe from the toes. This can be quite distracting and, as it is a gesture often used to signal physical attraction, has no place in a job interview. Likewise, avoid compulsive jabbing of floor, desk or chair with your foot. This can be perceived as a hostile and angry motion and is likely to annoy the interviewer.

Walking

Many interviews will require that you walk from point A to point B with the interviewer, either on a guided tour of facilities or to move from one office to another. Of course, if you are interviewing in a restaurant, you will have to walk with your interviewer to and from where you are dining. How long these walks last is not as important as how you use them to reinforce positive traits and impressions.

Posture is the first concern. Keep your shoulders back, maintain an erect posture, smile and make eye contact when appropriate. Avoid fidgeting with your feet as you move, rubbing one shoe against the other or kicking absentmindedly at the ground as you stand. These signals will lead others to believe that you are anxious and/or insecure. Crossing your arms or legs while standing carries the same negative connotations as it does when you are sitting. Putting your hands in your pockets is less offensive – assuming you don't jangle keys or coins – but men must be careful not to employ the hands-on-hips or thumbs-in-belt postures discussed earlier. These send messages that they are aggressive and dominating.

Seven signals for success

So far we have focused primarily on the pitfalls to avoid, but what messages should be sent and how? Here are seven general suggestions on good body language for an interview.

1. Walk slowly, deliberately and tall on entering the room.

2. On greeting your interviewer, give (and, hopefully, receive) a friendly 'eyebrow flash' – that brief, slight raising of the brows that calls attention to the face, encourages eye contact and, when accompanied by a natural smile, sends a strong, positive signal that the interview has got off to a good start.

3. Use mirroring techniques. In other words, make an effort – subtly – to reproduce the positive signals your interviewer sends. Of course, you should never mirror negative body signals. Say the interviewer leans forwards to make a point. A few moments later, you lean forwards slightly in order to hear better. Say the interviewer leans back and laughs; you 'laugh beneath' the interviewer's laughter, taking care not to overwhelm your partner by using an inappropriate volume level. This technique may seem contrived at first, but you will learn that it is far from that, if only you experiment a little.

4. Maintain a naturally alert head position, keeping your head up and your eyes facing front at all times.

5. Remember to avert your gaze from time to time so as to avoid the impression that you are staring. When you do so, look confidently and calmly to the right or to the left; never look down.

6. Do not hurry any movement.

7. Relax with every breath.

Putting it all together

We have discussed the individual gestures that can either improve or diminish your chances of success at the interview. Working in our favour is the fact that positive signals reinforce one another; employing them in combination yields an overwhelming positive message that is truly greater than the sum of its parts. Now it is time to look at how to combine the various positive elements to send a message of competence and professionalism.

Here is the best posture to aim for during the interview.

■ Sit well back in the chair, allowing the back of it to support you and help you sit upright.

■ Increase the impression of openness ('I have nothing to hide!') by unbuttoning your jacket as you sit down.

■ Keep your head up and maintain eye contact a good proportion of the time, especially when the interviewer begins to speak and when you reply.

■ Smile naturally whenever the opportunity arises.

■ Avoid folding your arms – it is better to keep them on the arms of your chair.

■ Remember to show one or both of your palms occasionally as you make points, but do not overuse this gesture.

Open for business

The more open your body movements during the interview, the more you will be perceived as open yourself. Understanding and directing your body language will give you added power to turn interviews into cooperative exchanges between two professionals.

Just as you interpret the body language of others, both positive and negative, so your body language makes an indelible impression on those you meet. It tells them if you like and have confidence in yourself, whether or not you are pleasant to be around and whether you are more likely to be honest or deceitful. Like it or not, our bodies carry these messages for the world to see.

Job interviews are reliable in terms of one thing: they bring out insecurities in those who must undergo them. All the more reason to consciously manage the impressions the body sends!

12 *The curtain goes up*

First impressions are the strongest. Here are the small preparations you can make before you walk into the interviewer's office.

Backstage in the theatre, the announcement 'Places, please' is made five minutes before the curtain goes up. It's the performers' signal to psych themselves up, complete final costume adjustments and make time to reach the stage. They are getting ready to go on stage and knock 'em dead. You should go through a similar process.

Winning that job offer depends not only on the things you do well but also on the absence of things you do poorly. As the interview date approaches, settle down with your CV and the exercises you performed in building it. Immerse yourself in your past successes and strengths. This is a time for building confidence. A little nervousness is perfectly natural and healthy, but channel the extra energy you have in a positive direction by beginning your physical and mental preparations.

First, you should assemble your interview kit.

▌ **The company dossier**

▌ **Two or three copies of your CV and executive briefing – one for you and one or two for the interviewer** It is perfectly all right to have your CV in front of you at the interview; it shows that you are organized. It also makes a great cheat sheet (after all, the interviewer is using it for that reason) – you can keep it on your lap during the interview with pad and pencil. It is not unusual to hear, 'Mr Jones wasn't given the job because he didn't pay attention to detail and could not even remember his employment dates.' Those are just the kinds of things you are likely to forget in the heat of the moment.

■ **A pad of paper and writing instruments** These articles have a twofold purpose. They demonstrate your organization and interest in the job and they give you something constructive to do with your hands during the interview. Bring along a blue or black ballpoint pen for filling out applications.

■ **Contact telephone numbers** If you get detained on the way to the interview, you can call and let the person you are going to meet know.

■ **Reference letters** Take the sensible precaution of gathering these from your employers on the off-chance that they are requested.

■ **A list of job-related questions** During the interview is the time when you gather information to evaluate a job (the actual evaluation comes when you have an offer in hand). At the end of the interview, you will be given the opportunity to ask additional questions. Develop some questions that help you understand the job's parameters and potential. You might ask, 'Why is the job open?' 'Where does the job lead?' 'What is the job's relationship to other departments?' 'How do the job and the department relate to the corporate mission?'

For a longer list of questions along those lines that it might be valuable to ask, see Chapter 23, Negotiating the offer. Understand, though, that some of those will obviously only be appropriate in the context of a serious negotiation talk. You can also find good questions to ask in the answer to 'Do you have any questions?' at the end of Chapter 15, How to knock 'em dead.

■ **Any additional information you have about the company or the job.** If time permits, ask the interviewer's secretary to send you some company literature. Absorb whatever you can.

■ **Directions to the interview.** Decide on your form of transportation and finalize your time of departure. Check the route, distance and travel time. Write it all down legibly and put it with the rest of your interview kit. If you forget to verify date, time and place (including floor and room number), you might not even arrive at the right place or on the right day for your interview.

First impressions are the strongest you make and they are based on your appearance. There is only one way to dress for the first meeting: clean-cut and conservative. You may or may not see yourself that way, but how *you* see yourself is not important now – your only concern is how *others* see you. As you could be asked to appear for an interview at a scant couple of hours notice, you must be in a constant state of readiness. Keep your best two suits freshly pressed, your shirts or blouses wrinkle-free and your shoes polished. If possible, don't wear these outfits unless you are interviewing.

Here are some more tips:

▌ regardless of sex or hairstyle, get a trim once a month;

▌ while a shower or bath prior to an interview is most desirable and the use of an unscented deodorant advisable, the wearing of after-shave or perfume should be avoided – you are trying to get a job, not a date;

▌ you should never drink alcohol the day before an interview – it affects eyes, skin colour and your wits;

▌ nails should be trimmed and manicured at all times, even if you work with your hands.

To arrive at an interview too early indicates overanxiousness; to arrive late is inconsiderate. The only sensible solution is to arrive at the interview on time, but at the location early. That allows you time to visit the toilets and make the necessary adjustments to your appearance. Take a couple of minutes in this temporary sanctuary to perform your final mental preparations:

▌ review the company dossier;

▌ recall the positive things you will say about past employers;

▌ breathe deeply and slowly for a minute – this will dispel your natural physical tension;

▌ repeat to yourself that the interview will be a success and that afterwards the interviewer will wonder how he or she ever managed without you;

▌ smile and head for the interview.

Under no circumstances back out because you do not like the receptionist or the look of the office – that would be allowing interview nerves to get the better of you. As you are shown into the office, you are on!

This potential new employer wants a confident and dynamic employee, but someone who is less confident and dynamic than he or she is, so take your lead from the interviewer. Do:

▌ give a firm handshake – once is enough;

▌ make eye contact and smile, saying, 'Hello, Mrs Smith, I am John Jones. I have been looking forward to meeting you.'

Do not:

▌ use first names, unless asked;

▌ smoke, even if invited;

▌ sit down, until invited;

▌ show anxiety or boredom;

▌ look at your watch;

▌ discuss equal rights, sex, race, national origin, religion or age;

▌ show samples of your work, unless requested;

▌   ask about benefits, salary or holidays;

▌   assume a submissive role – treat the interviewer with respect, but as an equal.

Now you are ready for anything – except for the tough questions that are going to be thrown at you next.

Part III

Great Answers to Tough Interview Questions

This section tells you not only what to answer but also how to answer. It provides the real preparation for getting the job you want and deserve.

'Like being on trial for your life' is how many people look at a job interview. They are probably right. With the interviewer as judge and jury, you are at least on trial for your livelihood. Therefore, you must lay the foundation for a winning defence. F Lee Bailey, one of the United States' most celebrated defence attorneys, attributes his success in the courtroom to preparation. He likens himself to a magician going into court with 50 rabbits in his hat, not knowing which one he'll really need, but ready to pull out any single one. Bailey is successful because he is ready for any eventuality. He takes the time to analyse every situation and every possible option. He never underestimates his opposition. He is always prepared. F Lee Bailey usually wins.

Another famous attorney, Louis Nizer, successfully defended all of his 50-plus capital offence clients. When lauded as the greatest courtroom performer of his day, Nizer denied the accolade. He claimed for himself the distinction of being the *best prepared*.

You won't win your day 'in court' just based on your skills. As competition for the best jobs increases, employers are comparing more and more applicants for every opening and asking more and more questions. To win against stiff competition, you need more than just your merits. When the race is close, the final winner is, as often as not, picked for a comparative lack of negatives when ranged against the other contenders. Like Bailey and Nizer, you can prove to yourself that the prize always goes to the best prepared.

During an interview, employers ask you dozens of searching questions – questions that test your confidence, poise and desirable personality traits. Questions that trick you into contradicting yourself. Questions that probe your quick thinking and job skills. They are all designed so that the interviewer can make decisions regarding some critical areas.

▌ Can you do the job?

▌ Will you complement or disrupt the department?

▌ Are you willing to take the extra step?

▌ Are you manageable?

▌ Is the money right?

Notice that only one of the critical areas has anything to do with your actual job skills. Being able to do the job is only a small part of getting an offer. Whether you will fit in and make a contribution or not and if you are manageable are just as important to the interviewer. Those traits that companies probe for during the interview are the same that will mark a person for professional growth when on board. In this era of high unemployment and high specialization, companies become more critical in the selection process and look more actively for certain traits, some of which cannot be ascertained by a direct question or answer. Consequently, the interviewer will seek a pattern in your replies that shows your possession of such traits – I discuss them in detail in the next chapter.

The time spent 'in court' on trial for your livelihood contains four deadly traps:

▌ failure to listen to the question;

▌ annoying the interviewer by answering a question that was not asked;

▌ providing superfluous information – you should keep answers brief, thorough, and to the point;

▌ attempting the interview without preparing for it.

The effect of such blunders is cumulative, and each reduces your chances of receiving a job offer.

The number of offers you win in your search for the ideal job depends on your ability to answer a staggering array of questions in terms that have value and relevance to the employer, such as 'Why do you want to work here?', 'What are your biggest accomplishments?', 'How long will it take you to make a contribution?', 'Why should I employ you?', 'What can you do for us that someone else cannot do?', 'What is your greatest weakness?', 'Why aren't you earning more?' and 'What interests you least about this job?' are just some of the questions you will be asked.

The examples of answers to these kinds of questions in the following chapters come from across the job spectrum. Though the examples of answers might come from the mouth of an administrator, while you are a scientist or in one of the service industries, the commonality of all job functions in contributing to the bottom line will help you draw the correct parallel for your job.

You will also notice that each example teaches a small yet valuable lesson in good business behaviour – something you can use both to get the job and make a good impression when you are on board.

Remember, the answers provided in the following chapters should not be repeated word for word, exactly as they come off the page. You have your own style of speech (not to mention your own kind of business experience), so try to put the answers in your own words.

13 The five secrets of securing a job offer

Knowing how an interviewer thinks is a critical element of the job search that is too frequently overlooked.

Before we examine the 'dos and don'ts' advice on interviewing contained in the next chapter, it's a good idea to review the interview process from the employer's perspective. As we have observed, there is a fallacy that all that is necessary for success at the interview is for you to show that you have what it takes to do the job. There's a lot more to it than that.

The first secret: ability and suitability

Saying, 'Hey, I can do this job – give me a shot and I'll prove it to you' is not enough any more. Today you have to *prove* your ability and suitability.

Every working professional has a combination of skills that broadly defines his or her ability and suitability. How well you program that computer, service that client or sew up that appendix is part of the picture; knowing the steps involved well enough *to be able to explain them clearly and simply to others* is another part.

Itemize your technical/professional skills as they parallel the requirements of the job. Then recall an incident to illustrate each of those skills. When you have done this, and not before, you will be in a position to begin justifying your ability and suitability to an employer.

If you are applying for a job in an industry with which you are familiar, you should also consider highlighting your industry sensibilities. Industry sensibilities means knowing 'how we do things here.' For example, a good computer programmer working in a bank has technical and professional skills – that is, the ability to program a computer is required by the employer. That same programmer has knowledge of how to get things done in the industry in which he or she operates – that is, the ability to work well with bankers, which is quite different from being able to work well with, say, television fundraisers.

Demonstrating both professional/technical *and* industry skills will set you apart from the vast majority of candidates. Show that you understand these combinations and you will stand out from the pack.

The second secret: willingness

You may find your interviewer asking you such questions as, 'Are you willing to make tea and coffee?' or, if you are in a small office, 'Are you willing to wash up or answer the phones?' You may want to ask if these duties are part of your job description, but doing so may lose you the opportunity to demonstrate your readiness to pitch in with any task. These questions are being used more and more by potential employers who want to gauge *willingness* – and have no intention of having you brew the perfect cup of tea or coffee.

The issue isn't whether or not you are prepared to do demeaning tasks. It is whether or not you are the kind of person who is prepared to do whatever it takes to help the team survive and prosper. Can you take the rough with the smooth? Are you prepared to go that extra mile? You are? Great. Think of a time when you did. Figure out how your doing so helped the company. Now rehearse the story until you can tell it in about 90 seconds.

The third secret: manageability and teamwork

There isn't a manager in the world who enjoys a sleepless night caused by an unmanageable employee. Avoiding such nights is a major concern for managers, who develop, over time, a remarkable sixth sense when it comes to spotting and weeding out mavericks.

Manageability is defined in different ways:

▌ the ability to work alone;

▌ the ability to work with others;

▌ a willingness to work with others regardless of their sex, age, religion, physical appearance, abilities or disabilities, skin colour or national origin;

▌ the ability to take direction and criticism when it is carefully and considerately given;

▌ last, but perhaps dearest to the manager's heart, the ability to take direction when it *isn't* carefully and considerately given, often because of a crisis.

Such 'manageability' considerations make a job interview tricky. Yes, you should certainly state your strongly held convictions – after all, you don't want to appear wishy-washy – but you should do so *only* as long as they are professional in nature and relate to the job at hand.

Let me give you an example of what I mean. A number of people have asked me about what they perceive as discrimination as a result of their being born-again Christians. However, each discussion invariably ends in the conclusion that a job interview is simply no place to bring up personal beliefs. Today's managers will usually go well out of their way to avoid even the perception of intolerance towards sincerely held spiritual beliefs. Yet, by the same token, they are deeply suspicious of any strident religious rhetoric that surfaces in a professional setting. (This also holds true of political, ethnic or other inappropriate issues raised by a candidate during an interview.) The potential employer's caution in these circumstances, far from representing discrimination, is a sign of concern that the candidate might not be tolerant of the views of others and might thereby become an obstacle to a harmonious work group.

The rules here are simple. Don't bring up religious, political or racial matters during the job interview. Even a casual reference to such topics can put a potential employer on the spot as he or she could subject the company to a lawsuit if a racial or religious topic is perceived as having influenced an employment decision. The interview is a potential payslip; don't mess with it.

You're a team player, someone who gets along well with others and has no problem tolerating other opinions or beliefs. Demonstrate that with your every word and action.

The fourth secret: professional behaviour

I emphasize *professional* behaviour throughout this book because, to a large extent, the traits that are most desirable to employers are learnt and developed as a result of our experiences in the workplace.

As you will see in Chapter 15, there are 20 universally admired behavioural traits common to successful people in all fields. Once you review them, you will no doubt find that they are important to you, too, as just understanding what they are will give you up to 20 unique points to make about your candidacy. However, understanding the traits is only part of the secret.

Harry works in imports and exports. He reads the list of traits, comes across the category 'Determination' and thinks, 'Yeah, that's me. I'm a determined guy.' On its own, though, he knows this is not enough. Then Harry recalls the time he came in over the weekend to clear the warehouse in time to make room for the 20-ton press due in Monday morning at 7 am. When he tells this story to the interviewer, he gets a lot further than he would if he simply said, 'Give the job to me; I'm determined.' Instead of a bland, unsubstantiated claim that would be forgotten almost the instant it left Harry's mouth, the interviewer gets a mental film of the event that's hard to forget: Harry coming in at the weekend to make room for that press. Actually, the interviewer *really* sees something much more important, namely, Harry applying the same level of determination and extra effort on behalf of the interviewer's company.

Simple statements don't leave any lasting impression on employers. Anecdotes that prove a point do.

The fifth secret: everyone employs people for the same job

Surprised? Here's another: No one in the history of industry and commerce has ever been added to a payroll for the love of mankind.

Regardless of job or profession, we are all, at some level, *problem solvers*. That's the first and most important part of the job description for anyone who has ever been taken on for any job, at any level, in any organization, anywhere in the world. This fifth secret is absolutely key to job hunting and career success in any field.

Think of your profession in terms of its problem-solving responsibilities. Once you have identified the particular problem-solving business you are in, you will have gone a long way towards isolating what the interviewer will want to talk about. Identify and list for yourself the typical problems you tackle for employers on a daily basis. Come up with plenty of specific examples. Then move on to the biggest and dirtiest problems you've been faced with. Again, recall specifically how you solved them.

Here's a technique used by HR professionals to help people develop examples of their problem-solving skills and the resultant achievements.

❚ **State the problem** What was the situation? Was it typical of your job or had something gone wrong? If the latter, be wary of apportioning blame.

❚ **Isolate relevant background information** What special knowledge or education were you armed with to tackle this dilemma?

❚ **List your key qualities** What professional skills and personal behaviour traits did you bring into play to solve the problem?

❚ **Recall the solution** How did things turn out in the end? (If the problem did not have a successful resolution, do not use it as an example.)

▌ **Determine what the solution was worth** Quantify the solution in terms of money earned, money saved or time saved. Specify your role as a team member or as a lone gun, as the facts demand.

With an improved understanding of what employers seek in employees, you will have a better understanding of yourself and what you have to offer in the way of specific problem-solving abilities. If you follow the steps outlined above, you will develop a series of illustrative stories for each key area. Remember, stories help interviewers visualize you solving *their* problems, as a paid member of the team.

Here's a story for you. It's based on a real-life interview pattern, although the names are fictional.

Mr Wanton Grabbit, 80-year-old senior partner at the revered law firm of Sue, Grabbit, and Runne, ran a 'wanted' advertisement in the paper for a word processing specialist. He was looking for someone with five years' experience in word processing and the same amount working in a legal environment. He also wanted someone with experience in using the office computer system.

Grabbit interviewed 10 candidates with exactly the experience the advertisement demanded. Each of them came away from the interview convinced that a job offer was imminent. None of them got the job. The person who did get the job had *three* years of experience and had never before set foot inside a law office.

Sue Sharp, the successful candidate, understood the fifth secret and asked a few intelligent questions of her own during the interview. Specifically, she asked, 'What are the first projects I will be involved with?' This led Mr Grabbit to launch into a long discourse on his desire to see the law firm rush headlong into the modern world. The first project, he explained, would be to load the firm's approximately 4,000 manual files on to the computer system.

Now, although Sue had never worked in a law firm before, she had, at her last job, automated a cumbersome manual filing system. Having faced the *problem* before, even though she had done so in the 'wrong' setting, she was able to demonstrate an understanding of the challenges the position presented. Furthermore, she was able to tell the illustrative stories from her last job that enabled Mr Grabbit to see her, in his mind's eye, tackling and solving his immediate, specific, short-term problems successfully.

We get two very special benefits when we understand and apply the fifth secret. First, we show that we possess the problem-solving abilities of a first-rate professional in the field. Second, when we ask about the problems, challenges, projects, deadlines and pressure points that will be tackled in the early months, we show that we will be able to hit the ground running on those first critical projects.

Integrate the five secrets as you read the following chapters. You will reap the rewards, while your competition will have to resign themselves to harvesting sour grapes.

14

Welcome to the real world

For the school or college leaver or graduate, here are some tough questions specifically tailored to discover your business potential.

Of all the steps a recent school or college leaver or graduate will take up the ladder of success over the years, none is more important or more difficult than getting a foot on the first rung. The interviewing process designed for recent graduates is particularly rigorous because management regards the taking on of entry-level professionals as one of its toughest jobs.

When a company employs experienced people, there is a track record to evaluate. With recent graduates, there is little or nothing. Often, the only solid things an interviewer has to go on are examination results. That's not much on which to base an employment decision – the results don't tell the interviewer whether or not you will fit in or make a reliable employee. Many recruiters liken the gamble of employing recent school and college leavers and graduates to laying down wines for the future: they know that some will develop into full-bodied, reliable vintages, but that others will be disappointments. So, recruiters have to find different ways to predict your potential accurately.

After relying, as best they can, on performance in exams to evaluate your ability, interviewers concentrate on questions that reveal how willing you are to learn and get the job done and how manageable you are likely to be, both on average days and when the going gets rough.

Your goal is to stand out from all the other entry-level candidates as someone altogether different and better. For example, don't be like thousands of others who, in answer to questions about their greatest strength, reply lamely, 'I'm good with people' or 'I like working with others.' As you know by now, such answers do not separate you from the herd. In fact, they brand you as average. To stand out, you must recount a past situation that illustrates exactly how good you are with people or one that demonstrates an ability to be a team player.

Fortunately, the key personality traits discussed throughout the book are just as helpful for getting your foot on the ladder as they are for aiding your climb to the top. They will guide you in choosing what aspects of your personality and background you should promote at an interview.

It isn't necessary to have snap answers ready for every question, because you never will. In fact, it is more important for you to pause after a question and collect your thoughts before answering: you must show that you think before you speak. That way, you will demonstrate your analytical abilities, which age feels youth has in short supply.

By the same token, occasionally asking for a question to be repeated is useful to gain time and is quite acceptable, as long as you don't do it with every question. If a question stumps you, as sometimes happens, do not stutter incoherently. It is sometimes best to say simply, 'I don't know' or you might say, 'I'd like to come back to that later' – the odds are even that the interviewer will forget to ask again; if he or she doesn't, at least you've had some time to come up with an answer.

Knowing everything about a certain entry-level position is not necessary, because business feels it can teach you most things. However, as a vice-president of Merrill Lynch once said, 'You must bring to the table the ability to speak clearly.' So, knowing what is behind those questions designed especially for entry-level applicants will give you the time to build informative and understandable answers.

'How did you get your summer jobs?'

All employers look favourably on recent graduates who have any work experience, no matter what it is. 'It is far easier to get a fix on someone who has worked while at school,' says Dan O'Brien, head of employment at Grumman. 'They manage their time better, are more realistic and more mature. Any work experience gives us much more in common.' So, as you make your answer, add that you learnt that business is about making a profit, doing things more efficiently, adhering to procedures and putting in whatever effort it takes to get the job done. In short, treat your summer jobs, no matter how humble, as any other business experience.

With this particular question, the interviewer is looking ideally for something that shows initiative, creativity and flexibility. Here's an example: 'In my town, summer jobs were hard to come by, but I applied to each local restaurant for a position waiting tables, called the manager at each one to arrange an interview and finally landed a job at one of the most prestigious. I was assigned to the afternoon shift, but with my quick work, accurate billing and ability to keep customers happy, they soon moved me to the evening shift. I worked there for three summers and, by the time I left, I was responsible for the training and management of the night-shift waiters, the allotment of tips and the evening's final closing and accounting. All in all, my experience showed me the mechanics of a small business and of business in general.'

'Which of the jobs you have held have you liked least?'

The interviewer is trying to trip you up. It is likely that your work experience contained a certain amount of repetition and drudgery, as all early jobs in the business world do. So, beware of saying that you hated a particular job 'because it was boring'. Avoid the negative and say something along these lines: 'All of my jobs had their good and bad points, but I've always found that if you want to learn, there's plenty to be picked up every day. Each experience was valuable.' Then describe a seemingly boring job, but show how it taught you valuable lessons or helped you hone different aspects of your personality profile.

'What are your future vocational plans?'

This is a fancy way of asking, 'Where do you want to be five years from now?' The trap all entry-level professionals make is to say, 'In management' because they think that shows drive and ambition. It has become such a trite answer, though, that it immediately generates a string of questions that most recent graduates can't answer. What is the definition of management? What is a manager's prime responsibility? A manager in what area?

Your safest answer identifies you with the profession you are trying to break into and shows you have your feet on the ground. 'My vocational plans are that I want to get ahead. To do that I must be able to channel my energies and expertise into those areas my industry and employer need. So, in a couple of years I hope to have become a thorough professional with a clear understanding of the company, the industry and where the biggest challenges, and therefore opportunities, lie. By that time, my goals for the future should be sharply defined.' An answer like that will set you far apart from your contemporaries.

'What university did you attend and why did you choose it?'

The university you attended isn't as important as your reasons for choosing it – the question is trying to examine your reasoning processes. Emphasize that it was your choice and that you didn't go there as a result of your parents' desires or because generations of your family have always gone there. Focus on the practical. 'I went to X University in London – it was a choice based on practicality. I wanted a university that would give me a good education and prepare me for the real world. It has a good record for turning out students fully prepared to take on responsibilities in the real world. It is [or isn't] a big university, but/and it has certainly taught me some big lessons about the value of [whatever personality values apply] in the real world of business.'

If the interviewer has a follow-up question about the role your parents played in selection of your college or university, be wary – he or she is plumbing your maturity. It is best to reply that the choice was yours, though you did seek the advice of your parents once you had made your selection and that they supported your decision.

'Are you looking for a permanent or temporary job?'

The interviewer wants reassurance that you are genuinely interested in the position and won't disappear in a few months to pursue postgraduate studies in Paris. Try to go beyond saying simply 'yes'. Explain why you want the job. You might say, 'Of course, I am looking for a permanent job. I intend to make my career in this field and I want the opportunity to learn the business, face new challenges and learn from experienced professionals.' You will also want to qualify the question with one of your own at the end of your answer: 'Is this a permanent or a temporary position you are trying to fill?' Don't be scared to ask. The occasional unscrupulous employer will hire someone fresh out of college or university for a short period of time – say, for one particular project – and then let him or her go.

'How did you pay for university?'

Avoid saying, 'Oh, Dad handled all of that', as it probably won't create quite the impression you'd like. Your parents may well have helped you out, but you should explain, if it's appropriate, that you worked part-time and took out loans (as most of us must during university).

'We have tried to hire people from your university before and they never seem to work out. What makes you different?'

Here's a stress question to test your poise and analytical skills. You can shout that, yes, of course you are different and can prove it. So far, though, all you know is that there was a problem, not what caused the problem. Respond this way: 'First, may I ask you exactly what problems you've had with people from this background?' Once you know what the problem is (if one really exists at all – it may just be a ploy to test your poise), then you can illustrate how you are different, but only then. Otherwise, you run the risk of your answer being interrupted with, 'Well, that's what everyone else said before I employed them. You haven't shown me that you are different.'

'I'd be interested to hear about some things you learnt at university that could be used on the job'

While specific job-related courses could form part of your answer, they cannot be all of it. The interviewer wants to hear about 'real-world' skills, so oblige by explaining what the experience of college taught you rather than a specific course. In other words, explain how the experience honed your relevant personality profiles. 'Within my subject, I tried to pursue those courses that had most practical relevance, such as… However, the greatest lessons I learnt were the importance of…' and then list your personality profile strengths.

'Do you like routine tasks/regular hours?'

A trick question. The interviewer knows from bitter experience that most recent graduates hate routine and are hopeless as employees until they come to an acceptance of such facts of life. Explain that, yes, you appreciate the need for routine, that you expect a fair amount of routine assignments before you are entrusted with the more responsible ones and that that is why you are prepared to accept it as necessary. As far as regular hours go you could say, 'No, there's no problem there. A company expects to make a profit, so the doors have to be open for business on a regular basis.'

'What have you done that shows initiative and willingness to work?'

Again, tell a story about how you landed or created a job for yourself or even got involved in some volunteer work. Your answer should show initiative in that you both handled unexpected problems calmly and anticipated others. Your willingness is demonstrated by the ways you overcame obstacles. For example, 'I worked for a summer in a small warehouse. I found out that a large shipment was due in a couple of weeks and I knew that room had to be made. The inventory system was outdated and the rear of the warehouse was disorganized, so I came in on a Saturday, figured out how much room I needed, cleaned up the mess at the rear and catalogued it all on the new inventory forms. When the shipment arrived, the truck just backed in. There was even room to spare.'

Often after an effort above and beyond the call of duty, a manager might congratulate you and, if it had happened to you in this instance, you might conclude your answer with the verbal endorsement 'The divisional manager happened along just when I was finishing the job and said he wished he had more people who took such pride in their work.'

'Can you take instructions without feeling upset or hurt?'

This is a manageability question. If you take offence easily or bristle when your mistakes are pointed out, you won't last long with any company. Competition is fierce at entry level, so take this as another chance to set yourself apart. 'Yes, I can take instruction – and, more important, I can take constructive criticism without feeling hurt. Even with the best intent, I will still make mistakes and at times someone will have to put me back on the right track. I know that if I ever expect to rise in the company, I must first prove myself to be manageable.'

'Have you ever had difficulties getting along with others?'

This is a combination question, probing for willingness *and* manageability. Are you a team player or are you going to disrupt the department and make the interviewer's life miserable? This is a closed question that requires only a yes/no answer, so give one and shut up.

'What type of position are you interested in?'

This again is one of those questions that tempts you to mention management. Don't. Say you are interested in what you will be offered, which is an entry-level job. 'I am interested in an entry-level position that will enable me to learn this business inside and out and will give me the opportunity to grow when I prove myself, either on a professional or a managerial ladder.'

'What qualifications do you have that will make you successful in this field?'

There is more to answering this question than reeling off your academic qualifications. In addition, you will want to stress relevant work experience and illustrate your strong points as they match the key personality traits that apply to the position you seek. It's a simple, wide-open question that says, 'Hey, we're looking for an excuse to employ you. Give us some help.'

'Why do you think you would like this type of work?'

This is a deceptively simple question because there is no pat answer. It is usually asked to see if you really understand what the specific job and profession entails on a day-to-day basis. So, to answer it requires you to have researched the company and job functions as carefully as possible. Preparation for this should include a call to another company in the field and a request to speak to someone doing the job you hope to get. Ask what the job is like and what that person does day to day. How does the job fit into the department? What contribution does it make to the overall efforts of the company? Why does he or she like that type of work? Armed with that information, you will show that you understand what you are getting into; most recent graduates do not.

'What's your idea of how industry works?'

The interviewer does not want a long dissertation, just the reassurance that you don't think it works along the same lines as a registered charity. Your understanding should be something like this: 'The role of any company is to make as much money as possible, as quickly and efficiently as possible and in a manner that will encourage repeat business from the existing client base and new business as a result of word of mouth and reputation.' Finish with the observation that it is every employee's role to play as a team member in order to achieve these goals.

'What do you know about our company?'

You can't answer this question unless you have enough interest to research the company thoroughly. If you don't have that interest, you should expect someone who has made the effort to get the job instead of you.

'What do you think determines progress in a good company?'

Your answer will include all the positive personality traits you have been illustrating throughout the interview. Include allusions to the listening profile, determination, ability to take the rough with the smooth, adherence to systems and procedures and the good fortune to have a manager who wants you to grow.

'Do you think your exam results should be considered by first employers?'

If your results were good, the answer is obviously 'yes'. If they weren't, your answer needs a little more thought. 'Of course, an employer should take everything into consideration and, along with results, will be an evaluation of willingness and manageability, an understanding of how business works and actual work experience. Combined, such experience and professional skills can be more valuable than results alone.'

Many virtuous candidates are called for entry-level interviews, but only those who prepare themselves to answer the tough questions will be chosen. Interviews for recent school and college leavers and graduates are partly sales presentations. The more you interview, the better you get, so don't leave preparing for them until the last minute. Start now and hone your skills to get a head start on your peers. Finally, here's what a professor from a top-notch business school once told me: 'You are taking a new product to market. Accordingly, you've got to analyse what it can do, who is likely to be interested and how you are going to sell it to them.' Take some time to get to know yourself and your particular values as they will be perceived in the world of business.

15 How to knock 'em dead

The basics of interviewing are found in the basics of business – each question is asked to find out whether or not you have the right stuff. Discover the 20 key personality traits of the most successful businesspeople and how to convey them.

■ 'Describe a situation where your work or an idea was criticized.'

■ 'Have you done the best work you are capable of doing?'

■ 'What problems do you have getting along with others?'

■ 'How long will you stay with the company?'

■ 'I'm not sure you're suitable for the job.'

■ 'Tell me about something you are not very proud of.'

■ 'What are some of the things your supervisor did that you disliked?'

■ 'What aspects of your job do you consider most crucial?'

Can you answer all these questions off the top of your head? Can you do it in a way that will set your worth above that of the other job candidates? I doubt it – they were *designed* to catch you off-guard. They won't, though, after you have read the rest of this book.

Even if you could answer some of them, this would not be enough to assure you of victory: the employer is looking for certain intangible assets as well. Think back to your last job for a moment. Can you recall someone with fewer skills, less professionalism and less dedication who somehow leveraged his or her career into a position of superiority to you? He or she was able to do that only by cleverly projecting a series of personality traits that are universally sought by all successful companies. Building those key traits into your answers to the interviewer's questions will win you any job and set the stage for your career growth at the new company.

There are 20 universally admired key personality traits; they are your passport to success at any interview. Use them for reference as you customize your answers to the tough questions in the following chapters.

Personal profile

The interviewer searches for personal profile keys to determine what type of person you really are. The presence of these keys in your answers tells the interviewer how you feel about yourself, your chosen career and what you would be like to work with. Few of them will arise from direct questions – your future employer will search for them in your answers to specific job-performance probes. The following words and phrases are those you will project as part of your successful, healthy personal profile.

■ **Drive** A desire to get things done. Goal-oriented.

■ **Motivation** Enthusiasm and a willingness to ask questions. A company realizes that a motivated person accepts added challenges and gives that little bit extra on every job.

■ **Communication skills** More than ever, the ability to talk and write effectively to people at all levels in a company is a key to success.

■ **Chemistry** The interviewer is looking for someone who does not get rattled, wears a smile, is confident without self-importance, gets along with others – who is, in short, a team player.

▌ **Energy** Someone who always gives that extra effort in the little things as well as important matters.

▌ **Determination** Someone who does not back off when a problem or situation gets tough.

▌ **Confidence** Not braggadocio. Poise. Friendly, honest and open to employees high or low. Not intimidated by the big fish, nor overly familiar.

Professional profile

All companies seek employees who respect their profession and employer. Projecting these professional traits will identify you as loyal, reliable and trustworthy.

▌ **Reliability** Following up on yourself, not relying on anyone else to ensure the job is well done and keeping management informed every step of the way.

▌ **Honesty and integrity** Taking responsibility for your actions, both good and bad. Always making decisions in the best interests of the company, never on whim or personal preference.

▌ **Pride** Pride in a job well done. Always taking the extra step to make sure the job is done to the best of your ability. Paying attention to the details.

▌ **Dedication** Whatever it takes in time and effort to see a project through to completion, on deadline.

▌ **Analytical skills** Weighing the pros and cons. Not jumping at the first solution to a problem that presents itself. Weighing the short- and long-term benefits of a solution against all its possible negatives.

▌ **Listening skills** Listening and understanding, as opposed to waiting your turn to speak.

Achievement profile

Earlier, I discussed that companies have very limited interests – making money, saving money (the same as making money) and saving time (which does both). Projecting your achievement profile in terms of these interests, in however humble a fashion, is the key to winning any job.

▌ **Money saved** Every penny saved by your thought and efficiency is a penny earned for the company.

▌ **Time saved** Every moment saved by your thought and efficiency enables your company to save money and make more in the additional time available. Double bonus.

▌ **Money earned** Generating revenue is the goal of every company.

Business profile

Projecting your business profile is important on those occasions when you cannot demonstrate ways in which you have made money, saved money or saved time for previous employers. These keys demonstrate that you are always on the lookout for opportunities to contribute and keep your boss informed when an opportunity arises.

▌ **Efficiency** Always keeping an eye open for wastage of time, effort, resources and money.

▌ **Economy** Most problems have two solutions: an expensive one and one the company would prefer to implement.

▌ **Procedures** Procedures exist to keep the company profitable. Don't work around them. That also means keeping your boss informed. You tell your boss about problems or good ideas, not his or her boss. Follow the chain of command. Do not implement your own 'improved' procedures or organize others to do so.

▌ **Profit** All the above traits are universally admired in the business world because they relate to profit.

As the requirements of the job are unfolded for you at the interview, meet them point by point with your qualifications. If your experience is limited, stress the appropriate key profile traits (such as energy, determination, motivation), your relevant interests and desire to learn. If you are weak in just one particular area, keep your mouth shut – perhaps that dimension will not be mentioned. If the area is probed, be prepared to handle and overcome the negative by stressing skills that compensate and/or demonstrate that you will experience a fast learning curve.

Do not show discouragement if the interview appears to be going poorly. You have nothing to gain by showing defeat and it could merely be a stress interview tactic to test your self-confidence.

If for any reason you get flustered or lost, keep a straight face and posture; gain time to marshal your thoughts by asking, 'Could you help me with that?' or 'Would you run that by me again?' or 'That's a good question; I want to be sure I understand. Could you please explain it again?'

Now it is time for you to study the tough questions. Use the examples and explanations to build answers that reflect your background and promote your skills and attributes.

'What are the reasons for your success in this profession?'

With this question, the interviewer is not so much interested in examples of your success – he or she wants to know what makes you tick. Keep your answers short, general and to the point. Using your work experience, personalize and use value keys from your personal, professional and business profiles. For example, 'I attribute my success to three things. First, I've always received support from colleagues, which encourages me to be cooperative and look at my specific job in terms of what we as a department are trying to achieve. That gives me great pride in my work and its contri-

bution to the department's efforts, which is the second factor.
Finally, I find that every job has its problems and, while there's
always a costly solution, there's usually an economical one as
well, whether it's in terms of time or money.' Then give an example from your experience that illustrates those points.

'What is your energy level like? Describe a typical day'

You must demonstrate good use of your time, that you believe in
planning your day beforehand and that, when it is over, you
review your own performance to make sure you are reaching the
desired goals. No one wants a part-time employee, so you should
sell your energy level. For example, your answer might end with,
'At the end of the day when I'm ready to go home, I make a rule
always to type one more letter [make one more call, etc.] and clear
my desk for the next day.'

'Why do you want to work here?'

To answer this question, you must have researched the company
and built a dossier about it. Your research work in Chapter 1 is
now rewarded. Reply with the company's attributes as you see
them. Cap your answer with reference to your belief that the
company can provide you with a stable and happy work environment – the company has that reputation – and that such an
atmosphere would encourage your best work.

'I'm not looking for just another pay cheque. I enjoy my work
and am proud of my profession. Your company produces a superior product/provides a superior service. I share the values that
make this possible, which should enable me to fit in and complement the team.'

'What kind of experience do you have for this job?'

This is a golden opportunity to sell yourself, but, before you do, be
sure you know what is most critical to the company. The interviewer is not just looking for a competent engineer, typist or
what-have-you, but looking for someone who can contribute
quickly to the current projects. When interviewing, companies

invariably give everyone a broad picture of the job, but the person they employ will be a problem solver, someone who can contribute to the specific projects in the first six months. Only by asking will you identify the areas of your interviewer's greatest urgency and therefore interest.

If you do not know the projects you will be involved with in the first six months, you must ask. Level-headedness and analytical ability are respected and the information you get will naturally let you answer the question more appropriately. For example, a company experiencing shipping problems might appreciate this answer, 'My high-speed machining background and familiarity with your equipment will allow me to contribute quickly. I understand deadlines, delivery schedules and the importance of getting the product shipped. Finally, my awareness of economy and profit has always kept reject parts to a bare minimum.'

'What are the broad responsibilities of a ...?'

This is suddenly becoming a very popular question with interviewers and rightly so. There are three layers to it. First, it acknowledges that all employees nowadays are required to be more efficiency and profit-conscious and need to know how individual responsibilities fit into the big picture. Second, the answer provides some idea of how much you will have to be taught or reoriented if and when you join the company. Third, it is a very effective knock-out question – if you lack a comprehensive understanding of the job, that's it! You'll be knocked out then and there.

While your answer must reflect an understanding of the responsibilities, be wary of falling foul of differences in corporate jargon. A systems analyst in one company, for instance, may be only a trainee programmer in another. With this in mind, you may wish to preface your answer with, 'While the responsibilities of my job title vary somewhat from company to company, at my current/last job, my responsibilities include/included…' Then, in case your background isn't an exact match, ask, 'Which areas of relevant expertise haven't I covered?' That will give you the opportunity to recoup.

'Describe how your job relates to the overall goals of your department and company'

This not only probes your understanding of departmental and corporate missions, but also obliquely checks into your ability to function as a team member to get the work done. Consequently, whatever the specifics of your answer, include words to this effect: 'The quality of my work directly affects the ability of others to do their work properly. As a team member, one has to be aware of the other players.'

'What aspects of your job do you consider most crucial?'

A wrong answer here can knock you out of the running very quickly. The executive who describes expenses reports as the job's most crucial aspect is a case in point. The question is designed to determine time management, prioritization skills and any inclination for task avoidance.

'Are you willing to go where the company sends you?'

Unfortunately with this one, you are, as the saying goes, damned if you do and damned if you don't. What is the real question? Do they want you to relocate or just travel on business? If you simply answer 'no', you will not get the job offer, but if you answer 'yes', you could end up anywhere. So, play for time and ask, 'Are you talking about business travel or is the company relocating?' In the final analysis, your answer should be 'yes'. You don't have to accept the job, but without the offer you have no decision to make. Your single goal at an interview is to sell yourself and win a job offer. Never forget, only when you have the offer is it possible to make a decision about that particular job.

'What did you like/dislike about your last job?'

The interviewer is looking for incompatibilities. If a trial lawyer says he or she dislikes arguing a point with colleagues, such a statement will only weaken – if not immediately destroy – his or her candidacy.

Most interviews start with a preamble by the interviewer about the company. Pay attention: that information will help you answer this question. In fact, any statement the interviewer makes about the job or company can be used to your advantage.

So, in answer, you liked everything about your last job. You might even say your company taught you the importance of certain key areas of your business, achievement or professional profile. Criticizing a prior employer is a warning flag that you could be a problem employee. No one intentionally hires trouble and that's what's behind the question. Keep your answer short and positive. You are allowed only one negative about past employers and then only if your interviewer has a 'hot button' about his or her department or company; if so, you will have written it down on your notepad. For example, the only thing your past employer could not offer might be something like 'the ability to contribute more in different areas in the smaller environment you have here.' You might continue with, 'I really liked everything about the job. The reason I want to leave it is to find a position where I can make a greater contribution. You see, I work for a large company that encourages specialization of skills. The smaller environment you have here will, as I said, allow me to contribute far more in different areas.' Tell them what they want to hear – replay the hot button.

Of course, if you interview with a large company, turn it around. 'I work for a small company and don't get the time to specialize in one or two major areas.' Then replay the hot button.

'What is the least relevant job you have held?'

If your least relevant job is not on your CV, it shouldn't be mentioned. Some people skip over those six months between jobs when they worked as waiting staff just to pay the bills and would rather not talk about it, until they hear a question like this one. However, mention of a job that, according to all chronological records, you never had, will throw your integrity into question and your candidacy out the door.

Apart from that, no job in your profession has been a waste of time if it increases your knowledge about how the business works and makes money. Your answer will be along the lines, 'Every job

I've held has given me new insights into my profession and the higher one climbs, the more important the understanding of the lower-level, more menial jobs. They all play a role in making the company profitable. Anyway, it's certainly easier to schedule and plan work when you have first-hand knowledge of what others will have to do to complete their tasks.'

'What have you learnt from jobs you have held?'

Tie your answer to your business and professional profile. The interviewer needs to understand that you seek and can accept constructive advice, and that your business decisions are based on the ultimate good of the company, not your personal whim or preference. 'More than anything, I have learnt that what is good for the company is good for me. So I listen very carefully to directions and always keep my boss informed of my actions.'

'How do you feel about your progress to date?'

This question is not geared solely to rating your progress; it also rates your self-esteem (personal profile keys). Be positive, yet do not give the impression you have already done your best work. Make the interviewer believe you see each day as an opportunity to learn and contribute and that you see the environment at this company as conducive to your best efforts.

'Given the parameters of my job, my progress has been excellent. I know the work, and I am just reaching that point in my career when I can make significant contributions.'

'Have you done the best work you are capable of doing?'

Say 'yes' and the interviewer will think you're a has-been. As with all these questions, personalize your work history. For this particular question, include the essence of this reply: 'I'm proud of my professional achievements to date, especially [give an example]. However, I believe the best is yet to come. I am always motivated to give of my best and in this job there are always opportunities to contribute when you stay alert.'

'How long would you stay with the company?'

The interviewer might be thinking of offering you a job, so you must encourage him or her to sell you on the job. With a tricky question like this, end your answer with a question of your own that really puts the ball back in the interviewer's court. Your reply might be, 'I would really like to settle down with this company. I take direction well and love to learn. As long as I am growing professionally, there is no reason for me to make a move. How long do you think I would continue to be challenged here?'

'How long would it take you to make a contribution to our company?'

Again, be sure to qualify the question – in what area does the interviewer need rapid contributions? You are best advised to answer this with a question, such as 'That is an excellent question. To help me answer, what do you anticipate my responsibilities will be for the first six or seven months?' or 'What are your greatest areas of need right now?' You give yourself time to think while the interviewer concentrates on images of you working for the company. When your time comes to answer, start with, 'It would take me a few weeks to settle down and learn the ropes. I'd be earning my keep very quickly, but making a real contribution... [give a hesitant pause]. Do you have a special project in mind you would want me to get involved with?' That response could lead directly to a job offer, but, if not, you already have the interviewer thinking of you as an employee.

'What would you like to be doing five years from now?'

The safest answer contains a desire to be regarded as a true professional and team player. As far as promotion goes, that depends on finding a manager with whom you can grow. Of course, you will ask what opportunities exist within the company before being any more specific: 'From my research and what you have told me about growth here, it seems that operations is where the heavy emphasis is going to be. It seems that's where you need the effort and where I could contribute towards the company's goals.' Alternatively, you could say, 'I have always felt that first-hand knowledge and experience open up opportunities that one might never have considered, so while, at this point in time, I plan to be a part of [for example] operations, it is reasonable to expect that other exciting opportunities will crop up.'

'What are your qualifications?'

Be sure you don't answer the wrong question. Does the interviewer want job-related or academic job qualifications? Ask. If the question concerns job-related information, you need to know what problems must be tackled first before you can answer adequately. If you can determine this, you will also know what is causing the manager most concern. Then, if you can show yourself as someone who can contribute to the solution of those projects or problems, you have taken a dramatic step ahead in the race for the job offer. Ask for clarification, then use appropriate value keys from all four categories tied in with relevant skills and achievements. You might say, 'I can give you a general answer, but I feel my answer might be more valuable if you could tell me about specific work assignments in the early months.' Another good answer is, 'If the major task right now is to automate the filing system, I should tell you that, in my last job, I was responsible for creating a computerized database for a previously uncomputerized firm.'

'What are your biggest accomplishments?'

Keep your answers job-related – from earlier exercises, a number of achievements should spring to mind. If you exaggerate contributions to major projects, you will be accused of suffering from 'coffee machine syndrome', the affliction of a junior clerk who claimed success for an Apollo space mission based on his relationships with certain scientists, established at the coffee machine. You might begin your reply with, 'Although I feel my biggest achievements are still ahead of me, I am proud of my involvement in… I made my contribution as part of that team and learnt a lot in the process. We did it with hard work, concentration and an eye for the bottom line.'

'How do you organize and plan for major projects?'

Effective planning requires both forward thinking – 'Who and what am I going to need to get this job done?' – and backwards thinking – 'If this job must be completed by the 20th, what steps must be made, and at what time, to meet that deadline?' Effective planning also includes contingencies and budgets for time and cost overruns. Show that you cover all the bases.

'How many hours a week do you find it necessary to work to get your job done?'

There is no absolutely correct answer here, so, again, you have to cover all the bases. Some managers pride themselves on working nights and weekends or never taking their full holiday quota. Others pride themselves on their excellent planning and time management that allows them never to work more than the usual office hours. You must pick the best of both worlds: 'I try to plan my time effectively and usually can. Our business always has its rushes, though, so I put in whatever effort it takes to get the job finished.' It is rare that the interviewer will then come back and ask for a specific number of hours. If that does happen, turn the question around: 'It depends on the projects. What is typical in your department?' The answer will give you the right cue, of course.

'Tell me how you've moved up through the organization'

A fast-track question, the answer to which tells a lot about your personality, goals, past, future and whether or not you still have any steam left in you. The answer might be long, but try to avoid rambling. Include a fair sprinkling of your key personality traits in your stories (because this is the perfect time to do it). As well as listing the promotions, you will want to demonstrate that they came as a result of dedicated, long-term effort, substantial contributions and flashes of genius.

'Can you work under pressure?'

You might be tempted to give a simple 'yes' or 'no' answer, but don't. It reveals nothing and you lose the opportunity to sell your skills and value profiles. Actually, this common question often comes from an unskilled interviewer, because it is closed. (How to handle different types of interviewers is covered in Chapter 17, The other side of the desk.) As such, the question does not give you the chance to elaborate. Whenever you are asked a closed question, mentally add, 'Please give me a brief yet comprehensive answer.' Do that and you will give the information requested and seize an opportunity to sell yourself. For example, you could say, 'Yes, I usually find it stimulating. However, I believe in planning and proper management of my time to reduce panic around deadlines within my area of responsibility.'

'What is your greatest strength?'

Isolate high points from your background and build in a couple of the key value profiles from different categories. You will want to demonstrate pride, reliability and the ability to stick with a difficult task yet change course rapidly when required. You can rearrange the previous answer here. Your answer in part might be, 'I believe in planning and proper management of my time, yet I can still work under pressure.'

'What are your outstanding qualities?'

This is essentially the same as an interviewer asking you what your greatest strengths are. While in the former question you might choose to pay attention to job-specific skills, this question asks you to talk about your personality profile. Now, while you are fortunate enough to have a list of the business world's most desirable personality traits at the beginning of this chapter, try to do more than just list them. In fact, rather than offering a long 'shopping list', you might consider picking out just two or three and giving an illustration of each.

'What interests you most about this job?'

Be straightforward, unless you haven't been given adequate information to determine an answer, in which case you should ask a question of your own to clarify. Perhaps you could say, 'Before answering, could I ask you to tell me a little more about the role this job plays in relation to departmental goals?' or 'Where is the biggest vacuum in your department at the moment?' or 'Could you describe a typical day for me?' The additional information you gather with these questions provides the appropriate slant to your answer – that is, what is of greatest benefit to the department and the company. Career-wise, that obviously has the greatest benefit to you, too. Your answer then displays the personality traits that support the existing need. Your answer in part might include, 'I'm looking for a challenge and an opportunity to make a contribution, so if you feel the biggest challenge in the department is X, I'm the one for the job.' Then, include the personality traits and experience that support your statements. Perhaps, 'I like a challenge, my background demonstrates excellent problem-solving abilities [give some examples] and I always see a project through to the finish.'

'What are you looking for in your next job?'

You want a company where your personal and professional profile keys will allow you to contribute to the business value keys. Avoid saying what you want the company to give you; you must say what you want in terms of what you can give to your employer. The key word in the following example is 'contribution': 'My experience at XYZ Limited has shown me I have a talent for motivating people. That is demonstrated by my team's absenteeism rate dropping by 20 per cent, turnover steadying at 10 per cent and production increasing by 12 per cent. I am looking for an opportunity to continue that kind of contribution and a company and supervisor who will help me develop in a professional manner.'

'Why should I give you the job?'

Your answer will be short and to the point. It will highlight areas from your background that relate to current needs and problems. Recap the interviewer's description of the job, meeting it point by point with your skills. Finish your answer with 'I have the qualifications you need [itemize them], I'm a team player, I take direction and I have the desire to make a thorough success of it.'

'What can you do for us that someone else cannot?'

This question should come only after a full explanation of the job has been given. If not, qualify the question with, 'What voids are you trying to fill when you appoint someone to this position?' Then recap the interviewer's job description, followed with, 'I can bring to this job a determination to see projects through to a proper conclusion. I listen and take direction well. I am analytical and don't jump to conclusions. Finally, I understand we are in business to make a profit, so I keep an eye on costs and returns.' End with, 'How do these qualifications fit your needs?' or 'What else are you looking for?'

You finish with a question that asks for feedback or a powerful answer. If you haven't covered the interviewer's hot buttons, he or she will cover them now and you can respond accordingly.

'Describe a difficult problem you've had to deal with'

This is a favourite tough question. It is not so much the difficult problem that's important, it's the approach you take to solving problems in general. It is designed to probe your professional profile – specifically, your analytical skills.

'Well, I always follow a five-step format with a difficult problem. One, I stand back and examine the problem. Two, I recognize the problem as the symptom of other, perhaps hidden, factors. Three, I make a list of possible solutions to the problem. Four, I weigh both the consequences and costs of each solution and determine the best solution. Five, I go to my boss, outline the problem, make my recommendation and ask for my superior's advice and approval.'

Then give an example of a problem and your solution. Here is a thorough example: 'When I joined my present company, I filled the shoes of a manager who had been fired. Staff turnover was very high. My job was to reduce turnover and increase performance. Sales of our new copier had slumped for the fourth quarter in a row, partly due to ineffective customer service. The new employer was very concerned and he even gave me permission to sack any or all of the sales team. The cause of the problem? The customer service team had never had any training. All my people needed was some intensive training. My boss gave me permission to speak to a training specialist. With what I learnt from her, I turned the department around. Sales continued to slump in my first quarter. Then they skyrocketed. Management was pleased with the sales and felt my job in customer service had played a real part in the turnaround. My boss was pleased because the solution was effective and cheap. I only had to replace two customer service people.'

'What would your references say?'

You have nothing to lose by being positive. If you demonstrate how well you and your boss got along, the interviewer does not have to ask, 'What do you dislike about your current manager?'

It is a good idea to ask past employers to give you a letter of recommendation. That way, you know what is being said. It reduces the chances of the interviewer checking up on you and, if you are asked this question, you can pull out a sheaf of rousing accolades and hand them over. If you are unable to obtain references in advance of a job offer, and the interviewer wishes to see them, he or she should ask your permission before writing to your referees. All that said, never offer references or written recommendations unless they are requested.

'Can we check your references?'

This question is frequently asked as a stress question to catch the too smooth candidate off-guard. It is also one that occasionally is asked in the general course of events. Comparatively few managers or companies ever check references – this astounds me, yet it's a fact of life. On the other hand, the higher up the corporate ladder you go, the more likely it is that your references will be checked. There is only one answer to this question if you ever expect to get an offer: 'Yes'.

Your answer may include, 'Yes, of course you can check my references. However, at present, I would like to keep matters confidential, until we have established a serious mutual interest [an offer]. At such time I will be pleased to furnish you with whatever references you need from prior employers. I would expect you to wait to check my current employer's references until you have extended an offer in writing, I have accepted, we have agreed on a start date and I have had the opportunity to resign in a professional manner.' You are under no obligation to give references from a current employer until you have a written offer in hand. You are also well within your rights to request that reference checks of current employers wait until you have started your new job.

'What types of decisions did you make in your last job?'

Your answer should include reference to the fact that your decisions were all based on appropriate business profile keys. The interviewer may be searching to define your responsibilities or want to know that you don't overstep yourself. It is also an opportunity, however humble your position, to show your achievement profile. For example, 'Being in charge of the company's post, my job is to make sure people get information in a timely manner. The job is well defined and my decisions aren't that difficult. I noticed a year or two ago that when I took the post around at 10 am, everything stopped for 20 minutes. I had an idea and gave it to my boss. She got it cleared by the MD and, ever since, we take the post around just before lunch. Mr Gray, the MD, told me my idea improved productivity, saved time and that he wished everyone was as conscientious.'

'What was the last book you read/film you saw? How did it affect you?'

It doesn't really matter what you say about the latest book or film, just as long as you have read or seen it. Don't be like the interviewee who said the name of the first book that came to mind – *In Search of Excellence* – only to be caught by the follow-up question, 'To what extent do you agree with Peters' simultaneous loose/tight pronouncements?' Also, by naming such a well-known book, you have managed only to say that you are like millions of others, which doesn't make you stand out in the crowd. Better that you should name something less faddish – that helps to avoid nasty follow-up questions. You needn't mention the most *recent* book or film you've seen either. Your answer must simply make a statement about you as a potential employee. Come up with a response that will set you apart and demonstrate your obvious superiority. Ideally you want to mention a work that in some way has helped you improve yourself – anything that has honed any of the 20 key personality traits will do.

'How do you handle tension?'

This question is different from 'Can you handle pressure?' It asks *how* you handle it. You could reply, 'Tension is caused when you let things pile up. It is usually caused by letting other areas of responsibility slip by for an extended period. For instance, if you have a difficult presentation coming up, you may procrastinate in your preparations for it. I've seen lots of people do things like that – a task seems so overwhelming they don't know where to begin. I find that if you break those overwhelming tasks into little pieces, they aren't so overwhelming any more. So I suppose I don't so much handle tension as handle the causes of it, by not letting things slip in areas that can give rise to it.'

'How long have you been looking for another position?'

If you are employed, your answer isn't that important – a short or long time is irrelevant to you in any follow-up probes because you are just looking for the right job, with the right people and company that offers you the right opportunities.

If, on the other hand, you are unemployed at the time, how you answer becomes more important. If you say, 'Well, I've been looking for two years now', this isn't going to score you any points. The interviewer thinks, 'Two years? No one else wanted him in that time, so I certainly don't.' So, if you must talk of months or more, be careful to add something like, 'Well, I've been looking for about a year now. I've had a number of offers in that time, but I have determined that, as I spend most of my waking hours at work, the job I take and the people I work with have got to be people with values I can identify with. I made the decision that I just wasn't going to suffer clockwatchers and jobsworths any more.'

'Have you ever been fired?'

Say 'no' if you can. If you can't, act on the advice given for the next question.

'Why were you fired?'

If you were laid off as part of a general reduction of the workforce, be straightforward and move on to the next topic as quickly as possible. If you have been terminated with cause, however, this is a very difficult question to answer. Like it or not, termination with cause is usually justified because the most loathed responsibility of any manager is to take away someone's livelihood. Virtually no one fires an employee just for the heck of it.

Looking at that painful event objectively, you will probably find the cause of your dismissal rooted in the absence of one or more of the 20 attributes. Having been fired also creates instant doubt in the mind of the interviewer and greatly increases the chances of your references being checked. So, if you have been fired, the first thing to do is bite the bullet and call the person who fired you, find out why it happened, if you don't know already, and learn what he or she would say about you today.

Your aim is to clear the air, so, whatever you do, don't be antagonistic. Reintroduce yourself, explain that you are looking (or, if you have been unemployed for a while, say you are 'still looking') for a new job. Say that you appreciate that the manager had to do what he or she did and that you learnt from the experience. Then, ask, 'If you were asked as part of a pre- or post-employment references check, how would you describe my leaving the company? Would you say that I was fired or that I simply resigned?

You see, every time I tell someone about my termination, whoosh, there goes another chance of getting another job!' Most managers will plump for the latter option, describing your departure as a resignation. After all, even testy managers tend to be humane after the fact and such a response saves them potential headaches and even lawsuits.

Whatever you do, don't advertise the fact you were fired. If you are asked, be honest, but make sure you have packaged the reason in the best light possible. Perhaps, 'I'm sorry to say, but I deserved it. I was having some personal problems at the time and I let them affect my work. I was late to work and lost my motivation. My supervisor (who, by the way, I still speak to) had directions to trim the workforce anyway and, as I was hired only a couple of years previously, I was one of the first to be let go.'

If you can find out the staff turnover figures, voluntary or otherwise, you might add, 'Fifteen other people have left so far this year.' A combination answer of this nature minimizes the stigma. You have even managed to demonstrate that you take responsibility for your actions, which shows your analytical and listening skills. If one of your past managers will speak well of you, there is nothing to lose and everything to gain by finishing with, 'Jill Johnson, at the company, would be a good person to check for a reference on what I have told you.'

I would never advise you to be anything but honest in your answers to any interview question. If, however, you have been terminated by a manager who is still vindictive, take heart: only about 10 per cent of all successful job candidates ever find that their references have been checked.

'Have you ever been asked to resign?'

When someone is asked to resign, it is a gesture on the part of the employer: 'You can quit or we will sack you, so which do you want it to be?' Because you were given the option, though, that employer cannot later say, 'I had to ask him to resign' – that is tantamount to firing and could lead to legal problems. In the final analysis, it is safe to answer 'no'.

'Were you ever dismissed from your job for a reason that seemed unjustified?'

Another sneaky way of asking, 'Were you ever fired?' The sympathetic phrasing is geared to getting you to reveal all the sordid details. The cold hard facts are that hardly anyone is ever fired without cause and you're kidding yourself if you think otherwise. With that in mind, you can quite honestly say 'no' and move on to the next topic.

'In your last job, what were some of the things you spent most of your time on and why?'

Employees come in two categories: goal-oriented (those who want to get the job done) and task-oriented (those who believe in 'busy' work). You must demonstrate good time management and that you are, therefore, goal-oriented, for that is what this question probes for.

You might reply, 'I work on the telephone, like a lot of businesspeople; meetings also take up a great deal of time. What is more important to me is effective time management. I find more gets achieved in a shorter time if a meeting is scheduled, say, immediately before lunch or at the close of business. I try to block my time in the morning. At 4 pm, I review what I've achieved, what went right or wrong and plan adjustments and my main thrust of business for tomorrow.'

'In what ways has your job prepared you to take on greater responsibility?'

This is one of the most important questions you will have to answer. The interviewer is looking for examples of your professional development, perhaps to judge your future growth potential, so you must tell a story that demonstrates it. The following example shows growth, listening skills, honesty and adherence to procedures. Parts of it can be adapted to your personal experience. Notice the 'then and now' aspect of the answer.

'When I first started my last job, my boss would brief me morning and evening. I made some mistakes, learnt a lot and got the jobs done on time. As time went by, I took on greater responsibilities [list some of them]. Nowadays, I meet with her every Monday for breakfast to discuss any major directional changes, so that she can keep management informed. I think that demonstrates not only my growth, but also the confidence my management has in my judgement and ability to perform consistently above standard.'

'In what ways has your job changed since you originally joined the company?'

You can use the same answer here as for the previous question.

'How does this job compare with others you have applied for?'

This is a variation on more direct questions, such as 'How many other jobs have you applied for?' and 'Who else have you applied to?', but it is a slightly more intelligent question and therefore more dangerous. It asks you to compare. Answer the question and sidestep at the same time: 'No two jobs are the same and this one is certainly unlike any other I have applied for.'

If you are pressed further, say, 'Well, to give you a more detailed answer, I would need to ask you a number of questions about the job and the company. Would now be a good time to do that or would it be better later in the interview process?'

'What makes this job different from your current/last one?'

If you don't have enough information to answer the question, say so, and ask some of your own. Behind the question is the interviewer's desire to uncover experience you are lacking – your answer could be used as evidence against you. Focus on the positive: 'From what I know of the job, I seem to have all the experience required to make a thorough success of it. I would say that the major differences seem to be…' and here you play back the positive attributes of the department and company as the interviewer gave them to you, either in the course of the interview or in answer to your specific questions.

'Do you have any questions?'

A good question. Almost always, this is a sign that the interview is drawing to a close and that you have one more chance to make an impression. Remember the adage: people respect what you inspect, not what you expect. Create questions from any of the following.

▌ Find out why the job is open, who had it last and what happened to him or her. Was he or she promoted or fired? How many people have held this position in the last couple of years? What happened to them subsequently?

▌ Why did the interviewer join the company? How long has he or she been there? What is it about the company that keeps him or her there?

▌ To whom would you report? Will you get the opportunity to meet that person?

▌ Where is the job located? What are the travel requirements, if any?

▌ What type of training is required and how long is it? What type of training is available?

▌ What would your first assignment be?

▌ What are the realistic chances for growth in the job? Where are the opportunities for greatest growth within the company?

▌ What are the skills and attributes most needed to get ahead in the company?

■ Who will be the company's major competitor over the next few years? How does the interviewer feel the company stacks up against them?

■ What has been the growth pattern of the company over the last five years? Is it profitable? How profitable?

■ If there is a written job description, could you see it?

■ How regularly do performance evaluations occur? What model do they follow?

Skills

If the job calls for you to be able to type 75 words a minute, then you may be given a typing test. If you are a programmer, you may be asked to take an objective test of programming skills or asked to debug a program. There are tests to measure every possible skill – filing, bookkeeping, mechanical comprehension, specific computer programs, mathematical ability and so on. Some of them are typical paper and pencil written tests. Newer tests present the information using a software program. Typing tests, for instance, have largely been replaced by keyboarding tests; you are still typing but there's no paper or correction fluid involved.

It's hard to argue against some of these tests. After all, if the job calls for you to type letters and reports all day, the boss wants to employ the best typist who applies. If you're supposed to use particular software on the PC all day, the employer will look for the person with the best knowledge of that program. As long as the employer is measuring an important skill, testing skills makes sense.

16

'What kind of person are you really, Mr Jones?'

Learn the techniques an interviewer uses to find out if you will fit into the company and the department and, most important, whether or not you are a good person to work with.

Will you reduce your new employer's life expectancy? The interviewer wants to know! If you are offered the job and accept, you will be working together up to 50 weeks of the year. Every employer wants to know whether or not you will fit in with the rest of the staff, if you are a team player and, most of all, are you manageable?

There are several questions the interviewer might use to probe this area. They will mainly be geared to your behaviour and attitudes in the past. Remember, it is universally believed that your past actions predict your future behaviour.

'How do you take direction?'

The interviewer wants to know if you are open-minded and can be a team player. Can you follow directions or are you a difficult, high-maintenance employee? It is hoped that you are a low-maintenance professional who is motivated to ask clarifying questions about a project before beginning and then gets on with the job at hand, coming back to initiate requests for direction as circumstances dictate.

This particular question can also be defined as 'How do you accept criticism?' Your answer should cover both points: 'I take direction well and recognize that it can come in two varieties, depending on the circumstances. There is carefully explained direction, when my boss has time to lay things out for me in detail; then there are those times when, as a result of deadlines and other pressures, the direction might be brief and to the point.

While I have seen some people get upset with that, personally I've always understood that there are probably other considerations I am not aware of. As such, I take the direction and get on with the job without taking offence, so my boss can get on with his or her job. It's the only way.'

'Would you like to have your boss's job?'

It is a rare boss who wants his or her livelihood taken away. On my own very first job interview, my future boss said, 'Mr Yate, it has been a pleasure to meet you. However, until you walked in my door, I wasn't out on the street looking for a new job.'

The interviewer wants to know if you are the type of person who will be confrontational, challenging, undermining or too ambitious or arrogant. He or she also seeks to determine how goal-oriented and motivated you are in your work life, so you may also want to comment on your sense of direction. However, remember that, while ambition is admired, it is admired most by the ambitious. Be cautiously optimistic, saying perhaps, 'Well, if my boss were promoted over the coming years, I would hope to have made a consistent enough contribution to warrant his recommendation. It is not that I am looking to take anyone's job; rather, I am looking for a manager who will help me develop my capabilities and grow with him.'

'What do you think of your current/last boss?'

Short, sweet and shut up. People who complain about their employers are recognized to be the same people who cause the most disruption in a department. This question means the interviewer has no desire to take on trouble. 'I liked her as a person, respected her professionally and appreciated her guidance.' This question is often followed by one that tries to validate your answer.

'Describe a situation where your work or an idea was criticized'

A doubly dangerous question. You are being asked to say how you handle criticism *and* detail your faults. If you are asked this question, describe a poor *idea* that was criticized, not poor work.

Poor work can cost money and is a warning sign, obviously, to the interviewer.

One of the wonderful things about a new job is that you can leave the past entirely behind, so it does not matter how you handled criticism in the past. What does matter is how the interviewer would like you to handle criticism, if and when it becomes his or her unpleasant duty to dish it out – that's what the question is really about. So, relate one of those it-seemed-like-a-good-idea-at-the-time ideas and finish with how you handled the criticism. You could say, 'I listened carefully and resisted the temptation to interrupt or defend myself. Then I fed back what I heard to make sure the facts were straight. I asked for advice, we bounced some ideas around, then I came back later and represented the idea in a more viable format. My supervisor's input was invaluable.'

'Tell me about yourself'

This is not an invitation to ramble on. If the context isn't clear, you need to know more about the question before giving an answer. In such a situation, you could ask, 'Is there a particular aspect of my background that would be most relevant to you?' This will enable the interviewer to help you find the appropriate focus and avoid discussing irrelevancies.

Whichever direction your answer ultimately takes, be sure that it has some relevance to the world of your professional endeavours. The tale you tell should demonstrate, or refer to, one or more of your key behavioural profiles in action – perhaps honesty, integrity, being a team player or determination. If you choose 'team player' (maybe you're the star player in a local football team), you can tell a story about yourself outside of work that also speaks volumes about you at work. In part, your answer should make the connection between the two, such as 'I put my heart into everything I do, whether it be sports or work. I find that getting along with teammates – or professional peers – makes life more enjoyable and productive.'

Alternatively, you might describe yourself as someone who is able to communicate with a variety of people and give an example from your personal life that indicates an ability to communicate that would also apply at work.

This isn't a question that you can answer effectively off the cuff. Take some time in advance to think about yourself and those aspects of your personality and/or background that you'd like to promote or feature for your interviewer.

'How do you get along with different kinds of people?'

You don't have to talk about respect for others, the need for diversity or how it took you 10 years to realize Jane was a different sex and Charlie a different colour, because that is not what this question is about. If you do respect others, then you will demonstrate this by explaining to your interviewer how you work in a team environment (because this is, in reality, a 'team player' question) and how you solicit and accept input, ideas, and viewpoints from a variety of sources. If you can give a quick, honest illustration of learning from a colleague who is obviously different from you in some way, it won't hurt.

'Rate yourself on a scale of 1 to10'

A stupid question. That aside, bear in mind that this is meant to plumb the depths of your self-esteem. If you answer 10, you run the risk of portraying yourself as insufferable. On the other hand, if you say less than 7, you might as well get up and leave. You are probably best claiming to be an 8 or 9, saying that you always give of your best, but that, in doing so, you always increase your skills and therefore always see room for improvement.

'What kinds of things do you worry about?'

Some questions, such as this one, can seem so off-the-wall that you might start treating the interviewer as a father confessor in no time flat. Your private phobias have nothing to do with your job and revealing them can get you labelled as unbalanced. It is best to confine your answer to the sensible worries of a conscientious professional: 'I worry about deadlines, staff turnover, tardiness, back-up plans for when the computer crashes or that one of my auditors burns out or defects to the competition – just the normal stuff. It goes with the territory, so I don't let it get me down.'

173

'What is the most difficult situation you have faced?'

This question looks for information on two fronts: how you define and how you handled the situation. You must have a story ready for this one in which the situation was both tough and allows you to show yourself in a good light. Avoid talking about problems that have to do with colleagues. You can talk about the difficult decision to fire someone, but emphasize that, once you had examined the problem and reached a conclusion, you acted quickly and professionally, with the best interests of the company at heart.

'What are some of the things that bother you?' 'What are your pet hates?' 'Tell me about the last time you felt anger on the job'

These questions are so similar that they can be treated in the same way. It is tremendously important that you show you can remain calm. Most of us have seen a colleague lose his or her cool on occasion – not a pretty sight and one that every sensible employer wants to avoid. This question comes up more and more often the higher up the corporate ladder you climb and the more frequent your contact with clients and the general public. To answer it, find something that angers conscientious workers: 'I enjoy my work and believe in giving value to my employer. Dealing with clock-watchers and the ones who regularly get sick on Mondays and Fridays really bothers me, but it's not something that gets me angry or anything like that.' An answer of this nature will help you much more than the kind given by one engineer who went on for some minutes about how he hated the small-mindedness of people who don't like pet rabbits in the office.

'What have you done that shows initiative?'

This question probes whether or not you are a doer, someone who will look for ways to increase sales and save time or money – the kind of person who gives a manager a pleasant surprise once in a while, who makes life easier for colleagues. Be sure, however, that your example of initiative does not show a disregard for company policies and procedures.

174

'My boss has to organize a lot of meetings. That means developing agendas, letting employees around the country know the dates well in advance, getting materials printed and so on. Most people in my position would wait for the work to be given to them. I don't. Every quarter, I sit down with my boss and find out the dates of all his meetings for the next six months. I immediately make the hotel and flight arrangements and then work backwards. I ask myself questions like, "If the agenda for the July meeting is to reach the field at least six weeks before the meeting, when must it be finished by?" Then I come up with a deadline. I do that for all the major activities for all the meetings. I put the deadlines in his diary and mine, only two weeks earlier in mine. That way I remind the boss that the deadline is getting close. My boss is the best-organized, most relaxed manager in the company. None of his colleagues can understand how he does it.'

'What are some of the things about which you and your supervisor disagreed?'

It is safest to state that you did not disagree.

'In what areas do you feel your supervisor could have done a better job?'

The same goes for this one. You could reply, though, 'I have always had the highest respect for my supervisor. I have always been so busy learning from Mr Jones that I don't think he could have done a better job. He has really brought me to the point where I am ready for greater challenges. That's why I'm here.'

'What are some of the things your supervisor did that you disliked?'

If you and the interviewer are both non-smokers, for example, and your boss isn't, use it. Apart from that, say something like, 'You know, I've never thought of our relationship in terms of like or dislike. I've always thought our role was to get along together and get the job done.'

175

'How well do you feel your boss rated your job performance?'

This is one very sound reason to ask for written evaluations of your work before leaving a company. Some performance review procedures include a written evaluation of your performance – perhaps your company employs it. If you work for a company that asks you to sign your formal review, you are quite entitled to request a copy of it. You should also ask for a letter of recommendation whenever you leave a job – you have nothing to lose. While I don't recommend thrusting recommendations under unwilling interviewers' noses (they smell a rat when written endorsements of any kind are offered unrequested), the time will come when you are asked and can produce them with a flourish. If you don't have written references, perhaps say, 'My supervisor always rated my job performance well. In fact, I was always rated as being capable of accepting further responsibilities. The problem was, there was nothing available in the company – that's why I'm here.'

If your research has been done properly, you can also quote verbal appraisals of your performance from prior jobs. 'In fact, my boss said only a month ago that I was the most valuable [for example] engineer in the work group, because...'

'How did your boss get the best out of you?'

This is a manageability question, geared to probing whether or not you are going to be a pain in the neck. Whatever you say, it is important for your ongoing happiness that you make it clear you don't appreciate being treated like a doormat. You can give a short, general answer: 'My last boss got superior effort and performance by treating me like a human being and giving me the same personal respect with which she liked to be treated herself.' This book is full of answers that get you out of tight corners and make you shine, but this is one instance in which you really should tell it like it is. You don't want to work for someone who is going to make life miserable for you.

'How interested are you in sports?'

A recently completed survey of middle and upper management personnel found that the executives who listed group sports/ activities among their extracurricular activities made quite a bit more money per year more than their sedentary colleagues. Don't you just love football suddenly? The interviewer is looking for your involvement in groups, as a signal that you know how to get along with others and pull together as a team.

'I really enjoy most team sports. Don't get a lot of time to indulge myself, but I am a regular member of my company's five-a-side team.' Apart from team sports, endurance sports are seen as a sign of determination – swimming, running, and cycling are all OK. Games of skill (bridge, chess, and the like) demonstrate analytical skills.

'What personal characteristics are necessary for success in your field?'

You know the answer to this one: it's a brief recital of your key personality profiles.

You might say, 'To be successful in my field? Drive, motivation, energy, confidence, determination, good communication and analytical skills. Combined, of course, with the ability to work with others.'

'Do you prefer working with others or alone?'

This question is usually used to determine whether or not you are a team player. Before answering, however, be sure you know whether or not the job requires you to work alone. Then answer appropriately. Perhaps, 'I'm quite happy working alone when necessary – I don't need much constant reassurance – but I prefer to work in a group as so much more is achieved when people pull together.'

'Explain your role as a group/team member'

You are being asked to describe yourself as either a team player or a loner. Most departments depend on harmonious teamwork for their success, so describe yourself as a team player, by all means: 'I perform my job in a way that helps others to do theirs in an efficient fashion. Beyond the mechanics, we all have a responsibility to make the workplace a friendly and pleasant place to be. That means everyone working for the common good and making the necessary personal sacrifices towards that good.'

'How would you define a conducive work atmosphere?'

This is a tricky question, especially because you probably have no idea what kind of work atmosphere exists in that particular office. So, the longer your answer, the greater your chances of saying the wrong thing. Keep it short and sweet: 'One where the team has a genuine interest in its work and desire to turn out a good product/deliver a good service.'

'Do you make your opinions known when you disagree with the views of your supervisor?'

If you can, state that you come from an environment where input is encouraged when it helps the team's ability to get the job done efficiently. 'If opinions are sought in a meeting, I will give mine, although I am careful to be aware of others' feelings. I will never criticize a colleague or a superior in open forum; besides, it is quite possible to disagree without being disagreeable. However, my past manager made it clear that she valued my opinion by asking for it. So, after a while, if there was something I felt strongly about, I would make an appointment to sit down and discuss it one-to-one.' You might choose to end by turning the tables with a question of your own: 'Is this a position where we work as a team to solve problems and get the job done or one where we are meant to get on independently and speak when spoken to?'

'What would you say about a supervisor who was unfair or difficult to work with?'

For this job, you'll definitely want to meet your potential supervisor – just in case you have been earmarked for the company ogre without warning. The response, 'Do you have anyone in particular in mind?' will probably get you off the hook. If you need to elaborate, try: 'I would make an appointment to see the supervisor and diplomatically explain that I felt uncomfortable in our relationship, that I felt he or she was not treating me as a professional colleague and therefore that I might not be performing up to standard in some way – that I wanted to right matters and ask for his or her input as to what I must do to create a professional relationship. I would enter into the discussion in the frame of mind that we were equally responsible for whatever communication problems existed and that this wasn't just the manager's problem.'

'Do you consider yourself a natural leader or a born follower?'

Ow! How you answer depends a lot on the job offer you are chasing. If you are a recent graduate, you are expected to have high aspirations, so go for it. If you are already on the corporate ladder with some practical experience in the school of hard knocks, you might want to be a little more cagey. Assuming you are up for (and want) a leadership position, you might try something like this: 'I would be reluctant to regard anyone as a natural leader. Hiring, motivating and disciplining other adults and, at the same time, moulding them into a cohesive team involves a number of delicately tuned skills that no honest people can say they were born with. Leadership requires, first of all, the desire; then it is a lifetime learning process. Anyone who reckons they have it all under control and have nothing more to learn isn't doing the employer any favours.'

Of course, a little humility is also in order because just about every leader in every company reports to someone and there is a good chance that you are talking to such a someone right now. So, you might consider including something like, 'No matter how well developed any individual's leadership qualities, an integral part of the skills of a leader is to take direction from his or her immediate boss and also to seek the input of the people being supervised. The wise leader will always follow good advice and sound business judgement wherever it comes from. I would say that, given the desire to be a leader, the true leader in the modern business world must embrace both.' How can anyone disagree with that kind of wisdom?

'Why do you feel you are a better [for example] assistant than some of your colleagues?'

If you speak disparagingly of your colleagues, you will not put yourself in the best light. That is what the question asks you to do, so it poses some difficulties. The trick is to answer the question but not accept the invitation to show yourself in anything other than a flattering light. 'I think that question is best answered by a manager. It is so difficult to be objective and I really don't like to slight my colleagues. I don't spend my time thinking about how superior I am because that would be detrimental to our working together as a team. I believe, however, some of the qualities that make me an outstanding assistant are...' and you can go on to illustrate job-related personal qualities that make you a beacon of productivity and a joy to work with.

'You have a doctor's appointment arranged for noon. You've waited two weeks to get in. An urgent meeting is scheduled at the last moment, though. What do you do?'

'What a crazy question,' you mutter. It's not. It is even more than a question, it is what I call a question shell. The question within the shell – in this instance, 'Will you sacrifice the appointment or your job?' – can be changed at will. This is a situational interviewing technique that poses an on-the-job problem to see how the prospective employee will respond. A company I know of asks this question as part of its initial screening and if you give the wrong answer, you never even get a face-to-face interview. So, what is the right answer to this or any similar shell question?

Fortunately, once you understand the interviewing technique, it is quite easy to handle – all you have to do is turn the question around: 'If I were the manager who had to schedule a really important meeting at the last moment and someone on my staff chose to go to the doctor's instead, how would I feel?'

It is unlikely that you would be an understanding manager unless the visit were for a triple bypass. To answer, you start with an evaluation of the importance of the problem and the responsibility of everyone to make some sacrifices for the organization and finish with: 'The first thing I would do is reschedule the appointment and save the doctor's office inconvenience. Then I would immediately make sure I was properly prepared for the emergency meeting.'

'How do you manage to interview while still employed?'

As long as you don't say that you faked a dentist appointment to make the interview you should be all right. Beware of revealing anything that might make you appear at all underhanded. Best to make the answer short and sweet and let the interviewer move on to richer areas of enquiry. Just explain that you had some holiday time due or took a day off in lieu of overtime pay. 'I had some holiday time, so I went to my boss and explained I needed a couple of days off for some personal business and asked her what days would be most suitable. Although I plan to change jobs, I don't in any way want to hurt my current employer in the process by being absent during a busy time.'

'When do you expect a promotion?'

Tread warily – show that you believe in yourself and have both feet firmly planted on the ground. 'That depends on a few criteria. Of course, I cannot expect promotions without the performance that marks me as deserving of promotion. I also need to join a company that has the growth necessary to provide the opportunity. I hope that my manager believes in promoting from within and will help me grow so that I will have the skills necessary to be considered for promotion when the opportunity comes along.'

If you are the only one doing a particular job in the company or are in management, you need to build another factor into your answer. For example, 'As a manager, I realize that part of my job is to have done my succession planning and that I must have someone trained and ready to step into my shoes before I can expect to step up. That way I play my part in preserving the chain of command.' To avoid being caught off-guard with queries about your having achieved that in your present job, you can finish with 'Just as I have done in my present job, where I have a couple of people capable of taking over the reins when I leave.'

'Tell me a story'

Wow. What on earth does the interviewer mean by this question? You don't know until you get him or her to elaborate. Ask, 'What would you like me to tell you a story about?' To make any other response is to risk making a fool of yourself. Very often the question is asked to see how analytical you are. People who answer the question without qualifying show that they do not think things through carefully. The subsequent question will be about either your personal or professional life. If it is about your personal life, tell a story that shows you like people and are determined. Do not discuss your love life. If the subsequent question is about your professional life, tell a story that demonstrates your willingness and manageability.

'What have your other jobs taught you?'

Talk about the professional skills you have learnt and the personality traits you have polished. Many interviewees have had success finishing their answer with 'There are two general things I have learnt from past jobs. First, if you are confused, ask – it's better to ask a silly question than make a stupid mistake. Second, it's better to promise less and produce more than to make unrealistic forecasts.'

'Define cooperation'

This question asks you to explain how to function as a team player in the workplace. Your answer could be, 'Cooperation is a person's ability to sacrifice personal wishes and beliefs whenever necessary to assure that the department reaches its goals. It is also a person's desire to be part of a team and, by hard work and goodwill, make the department greater than the sum of its parts.'

'What difficulties do you have tolerating people with different backgrounds and interests from yours?'

Another 'team player' question with the awkward implication that you do have problems. Give the following answer: 'I don't have any.'

'In hindsight, what have you done that was a little harebrained?'

You are never harebrained in your business dealings and you haven't been harebrained in your personal life since you left school, right? The only safe examples to use are ones from your deep past that ultimately turned out well. One of the best to use, if it applies to you, is this one: 'Well, I guess the time I bought my house. I had no idea what I was letting myself in for and, at the time, I really couldn't afford it. Still, I managed to make the payments, though I had to work like someone possessed. Yes, my first house – that was a real learning experience.' Not only can most people relate to this example, but it also gives you the opportunity to sell one or two of your very positive and endearing traits.

If you think the interview is only tough for the interviewee, it's time to take a look at things from the other side of the desk. Knowing what's going on can really help you shine.

17 The other side of the desk

Two types of interviewers can spell disaster for the unprepared: the highly skilled and the unconscious incompetent. Find out how to recognize and respond to each one.

There are two terrible places to be during an interview – sitting in front of the desk wondering what on earth is going to happen next and sitting behind the desk asking the questions. The average interviewer dreads the meeting almost as much as the interviewee, yet for opposite reasons.

Many businesses frequently yield to the mistaken belief that any person, on being promoted to the ranks of management, becomes mystically endowed with all necessary managerial skills. That is a fallacy. Comparatively few management people have been taught to interview; most just bumble along and pick up a certain proficiency over a period of time.

There are two distinct types of interviewers who can spell disaster for you if you are unprepared. One is the highly skilled interviewer, who has been trained in systematic techniques for probing your past for all the facts and evaluating your potential. The other is the totally incompetent interviewer, who may even lack the ability to phrase a question adequately. Both are equally dangerous when it comes to winning a job offer.

The skilful interviewer

Skilful interviewers know exactly what they want to discover. They have taken exhaustive steps to learn the strategies that will help them employ only the best for their company. They follow a set format for the interview process to ensure objectivity in selection and a set sequence of questions to ensure the facts are gathered. They will definitely test your mettle.

There are many ways for a manager to build and conduct a structured interview, but all have the same goals, which are to:

▊ ensure systematic coverage of your work history and applicable job-related skills;

▊ provide a technique for gathering all the relevant facts;

▊ provide a uniform strategy that objectively evaluates all job candidates;

▊ determine ability, willingness and manageability.

Someone using structured interview techniques will usually follow a standard format. The interview will begin with small talk and a brief introduction to relax you. Following close on the heels of that chit-chat comes a statement geared to assure you that baring your faults is the best way to get the job. Your interviewer will then outline the steps in the interview. That will include you giving a chronological description of your work history, then the interviewer asking specific questions about your experience. Then, prior to the close of the interview, you will be given an opportunity to ask your own questions.

Sounds pretty simple, huh? Well, watch out! The skilled interviewer knows exactly what questions to ask, why they will be asked, in what order they will be asked and what the desired responses are. He or she will interview and evaluate every applicant for the job in exactly the same fashion. You are up against a pro.

Like the hunter who learns to think like his or her prey, you will find that the best way to win over the interviewer is to think like the interviewer. In fact, take that idea a little further – you must win, but you don't want the other guys to realize you beat them at their own game. To do that, you must learn how the interviewer has prepared for you; and by going through the same process you will beat your competitors to the job offer.

The dangerous part of this type of structured interview is called 'skills evaluation'. The interviewer has analysed all the different skills it takes to do the job and all the personality traits that complement those skills. Armed with that data, he or she has developed a series of carefully sequenced questions to draw out your relative merits and weaknesses.

Graphically, it looks like this:

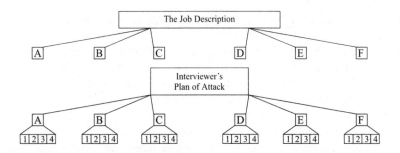

Letters A–F are the separate skills necessary to do the job; numbers 1–4 are questions asked to identify and verify each particular skill. This is where many of the tough questions will arise. The only way to prepare for them effectively is to take the interviewer's viewpoint and complete this exercise in its entirety. The effort requires a degree of objectivity, but will generate multiple job offers.

▌ Look at the position you seek. What role does it play in helping the company achieve its corporate mission and make a profit?

▌ What are the five most important duties of that job?

▌ From a management viewpoint, what are the skills and attributes necessary to perform each of these tasks?

Write it all down. Now, put yourself in the interviewer's shoes. What topics would you examine to find out if a person can really do the job? If, for some reason, you get stuck in the process, just use your past experience. You have worked with good and bad people and their work habits and skills will lead you to develop both the potential questions and the correct answers.

Each job skill you identify is fertile ground for the interviewer's questions. Don't forget the intangible skills that are so important to many jobs, like self-confidence and creativity, because the interviewer won't. Develop a number of questions for each job skill you identify.

Again, looking back at colleagues (and still wearing the manager's hat), what are the personal characteristics that would make life more comfortable for you as a manager? These are also dimensions that are likely to be probed by the interviewer. Once you have identified the questions you would ask in the interviewer's position, the answers should come easily.

That's the way managers are trained to develop structured interview questions – I just gave you the inside track. Complete the exercise by developing the answers you would like to hear as a manager. Take time to complete the exercise conscientiously, writing out both the questions and the appropriate answers.

These sharks have some juicy questions to probe your skills, attitude and personality. Would you like to hear some of them? Notice that these questions tend to lay out a problem for you to solve, but in no way lead you towards the answer. They are often two- and three-part questions as well. The additional question that can be tagged on to them all is, 'What did you learn from this experience?' Assume it is included whenever you get one of these questions – you'll be able to sell different aspects of your success profile.

'You have been given a project that requires you to interact with different levels within the company. How do you do this? What levels are you most comfortable with?'

This is a two-part question that probes communication and self-confidence skills. The first part asks how you interact with superiors and motivate those working with and for you on the project. The second part of the question is asking, 'Who do you regard as your peer group – help me categorize you.' To cover those bases, you will want to include the essence of this: 'There are essentially two types of people I would interact with on a project of this nature. First, there are those I report to, who bear the ultimate responsibility for its success. With them, I determine deadlines and how they will evaluate the success of the project. I outline my approach, breaking the project down into component parts, getting approval on both the approach and the costs. I would keep my supervisors up-to-date on a regular basis and seek input whenever needed. My supervisors would expect three things from me: the facts, an analysis of potential problems and that I will not be intimidated, as that would jeopardize the project's success. I would comfortably satisfy those expectations.

'The other people to interact with on a project like this are those who work with and for me. With those people, I would outline the project and explain how a successful outcome would benefit the company. I would assign the component parts to those best suited to each and arrange follow-up times to assure completion by deadline. My role here would be to facilitate, motivate and bring the different personalities together to form a team.

'As for comfort level, I find this type of approach enables me to interact comfortably with all levels and types of people.'

'Tell me about an event that really challenged you. How did you meet the challenge? In what way was your approach different from others'?'

This is a straightforward two-part question. The first probes your problem-solving abilities. The second asks you to set yourself apart from the herd. First of all, outline the problem. The blacker you make the situation, the better. Having done that, go ahead and explain your solution, its value to your employer and how it was different from other approaches.

'My company has offices all around the country; I am responsible for 70 of them. My job is to visit each office on a regular basis and build market penetration strategies with management and train and motivate the sales and customer service force. When the recession hit, the need to service those offices was more important than ever, yet the travelling costs were getting prohibitive.

'Morale was an especially important factor – you can't let outlying offices feel defeated. I reapportioned my budget and did the following: I dramatically increased telephone contact with the offices. I instituted a monthly sales technique letter – how to prospect for new clients, negotiate difficult sales and so forth. I bought and rented sales training and motivational tapes and sent them to my managers with instructions on how to use them in a sales meeting. I stopped visiting all the offices. Instead, I scheduled weekend training meetings in central locations throughout my area: one day of sales training and one day of management training, concentrating on how to run sales meetings, early termination of low producers and so on.

'While my colleagues complained about the drop in sales, mine increased, albeit by a modest 6 per cent. After two quarters, my approach was officially adopted by the company.'

'Give me an example of a method of working you have used. How did you feel about it?'

You have a choice of giving an example of either good or bad work habits. Give a good example, one that demonstrates your understanding of corporate goals, your organizational skills, analytical ability or time management skills.

You could say, 'I believe in giving an honest day's work for a day's pay. That requires organization and time management. I do my paperwork at the end of each day, when I review the day's achievements. With this done, I plan for tomorrow. When I come to work in the morning, I'm ready to get going without wasting time. I try to schedule meetings right before lunch – people get to the point more quickly if it's on their time. I feel that is an efficient and organized method of working.'

'When you joined your last company and met the group for the first time, how did you feel? How did you get on with them?'

Your answer should include: 'I naturally felt a little nervous, but I was excited about the new job. I shared that excitement with my new friends and told them that I was enthusiastic about learning new skills from them. I was open and friendly and, when given the opportunity to help someone myself, I jumped at it.'

'In your last job, how did you plan for the interview?'

That's an easy one. Just give a description of how the skilled interviewer prepares.

'How have you benefited from your disappointments?'

Disappointments are different from failures. It is an intelligent – probably trained – interviewer who asks this one. It is also an opportunity for the astute interviewee to shine. The question itself is very positive – it asks you to show how you benefited. Note also that it doesn't ask you to give details of specific disappointments, so you don't have to open your mouth and insert your foot. Instead, be general. Edison once explained his success as an inventor by claiming that he knew more ways not to do something than anyone else living; you can do worse than quote him. In any event, sum up your answer with, 'I treat disappointments as a learning experience – I look at what happened, why it happened and how I would do things differently in each stage should the same set of circumstances appear again. That way, I put disappointment behind me and am ready with renewed vigour and understanding to face the new day's problems.'

Incidentally, a person with strong religious beliefs may be tempted to answer a question like this in terms of religious values. If you benefit from disappointments in a spiritual way, remember that not everyone feels the same as you do. More important, making an interviewer feel awkward in any way is not the way to win a job offer.

'What would you do when you have a decision to make and no procedure exists?'

This question probes your analytical skills, integrity and dedication. Most of all, the interviewer is testing your manageability and adherence to procedures – the 'company way of doing things.' You need to cover that with: 'I would act without my manager's direction only if the situation were urgent and my manager was unavailable. Then, I would take command of the situation, make a decision based on the facts and implement it. I would update my boss at the earliest opportunity.' If possible, tell a story to illustrate.

'That is an excellent answer. Now to give me a balanced view, can you give me an example that didn't work out so well?'

There are two techniques that every skilled interviewer will use, especially if you are giving good answers. In this question, the interviewer looks for negative balance – that is, in the follow-up, the person will look for negative confirmation. Here, you are required to give an example of an inadequacy. The trick is to pull something from the past, not the present, and finish with what you learnt from the experience. For example, 'That's easy. When I first joined the workforce, I didn't really understand the importance of systems and procedures. There was one time when I was too anxious to contribute and didn't have the full picture. There was a sales visit report everyone had to fill out after visiting a customer. I always put a lot of effort into it until I realized it was never read – it just went in the files. So, I stopped doing it for a few days to see if it made any difference. I thought I was gaining time to make more sales for the company. I was so proud of my extra sales calls I told the boss at the end of the week. My boss explained that the records were for the long term, so that, should my job change, the next salesperson would have the benefit of a full client history. It was a long time ago, but I have never forgotten the lesson: there's always a reason for systems and procedures. I've had the best-kept records in the company ever since!'

To look for negative confirmation, the interviewer may then say something like, 'Thank you. Now, can you give me another example?' He or she is trying to confirm a weakness. If you help, you could well do yourself out of a job. Here's what your reaction should be: you sit deep in thought for a good 10 seconds, then look up and say firmly, 'No, that's the only occasion when anything like that happened.' Then shut up and refuse to be enticed further.

The unconscious incompetent

Now you should be ready for almost anything a professional interviewer could throw at you. Your foresight and strategic planning will generate multiple offers of employment for you in all circumstances except one – when you face the unconsciously incompetent interviewer. He or she is probably more dangerous to your job offer status than everything else combined.

The problem is embodied in the experienced manager who is a poor interviewer, but who does not know it. He or she, consciously or otherwise, bases employment decisions on 'experience' and 'knowledge of mankind' and 'gut feeling'. In any event, he or she is an unconscious incompetent. You have probably been interviewed by one in your time. Remember leaving an interview and, upon reflection, feeling the interviewer knew absolutely nothing about you or your skills? If so, you know how frustrating that can be. Here, you'll see how to turn that difficult situation to your advantage. In the future, good managers who are poor interviewers will be offering jobs with far greater frequency than ever before. Understand that a poor interviewer can be a wonderful manager – interviewing skills are learnt, not inherited or created as a result of a mystical corporate blessing.

The unconscious incompetents abound. Their heinous crime can only be exceeded by your inability to recognize and take advantage of the proffered opportunity.

As in handling the skilled interviewer, it is necessary to imagine how the unconscious incompetent thinks and feels. There are many manifestations of the poor interviewer. Each of the next examples is followed by instructions for appropriate handling of the unique problems posed for you.

Example 1

The interviewer's desk is cluttered and the CV or application that was handed to him or her a few minutes before cannot be found. (This example, by the way, is usually the most common sign of the unconscious incompetent.)

Response

Sit quietly through the bumbling and searching. Check out the surroundings. Breathe deeply and slowly to calm any natural interview nerves. As you bring your adrenaline under control, you bring a certain calming effect to the interviewer and the interview.

Example 2

The interviewer experiences constant interruptions from the telephone or people walking into the office.

Response

This provides good opportunities for selling yourself. Make notes on your pad of where you were in the conversation and refresh the interviewer on the point when you start talking again. He or she will be impressed with your level head and good memory. The interruptions also give time, perhaps, to find something of common interest in the office, something you can compliment. You will also have time to compose the suitable value key follow-up to the point made in the conversation prior to the interruption.

Example 3

The interviewer starts with an explanation of why you are both sitting there and then allows the conversation to degenerate into a lengthy diatribe about the company.

Response

Show interest in the company and the conversation. Sit straight, look attentive (the other applicants probably fall asleep), make appreciative murmurs and nod at the appropriate times until there is a pause. When it occurs, comment that you appreciate the background on the company, because you can now see more clearly how the job fits into the general scheme of things and that you see, for example, how valuable communication skills would be for the job. Could the interviewer please tell you some of the other job requirements? Then, as the job's functions are described, you can interject appropriate information about your background with 'Would it be of value, Mr Smith, if I described my experience with…?'

Example 4

The interviewer begins with, or quickly breaks into, the drawbacks of the job. The job may even be described in totally negative terms. That is often done without giving a balanced view of the duties and expectations of the position.

Response

An initial negative description often means that the interviewer has had bad experiences of employing people for the position. Your course is to empathize (not sympathize) with his or her bad experiences and make it known that you recognize the importance of (for example) reliability, especially in this particular type of job. (You will invariably find in these instances that what your interviewer has lacked in the past is someone with a serious understanding of value keys.) Illustrate your proficiency in that particular aspect of your profession with a short example from your work history. Finish your statements by asking the interviewer what some of the biggest problems to be handled in the job are. The questions demonstrate your understanding and the interviewer's answers outline the areas of your background and skills to which you should draw attention.

Example 5

The interviewer spends considerable time early on in the interview describing 'the type of people we are here at XYZ Limited.'

Response

Very simple. You have always wanted to work for a company with that atmosphere. It creates the type of work environment that is conducive to a person really giving his or her best efforts.

Example 6

The interviewer asks closed questions, which are ones that demand no more than a yes or no answer, such as, 'Do you pay attention to detail?' Such questions are hardly adequate to establish your skills, yet you must handle them effectively to secure the job offer.

Response

A 'yes' or 'no' answer to a closed question will not get you that offer. The trick is to treat each closed question as if the interviewer has added, 'Please give me a brief yet thorough answer.' Closed questions also are often mingled with statements followed by pauses. In those instances, agree with the statement in a way that demonstrates both a grasp of your job and the interviewer's statement. For example, 'That's an excellent point, Mr Smith. I couldn't agree more that the attention to detail you describe naturally affects cost containment. My track record in this area is…'

Example 7

The interviewer asks a continuous stream of negative questions (as described in Chapter 18, The stress interview).

Response

Use the techniques and answers described earlier. Give your answers with a smile and do not take the questions as personal insults as they are not intended that way. The more stressful the situations the job is likely to place you in, the greater the likelihood of your having to field negative questions. The interviewer wants to know if you can take the heat.

Example 8

The interviewer has difficulty looking at you while speaking.

Response

The interviewer is someone who finds it uncomfortable being in the spotlight. Try to help him or her to be a good audience. Ask specific questions about the job responsibilities and offer your skills in turn.

Often, the manager interviewing will arrange for you to meet with two or three other people. Frequently, the other interviewers have been neither trained in appropriate interviewing skills nor told the details of the job for which you are interviewing. So, take additional copies of your executive briefing with you to the interview to aid them in focusing on the appropriate job functions.

When you understand how to recognize and respond to these different types of interviewers, you will leave your interview having made a favourable first impression. No one forgets first impressions.

18 *The stress interview*

Your worst nightmare can come true at a stress interview, but, once you learn that these questions are just amplified versions of much simpler ones, you can remain cool and calm Also, a vital discussion on handling illegal interview questions.

To all intents and purposes, every interview is a stress interview – the interviewer's negative and trick questions can act as the catalyst for your own fear. The only way to combat this fear is to be prepared, to know what the interviewer is trying to do and anticipate the various directions he or she will take. Whenever you are ill-prepared for an interview, no one will be able to put more pressure on you than you do on yourself. Remember, a stress interview is just a normal interview with the volume turned all the way up – the music is the same, just louder. Only preparation will keep you cool and collected.

You've heard the horror stories. An interviewer demands of a hapless applicant, 'Sell me this pen' or asks, 'How would you improve the design of a teddy bear?' The candidate is faced with a battery of interviewers, all demanding rapid-fire answers to questions like, 'You're giving a dinner party. Which 10 famous people would you invite and why?' When the interviewee offers evidence of foot-in-mouth disease by asking, 'Living or dead?' he receives his just desserts in reply: 'Ten of each.'

Such awful-sounding questions are thrown in to test your poise, see how you react under pressure and plumb the depths of your confidence. Many people ruin their chances by reacting to them as personal insults rather than the challenges and opportunities to shine that they really are.

Previously restricted to the executive suite for the selection of high-powered executives, stress interviews are now widespread throughout the professional world. They can come complete with all the intimidating and treacherous tricks your worst nightmare can devise. Yet, a good performance at a stress interview can mean the difference between a job in the fast lane and a stalled career. The interviewers in a stress interview are invariably experienced and well organized and have developed tightly structured procedures and advanced interviewing techniques. The questions and tension they generate have the cumulative effect of throwing you off balance and revealing the 'real' you – rather than someone who can respond with last night's rehearsed answers to six or seven stock questions.

Stress questions can be turned to your advantage or merely avoided with nifty footwork. Whichever approach you choose, you will be among a select few who understand this line of questioning. As always, when addressing the questions in this chapter, remember to develop personalized answers that reflect your experience and profession. Practise your responses out loud – by doing that, they will become more natural and will help you feel more confident during an interview. You might even consider making a tape of tough questions, spacing them at intervals of 30 seconds to a couple of minutes. You can then play the tape back and answer the questions in real time.

As we will see in this chapter, reflexive questions can prove especially useful when the heat is on. Stress questions are designed to sort out the doers from those who freeze under pressure. Used with discretion, the reflexives – ' ...don't you think?' – will demonstrate to the interviewer that you are able to function well under pressure. At the same time, of course, you put the ball back in the interviewer's court.

One common stress interview technique is to set you up for a fall: a pleasant conversation, one or a series of seemingly innocuous questions to relax your guard, then a dazzling series of jabs and body blows that leave you gibbering. For instance, an interviewer might lull you into a false sense of security by asking some relatively stress-free questions: 'What was your initial starting salary at your last job?' then, 'What is your salary now?' then, 'Do you receive bonuses?' and so on. To put you on the ropes, he or she might then completely surprise you with, 'Tell me what sort of troubles you have living within your means' or 'Why aren't you earning more at your age?' Such interviewers are using stress in an intelligent fashion, to simulate the unexpected and sometimes tense events of everyday business life. Seeing how you handle simulated pressure gives a fair indication of how you will react to the real thing.

The sophisticated interviewer talks very little, perhaps only 20 per cent of the time, and that time is spent asking questions. Few comments and no editorializing on your answers means that you get no hint, verbal or otherwise, about your performance.

The questions are planned, targeted, sequenced and layered. The interviewer covers one subject thoroughly before moving on. Let's take the simple example of 'Can you work under pressure?' As a reader of this book, you will know to answer that question with an example and thereby deflect the main thrust of the stress technique. The interviewer will be prepared for a simple yes or no answer. What follows will keep the unprepared applicant reeling.

'Can you work under pressure?'

A simple, closed question that requires just a yes or no answer, but you won't get off so easy.

'Good, I'd be interested to hear about a time when you experienced pressure in your job'

An open-ended request to tell a story about a pressure situation. After this, you will be subjected to the layering technique – six layers in the following instance. Imagine how tangled you could get without preparation.

'Why do you think this situation arose?'

It's best if the situation you describe is not a peer's or manager's fault.

'When exactly did it happen?'

Watch out! Your story of saving thousands from the burning skyscraper may well be checked with your referees.

'What in hindsight were you most dissatisfied with about your performance?'

Here we go. You're trying to show how well you perform under pressure, then suddenly you're telling tales against yourself.

'How do you feel others involved could have acted more responsibly?'

An open invitation to criticize peers and superiors, which you should diplomatically decline.

'Who holds responsibility for the situation?'

Another invitation to point the finger of blame.

'Where in the chain of command could steps be taken to avoid that sort of thing happening again?'

This question probes your analytical skills and whether or not you are the type of person who always goes back to the scene of the crime to learn for the next time.

You have just been through an old reporter's technique of asking why, when, who, what, how and where. The technique can be applied to any question you are asked and is frequently used to probe those success stories that sound just too good to be true. You'll find them suddenly tagged on to the simple closed questions, as well as to the open-ended ones. Typically, they'll start with something like 'Share with me' 'Tell me about a time when' or 'I'm interested in finding out about' and then request specific examples from your work history.

After you've survived that barrage, a friendly tone may conceal another zinger: 'What did you learn from the experience?' This question is geared to probing your judgement and emotional maturity. Your answer should emphasize whichever of the key personality traits your story was illustrating.

When an interviewer feels you were on the edge of revealing something unusual in an answer, you may well encounter 'mirror statements'. Here, the last key phrase of your answer will be repeated or paraphrased and followed by a steady gaze and silence. For example, 'So, you learnt that organization is the key to management.' The idea is that the quiet and an expectant look will work together to keep you talking. It can be disconcerting to find yourself rambling on without quite knowing why. The trick is knowing when to stop. When the interviewer gives you an expectant look in this context, expand your answer (you have to), but by no more than a couple of sentences. Otherwise, you will get that creepy feeling that you're digging yourself into a hole.

There will be times when you face more than one interviewer at a time. When that happens, remember the story of a female attorney who had five law partners all asking questions at the same time. As the poor interviewee got halfway through one answer, another question would be shot at her. Pausing for breath, she smiled and said, 'Hold on, ladies and gentlemen. These are all excellent questions and, given time, I'll answer them all. Now who's next?' In so doing, she showed the interviewers exactly what they wanted to see and what, incidentally, is behind every stress interview and every negatively phrased question – finding the presence of poise and calm under fire, combined with a refusal to be intimidated.

You never know when a stress interview will raise its ugly head. Often it can be that rubber-stamp meeting with the senior manager at the end of a series of gruelling meetings. This is not surprising. While other interviewers are concerned with determining whether or not you are able, willing and a good fit for the job in question, the senior executive who eventually throws you for a loop may be probing you for potential promotability.

The most intimidating stress interviews are recognizable before the interviewer speaks – no eye contact, no greeting, either silence or a non-committal grunt and no small talk. You may also recognize such an interviewer by his or her general air of boredom, lack of interest or thinly veiled aggression. The first words you hear could well be, 'OK, so go ahead. I don't have all day.' In these situations, forewarned is forearmed, so here are some of the questions you can expect to follow such openings.

'What is your greatest weakness?'

This is a direct invitation to put your head in a noose. Decline the invitation.

If there is a minor part of the job at hand where you lack knowledge – but knowledge you will obviously pick up quickly – use that. For instance, 'I haven't worked with this type of spreadsheet program before, but, given my experience with six other types, I don't think it should take me more than a couple of days to pick it up.' Here you remove the emphasis from a weakness and put it on to a developmental problem that is easily overcome. Be careful, however – this very effective ploy must be used with discretion.

Another good option is to give a generalized answer that takes advantage of value keys. Design the answer so that your weakness is ultimately a positive characteristic. For example, 'I enjoy my work and always give each project my best shot. So, when sometimes I don't feel others are pulling their weight, I find it a little frustrating. I am aware of that weakness and, in those situations, I try to overcome it with a positive attitude that I hope will catch on.'

Also, consider the technique of putting a problem in the past. Here you take a weakness from way back and show how you overcame it. It answers the question but ends on a positive note. An illustration: 'When I first got into this field, I always had problems with my paperwork – you know, leaving an adequate paper trail. To be honest, I let it slip once or twice. My manager sat me down and explained the potential troubles such behaviour could cause. I really took it to heart and I think you will find my paper trails some of the best around today. You only have to tell me something once.' With that kind of answer, you also get the added bonus of showing that you accept and act on criticism.

Congratulations! You have just turned a pig of a question into an opportunity to sell yourself. In deciding on the particular answer you will give, remember that the interviewer isn't really concerned about your general weaknesses – no one is a saint outside of the interview room. He or she is simply concerned about any red flags that might signal your inability to perform the job or work well under supervision.

'With hindsight, how could you have improved your progress?'

Here's a question that demands, 'Tell me your mistakes and weaknesses.' If you can mention ways of improving your performance without damaging your candidacy, do so. The end of your answer should contain something like, 'Other than that, I don't know what to add. I have always given it my best shot.' Then shut up.

'What kinds of decisions are most difficult for you?'

You are human, admit it, but be careful what you admit. If you have ever had to fire someone, you are in luck, because no one likes to do that. Emphasize that, having reached a logical conclusion, you act. If you are not in management, tie your answer to the key profiles: 'It's not that I have difficulty making decisions – some just require more consideration than others. A small example might be holiday time. Now, everyone is entitled to it, but I don't believe you should leave your boss in a bind at short notice. I think very carefully at the beginning of the year when I'd like to take my holidays and then think of alternative dates. I go to my supervisor, tell him what I hope to do and see if there is any conflict. I wouldn't want to be out of the office for the two weeks prior to a project deadline, for instance. So, by carefully considering things far enough in advance, I don't procrastinate and make sure my plans fit in with my boss and the department for the year.'

Here you take a trick question and use it to demonstrate your consideration, analytical abilities and concern for the department – and for the company's bottom line.

'Tell me about the problems you have living within your means'

This is a twister to catch you off-guard. Your best defence is, first of all, to know that it exists and, second, give it short shrift. 'I know few people who are satisfied with their current earnings. As a professional, I am continually striving to improve my skills and improve my standard of living. My problems, though, are no different from those of this company or any other – making sure all the bills get paid on time and recognizing that every month and year there are some things that are prudent to do and other expenses that are best deferred.'

'What area of your skills/professional development do you want to improve at this time?'

Another 'tell me all your weaknesses' question. You should try to avoid damaging your candidacy by tossing around careless admissions. One effective answer to this is to say, 'Well, from what you told me about the job, I seem to have all the necessary skills and background. What I would really find exciting is the opportunity to work on a job where...' At this point, you replay the interviewer's hot buttons about the job. You emphasize that you really have all the job-related skills and also tell the interviewer what you find exciting about the job. It works admirably.

Another safe response is to reiterate one or two areas that combine personal strengths and the job's most crucial responsibilities, then finish by saying, 'These areas are so important that I don't think anyone can be too good or should ever stop trying to polish their skills.'

'Your application shows you have been with one company a long time without any appreciable increase in rank or salary. Tell me about this'

Ugh. A toughie. To start with, you should analyse why this state of affairs exists (assuming the interviewer's assessment is accurate). Then, when you have determined the cause, practise saying it out loud to yourself as you would say it during an actual interview. It may take a few tries. Chances are that, no matter how valid your explanation really is, it will come off sounding a little tinny or vindictive without some polishing. Avoid the sour grapes syndrome at all costs.

Here are some tactics you can use. First of all, try to avoid putting your salary history on application forms. No one is going to deny you an interview for lack of a salary history if your skills match those the job requires. Of course, you should never put such trivia on your CV.

If the interviewer is intent and asks you outright for this information, you'll find a great response in the section on salary histories in Chapter 23.

Now then, next we'll address the delicate matter of 'Hey, wait a minute, why no promotions?' This is one case where saying the wrong thing can get you in just as much trouble as failing to say the right thing. The interviewer has posed a truly negative enquiry. The more time either of you spend on it, the more time the interviewer gets to devote to concentrating on negative aspects of your candidacy. Make your answer short and sweet, then shut up. For instance, 'My current employer is a stable company with a good working environment, but there's minimal growth there in my area – in fact, there hasn't been any promotion in my area since _____. Your question is the reason I am meeting here with you; I have the skills and ability to take on more responsibility and I'm looking for a place to do that.'

'Are you willing to take calculated risks when necessary?'

First, qualify the question: 'How do you define calculated risks? What sorts of risks? Give me an example of a risk you have in mind; what are the stakes involved?' That will show you exactly the right analytical approach to evaluating a calculated risk and, while the interviewer is rattling on, you have bought time to come up with an answer. Whatever your answer, you will include, 'Naturally, I would never take any risk that would in any way jeopardize the safety or reputation of my company or colleagues. In fact, I don't think any employer would appreciate an employee at any level taking risks of any nature without first having a thorough briefing and chance to give input.'

'See this pen I'm holding? Sell it to me'

Not a request, as you might think, that would only be asked of a salesperson. In today's professional workplace, everyone is required to communicate effectively and sell appropriately – sometimes products, but more often ideas, approaches and concepts. As such, you are being examined about your understanding of features and selling of benefits, how quickly you think on your feet and how effective your verbal communication is. For example, the interviewer holds up a yellow highlighter. First, you will want to establish the customer's needs with a few questions such as, 'What sort of pens do you currently use? Do you use a highlighter? Do you read reports and need to recall important points? Is comfort important to you?' Then you will proceed calmly, 'Let me tell you about the special features of this pen and show you how they will satisfy your needs. First of all, it is tailor-made for highlighting reports and that will save you time in recalling the most important points. The case is wide for comfort and the base is flat so it will stand up and be visible on a cluttered work area. It's disposable and affordable enough to have a handful for desk, briefcase, car and home. Also, the bright yellow means you'll never lose it.' Then close with a smile and a question of your own that will bring a smile to the interviewer's face 'How many boxes of these shall we deliver?'

'How will you be able to cope with a change in environment after [say] five years with your current company?'

Another chance to take an implied negative and turn it into a positive. 'That's one of the reasons for my wanting to make a change. After five years with my current employer, I felt I was about to get stale. Everyone needs a change of scene once in a while. It's just time for me to make some new friends, face some new challenges and experience some new approaches; hopefully, I'll have the chance to contribute from my experience.'

'Why aren't you earning more at your age?'

Accept this as a compliment to your skills and accomplishments. 'I have always felt that solid experience would stand me in good stead in the long run and that earnings would come in due course. Also, I am not the type of person to change jobs just for the money. At this point, I have a solid background that is worth something to a company.' Now, to avoid the interviewer putting you on the spot again, finish with a question: 'How much should I be earning now?' The figure could be your offer.

'What is the worst thing you have heard about our company?'

This question can come as something of a shock. As with all stress questions, your poise here is vital and if you can carry off a halfway decent answer as well, you are a winner. The best response to this question is simple. Just say with a smile, 'You're a tough company to get into because your interviews and interviewers are so rigorous.' It's true, it's flattering, and it shows that you are not intimidated.

'How would you define your profession?'

With questions that solicit your understanding of a topic, no matter how good your answer, you can expect to be interrupted in mid-reply with 'That has nothing to do with it' or 'Whoever put that idea into your head?' While your response is a judgement call, 999 times out of a thousand these comments are not meant to be taken as serious criticisms. Rather, they are tests to see how well you would be able to defend your position in a no-holds-barred conversation with the chairman of the Board, who says exactly what he or she thinks at all times. So, go ahead and defend yourself, without taking or showing offence.

Your first response will be to gain time and get the interviewer talking. 'Why do you say that?' you ask, answering a question with a question. Turning the tables on your aggressor displays your poise, calm and analytical skills better than any other response.

'Why should I take on an outsider when I could fill the job with someone inside the company?'

The question isn't as stupid as it sounds. Obviously, the interviewer has examined existing employees with an eye towards their promotion or reassignment. Just as obviously, the job cannot be filled from within the company. If it could be, it would be and for two very good reasons: it is cheaper for the company to promote from within and it is good for employee morale.

Hiding behind this intimidating question is actually a pleasant invitation: 'Tell me why I should give you the job.' Your answer should include two steps. The first is a simple recitation of your skills and personality profile strengths, tailored to the specific requirements of the job.

For the second step, realize first that whenever a manager is filling a position, he or she is looking not only for someone who can do the job but also for someone who can benefit the department in a larger sense. No department is as good as it could be – each has weaknesses that need strengthening. So, in the second part of your answer, include a question of your own: 'Those are my general attributes. However, if no one is promotable from inside the company, that means you are looking to add strength to your team in a special way. In what ways do you hope the final candidate will be able to benefit your department?' The answer to this is your cue to sell your applicable qualities.

'Have you ever had any financial difficulties?'

The potential employer wants to know if you can control not only your own finances but also finances in general. If you are in the insurance field, for example – in claims, accounting, supervision or management – you can expect to hear this one. The question, though, is not restricted to insurance – anyone, especially a person who handles money in day-to-day business, is fair game.

The interviewer does not want to hear sob stories. If your credit history is not too good, concentrate on the information that will damage your candidacy the least and enhance it the most. You might find it appropriate to bring the matter up yourself if you work in an area where your credit history is likely to be checked. If you choose to wait until the interviewer brings it up, you might say (if you had to file for bankruptcy, for instance), 'I should tell you that some years ago, for reasons beyond my control, I was forced into personal bankruptcy. That has been behind me for some time. Today, I have a sound credit rating and no debts. Bankruptcy is not something I'm proud of, but I did learn from the experience and I feel it has made me a more proficient account supervisor.' The answer concentrates on today, not past history.

'How do you handle rejection?'

This question is common if you are applying for a job in sales, including face-to-face sales, telemarketing, public relations and customer service. If you are after a job in one of these areas and you really don't like the heavy doses of rejection that are any salesperson's lot, consider a new field. The anguish you will experience will not lead to a successful career or a happy life.

With that in mind, let's look behind the question. The interviewer simply wants to know if you take rejection as rejection of yourself or simply accept it as a temporary rejection of a service or product. Here is a sample answer that you can tailor to your particular needs and background: 'I accept rejection as an integral part of the sales process. If everyone said "yes" to a product, there would be no need for the sales function. As it is, I see every rejection as bringing me closer to the customer who will say "yes".' Then, if you are encouraged to go on, 'I regard rejection as simply a fact of life, that the customer has no need for the product today. I can go on to my next call with the conviction that I am a little closer to my next sale.'

'Why were you out of work for so long?'

You must have a sound explanation for any and all gaps in your employment history. If not, you are unlikely to receive a job offer. Emphasize that you were not just looking for another pay cheque, you were looking for a company with which to settle and make a long-term contribution.

'I made a decision that I enjoy my work too much just to accept another pay cheque. So, I determined that the next job I took would be one where I could settle down and do my best to make a solid contribution. From everything I have heard about this company, you are a group that expects people to pull their weight, because you've got a real job to do. I like that and I would like to be part of the team. What do I have to do to get the job?'

You answer the question, compliment the interviewer and shift the emphasis from your being unemployed to how you can get the job offer.

'Why have you changed jobs so frequently?'

If you have jumped around, blame it on youth (even the interviewer was young once). Now you realize what a mistake your job-hopping was and, with your added domestic responsibilities, you are now much more settled. Alternatively, you may wish to impress on the interviewer that your job-hopping was never as a result of poor performance and that you grew professionally as a result of each job change.

You could reply, 'My first job involved a long journey to and from work. It was hard, but I knew it would give me good experience in a very competitive field. Subsequently, I found a job much closer to home where commuting was only half an hour each way. I was very happy at my second job. However, I got an opportunity to really broaden my experience base with a new company that was just starting up. With the wisdom of hindsight, I realize that move was a mistake – it took me just six months to see that I couldn't make a contribution there. I've been with my current company a reasonable length of time. So, I have broad experience in different environments. I didn't just job-hop, I have been following a path to gain this broad experience. So, you see, I have more experience than the average person of my years and a desire to settle down and make it pay off for me and my employer.'

Alternatively, you can say, 'Now I want to settle down and make my diverse background pay off in my contributions to my new employer. I have a strong desire to contribute and am looking for an employer that will keep me challenged. I think this might be the company to do that – am I right?'

'Tell me about a time when you put your foot in your mouth'

Answer this question with caution. The interviewer is examining your ability and willingness to interact pleasantly with others. The question is tricky because it asks you to show yourself in a poor light. Your answer should downplay the negative impact of your action and end with positive information about your candidacy. The best thing to do is start with an example outside of the workplace and show how the experience improved your performance at work.

'About five years ago, I let the cat out of the bag about a surprise birthday party for a friend, a terrific *faux pas.* It was a mortifying experience and I promised myself not to let anything like that happen again.' Then, after this fairly innocuous statement, you can talk about communications in the workplace. 'As far as work is concerned, I always regard employer/employee communications on any matter as confidential unless expressly stated otherwise. So, putting my foot in my mouth doesn't happen to me at work.'

'Why do you want to leave your current job?' or 'Why did you leave your last job?'

This is a common trick question. You should have an acceptable reason for leaving every job you have held, but, if you don't, pick one of the six acceptable reasons from the employment industry formula, the acronym for which is CLAMPS:

- *C*hallenge – you weren't able to grow professionally in that position;
- *L*ocation – the journey to work was unreasonably long;
- *A*dvancement – there was nowhere for you to go, you had the talent, but there were too many people ahead of you;
- *M*oney – you were underpaid for your skills and contribution;
- *P*ride or *P*restige – you wanted to be with a better company;
- *S*ecurity – the company was not stable.

For example, 'My last company was a family-owned affair. I had gone as far as I was able. It just seemed time for me to join a more prestigious company and accept greater challenges.'

'What interests you least about this job?'

This question is potentially explosive, but easily defused. Regardless of your occupation, there is at least one repetitive, mindless duty that everyone groans about and that goes with the territory. Use that as your example in a statement of this nature: 'Filing is probably the least demanding part of the job. However, it is important to the overall success of my department, so I try to do it with a smile.' This shows that you understand that it is necessary to take the rough with the smooth in any job.

'What was there about your last company that you didn't particularly like or agree with?'

You are being checked out as a potential fly in the ointment. If you have to answer, you might say something about the way the company policies and/or directives were sometimes consciously misunderstood by some employees who disregarded the bottom line – the profitability of the company.

Alternatively, you could say, 'You know how it is sometimes with a big company. People lose awareness of the cost of things. There never seemed to be much concern about economy or efficiency. Everyone wanted his or her year-end bonus, but only worried about it just before it was going to be announced. The rest of the year, nobody gave a hoot. I think that's the kind of thing we could be aware of almost every day, don't you agree?'

Another is, 'I didn't like the way some people gave lip-service to "the customer comes first"', but really didn't go out of their way to keep the customer satisfied. I don't think it was a fault of management, just a general malaise that seemed to affect a lot of people.'

'What do you feel is a satisfactory attendance record?'

There are two answers to this question – one if you are in management, one if you are not. As a manager, 'I believe attendance is a matter of management, motivation and psychology. Letting the employees know you expect their best efforts and won't accept half-baked excuses is one thing. The other is to keep your employees motivated by a congenial work environment and the challenge to stretch themselves. Giving people pride in their work and letting them know you respect them as individuals have a lot to do with it, too.'

If you are not in management, the answer is even easier: 'I've never really considered it. I work for a living, I enjoy my job and I'm rarely ill.'

'What is your general impression of your last company?'

Always answer positively. Keep your real feelings to yourself, whatever they might be. There is a strong belief among the management fraternity that people who complain about past employers will cause problems for their new ones. Your answer is, 'Very good' or 'Excellent.' Then smile and wait for the next question.

'What are some of the problems you encounter in doing your job and what do you do about them?'

Note well the old saying, 'A poor workman blames his tools.' Your awareness that careless mistakes cost the company good money means you are always on the lookout for potential problems. Give an example of a problem you recognized and solved.

For example, 'My job is fairly repetitive, so it's easy to overlook problems. Lots of people do. However, I always look for them – it helps keep me alert and motivated, so I do a better job. To give you an example, we make computer memory disks. Each one has to be machined by hand and, once completed, the slightest abrasion will turn one into a reject. I have a steady staff and little turnover and everyone wears cotton gloves to handle the disks. Yet, about six months ago, the reject rate suddenly went through the roof. Is that the kind of problem you mean? Well, the cause was one that could have gone unnoticed for ages. Jill, the section head who inspects all the disks, had lost a lot of weight, her diamond engagement ring was slipping around her finger and it was scratching the disks as she passed them and stacked them to be shipped. Our main client was disatisfied over it, so my looking for problems and paying attention to detail really paid off.'

The interviewer was trying to get you to reveal weak points, but you avoided the trap.

'What are some of the things you find difficult to do? Why do you feel that way?'

This is a variation on a couple of earlier questions. Remember, anything that goes against the best interests of your employer is difficult to do. If you are pressed for a job function you find difficult, answer in the past tense as, that way, you show that you recognize the difficulty, but you obviously handle it well.

'That's a tough question. There are so many things that are difficult to learn in our business if you want to do the job right. I used to have 40 clients to sell to every month and I was so busy keeping in touch with all of them, I never got a chance to sell to any of them. So, I graded them into three groups. I called on the top 20 per cent with whom I did business every three weeks. The next group were those I sold to occasionally. I called on them once a month, but with a difference – each month, I marked 10 of them to spend time with and really get to know. I still have difficulty reaching all 40 of my clients in a month, but my sales have tripled and are still climbing.'

'Jobs have pluses and minuses. What were some of the minuses on your last job?'

A variation on the question, 'What interests you least about this job?' which was handled earlier. Use the same type of answer. For example, 'Like any salesperson, I enjoy selling, not doing the paperwork. However, as I cannot expect the customer to get the goods and me my commission without following through on this task, I grin and bear it. Besides, if I don't do the paperwork, that holds up other people in the company.'

If you are not in sales, use the salesforce as a scapegoat. 'In accounts receivable, it's my job to get the money in to make payroll and positive things like that. Half the time, the goods get shipped before I get the paperwork because sales say, "It's a rush order". That's a real minus to me. It was so bad at my last company, we tried a new approach. We met with sales and explained our problem. The result was that incremental commissions were based on cash in, not on bill date. They saw the connection and things are much better now.'

'What kinds of people do you like to work with?'

This is the easy part of a tricky three-part question. Obviously, you like to work with people who have pride, honesty, integrity and dedication to their work. On to part 2.

'What kinds of people do you find it difficult to work with?'

The second part of the same question. You could say, 'People who don't follow procedures or slackers – the occasional rotten apples who don't really care about the quality of their work. They're long on complaints, but short on solutions.' This brings us to the third part of the question.

'How have you successfully worked with this difficult type of person?'

This is the most difficult part to answer. You might reply, 'I stick to my guns, stay enthusiastic and hope some of it will rub off. I had a big problem with one guy – all he did was complain and always in my area. Eventually, I told him how I felt. I said if I were a millionaire, I'd have all the answers and wouldn't have to work, but, as it was, I wasn't, and had to work for a living. I told him that I really enjoyed his company, but I didn't want to hear it any more. Every time I saw him after that, I presented him with a work problem and asked his advice. In other words I challenged him to come up with positives, not negatives.'

You can go on to say that sometimes you've noticed that such people simply lack enthusiasm and confidence and that energetic and cheerful colleagues can often change that. If the interviewer follows up with an enquiry about what you would do if no amount of good effort on your part solved the problem, respond, 'I would maintain cordial relations, but not go out of my way to seek more than a business-like acquaintance. Life is too short to be demotivated by people who always think their cup is half empty.'

'How did you get your last job?'

The interviewer is looking for initiative. If you can, show it. At the least, though, show determination.

'I was actually turned down for my last job for having too little experience. I asked the manager to give me a trial before she offered it to anyone else. I went in and asked for a list of companies they'd never sold to, picked up the phone and, within that hour, I arranged two appointments. How did I get the job? In a word, determination!'

'How would you evaluate me as an interviewer?'

This question is dangerous – maybe more so than the one asking you to criticize your boss. Whatever you do, of course, don't tell the truth if you think the interviewer is an incompetent. It may be true, but it won't get you a job offer. This is an instance where honesty is not the best policy. It is best to say, 'This is one of the toughest interviews I have ever been through and I don't relish the prospect of going through another. Yet, I do realize what you are trying to achieve.' Then go on to explain that you understand the interviewer wants to know whether or not you can think on your feet, that there is pressure in the job and that he or she is trying to simulate some of that real-life pressure in the interview. You may choose to finish the answer with a question of your own: 'How do you think I fit the profile of the person you need?'

'I'm not sure you're suitable for the job'

Don't worry about the tone of the question – the interviewer's 'I'm not sure' really means, 'I'd like to take you on, so here's a wide-open opportunity to sell me on yourself.' He or she is probing three areas from your personal profile: your confidence, determination and listening profiles. Remain calm and put the ball straight back into the interviewer's court: 'Why do you say that?' You need both the information and time to think up an appropriate reply, but it is important to show that you are not intimidated. Work out a plan of action for this question. Even if the interviewer's point regarding your skills is valid, come back with value keys and alternative compatible skills. Counter with other skills that show your competence and learning ability and use them to show you can pick up the new skills quickly. Tie the two together and demonstrate that, with your other attributes, you can bring many pluses to the job. Finish your answer with a reflexive question that encourages a 'yes' answer.

'I admit my programming skills in that language are a little light. However, all languages have similarities and my experience demonstrates that, with competence in four other languages, getting up to speed with this one will take only a short while. Plus, I can bring a depth of other experience to the job.' Then, after you itemize your experience: 'Wouldn't you agree?'

If the reason for the question is not a lack of technical skills, it must be a question about one of your key profile areas. Perhaps the interviewer will say, 'You haven't convinced me of your determination.' This is an invitation to sell yourself, so tell a story that demonstrates determination.

For example: 'It's interesting you should say that. My present boss is convinced of my determination. About a year ago we were having some problems with a union organization in the plant. Management's problem was our 50 per cent Asian virtually monolingual production workforce. Despite the fact that our people had the best working conditions and benefits in the area, they were strongly pro-union. If they were successful, we would be the first unionized division in the company. No one in management spoke Hindi, so I took a crash course – two hours at home every night for five weeks. I got one of the maintenance crew to help me with my grammar and diction. Then a number of other production workers started saying simple things to me in Hindi and helping me with the answers. I opened the first meeting with the workforce to discuss the problems, greeting them in their own language – they really appreciated it. We had demonstrated that we cared enough to try to communicate. Our division never did unionize and my determination to take that extra step paid off and allowed my superiors to negotiate from a position of caring and strength. Wouldn't you agree that my work in that instance shows determination?'

'Wouldn't you feel better off in another firm?'

Relax, things aren't as bad as you might assume. This question is usually asked if you are really doing quite well or if the job involves a certain amount of stress. A lawyer, for example, might well be expected to face this one. The trick is not to be intimidated. Your first step is to qualify the question. Relax, take a breath, sit back, smile and say, 'You surprise me. Why do you say that?' The interviewer must then talk, giving you precious time to collect your wits and come back with a rebuttal.

Then answer 'no' and explain why. All the interviewer wants to see is how much you know about the company and how determined you are to join their ranks. Your earlier research and knowledge of personal profile keys (determination) will pay off again. Overcome the objection with an example and show how that will help you contribute to the company. End with a question of your own. In this instance, the question has a twofold purpose: one, to identify a critical area to sell yourself; and, two, to encourage the interviewer to consider an image of you working at the company.

You could reply: 'Not at all. My whole experience has been with small companies. I am good at my job and in time could become a big fish in a little pond, but that is not what I want. This company is a leader in its business. You have a strong reputation for encouraging skills development in your employees. This is the type of environment I want to work in. Now, coming from a small company, I have done a little bit of everything. This means that no matter what you throw at me, I will learn it quickly. For example, what would be the first project I would be involved with?'

End with a question of your own that gets the interviewer focusing on those immediate problems. You can then explain how your background and experience can help.

'What would you say if I told you your presentation this afternoon was pretty bad?'

'If' is the key word here, with the accusation there only for the terminally neurotic. The question is designed to see how you react to criticism and so tests your 'manageability.' No company can afford to employ the thin-skinned applicant today. You will come back and answer the question with a question of your own. An appropriate response would be, 'First of all, I would ask which aspects of my presentation were poor. My next step would be to find out where you felt the problem was. If there was miscommunication, I'd clear it up. If the problem was elsewhere, I would seek your advice and be sure that the problem was not recurrent.' This would show that when it is a manager's duty to criticize performance, you are an employee who will respond in a businesslike and emotionally mature manner.

The illegal question

Of course, one of the most stressful – and negative – questions is the illegal one, a question that delves into your private life or personal background. Such a question will make you uncomfortable if it is blatant and could also make you angry.

Your aim, however, is to overcome your discomfort and avoid getting angry. You want to be offered the job and any self-righteousness or defensive reaction on your part will ensure that you *don't* get it. You may feel angry enough to get up and walk out or say things like, 'These are unfair practices; you'll hear from my lawyer in the morning.' However, the result will be that you won't get the job and, therefore, won't have the leverage you need. Remember, no one is saying you can't refuse the job once it's offered to you.

So, what is an illegal question? The Sex Discrimination Act and the Race Relations Act forbid employers from discriminating against any person on the basis of sex, age, race, national origin or religion. In Northern Ireland, religious discrimination is also ruled out.

An interviewer may not ask about your religion, church, synagogue or parish, the religious holidays you observe or your political beliefs or affiliations. He or she may not ask, for instance, 'Does your religion allow you to work on Saturdays?' but may ask something like, 'This job requires work on Saturdays. Is that a problem?' Similarly, the interviewer may enquire if the usual number of hours a week required will be acceptable.

An interviewer may not ask about your ancestry, national origin or parentage. In addition, you cannot be asked about the naturalization status of your parents, spouse or children. The interviewer cannot ask about your birthplace, *but* may ask (and probably will, considering the current immigration laws) whether you are a citizen or resident with the right to work in this country.

An interviewer may not ask about your native language, the language you speak at home or how you acquired the ability to read, write or speak a foreign language. *However,* he or she may ask about the languages in which you are fluent, if knowledge of those languages is pertinent to the job.

An interviewer may not ask about your age, date of birth or the ages of your children. *However,* he or she may ask you if you are over 18 years old.

An interviewer may not ask about maiden names or if you have changed your name, your marital status, number of children or dependents or your spouse's occupation or, if you are a woman, whether you wish to be addressed as Miss, Mrs or Ms. *However,* the interviewer may ask about how you like to be addressed (a common courtesy) and if you have ever worked for the company before under a different name. If you have, you may want to mention that, especially as your prospective manager may check your references and additional background information.

As you consider a question that seems to verge on illegality, you should take into account that the interviewer may be asking it innocently and may be unaware of the laws on the matter. Your best bet is to be polite and straightforward, as you would in any other social situation. You also want to move the conversation on to an examination of your skills and abilities, not your status. Here are some sample illegal questions and some possible responses. Remember, your objective is to get job offers; if you later decide that this company is not for you, you are under no obligation to accept the position.

'How old are you?'

Age discrimination is still prevalent, but with older people joining the workforce every day and the increasing need for experienced workers, you will hear this question less and less. Answer the question in terms of your experience. For example, 'I'm in my fifties and have more than 25 years of experience in this field.' Then list your skills as they apply to the job.

'Are you married?'

If you are, the company is concerned with the impact your family duties and future plans will have on your time there. Your answer could be, 'Yes, I am. Of course, I make a separation between my work life and my family life that allows me to give my all to a job. I have no problem with travel or late hours – those things are part of this line of work. I'm sure my references will confirm this for you.'

'Do you plan to have children?'

This isn't any of the interviewer's business, but he or she wants to know whether or not you will leave the company early to raise a family. You can answer 'no' of course. If you answer 'yes' you might add, 'but those plans are for the future and they depend on the success of my career. Certainly, I want to do the best, most complete job for this company I can. I consider that my skills are right for the job and that I can make a long-term contribution. I certainly have no plans to leave the company just as I begin to make meaningful contributions.' However, unless this question is also asked of male applicants, it could be considered as discriminating against women. The skilful interviewer can usually elicit such information without asking a direct question.

If the questions become too pointed, you may want to ask, innocently, 'Could you explain the relevance of that issue to this position? I'm trying to get a handle on it.' That response, however, can seem confrontational, so you should only use it if you are *extremely* uncomfortable or are quite certain you can get away with it. Sometimes, the interviewer will drop the line of questioning.

Illegal questions tend to arise not out of brazen insensitivity, but, rather, out of an interest in you. The employer is familiar with your skills and background, feels you can do the job and wants to get to know you as a person. Outright discrimination these days is really quite rare. With illegal questions, your response must be positive – that's the only way you're going to be offered the job and winning that creates a platform for getting other jobs. You don't have to work for a discriminatory company, but you can certainly use the firm to get to something better.

Mock meetings, role plays and in-tray tests

Some employers use even more elaborate versions of the stress interview when selecting staff. Groups of candidates may be put in a room together and asked to stage a mock meeting or give an impromptu presentation. You may even be asked to demonstrate your organization and time management skills by sorting out and acting on an in-tray full of an overwhelming amount of supposedly urgent material, all the while being interrupted by telephone calls.

Collectively, these approaches are referred to as assessment centre techniques. They are frequently run – on an employer's behalf – by a third-party operation that specializes in this corporate manifestation of the Spanish Inquisition. Some companies use this approach when deciding on executives, some for choosing sales and customer service professionals and others for identifying the best candidates for administrative positions. Unfortunately, assessment centre techniques are so common today that anyone in the job market risks facing their myriad tortures. The good news is that I have one or two techniques that can help you face these latter-day dungeons of delight with equanimity.

One of the reasons that assessment centre techniques are growing in popularity is the corporate world's increasing focus on teamwork. Many employers think they can choose the best workers for a team environment by using group interviews. (Forget the fact that assessment centres haven't proved themselves better or worse than other selection methods!) As you may encounter this old–new approach during your job search, I want you to be ready for it.

Racks, beds of nails and iron maidens

Assessment centres use a broad variety of techniques, including:

▌ mock meetings;

▌ in-tray tests;

▌ role playing.

Let me give you some background on each of these techniques and show you how you can prepare yourself to make a great impression in any situation. With these selection techniques, forewarned is forearmed. With a little bit of time to prepare and an understanding of how these situations work, you can survive anything they might throw at you. Besides, it's only pretend, so there's no need to break out in a cold sweat.

Mock meetings: taking control, taking charge and being a team player

Some employers will want to see you take charge of, or perhaps take over, the leadership of the group, while others want to see your skills at interacting with people and some will want to see both. Your first step in preparing for a mock meeting is to outline the challenges you would face in the average daily routine of the job you've applied for. These challenges are likely to form the basis of the situations you'll be asked to respond to. For example, if your job will involve making sales presentations for expensive items to groups of people, you can expect the mock meeting to include all of the difficult questions, problems and people you would be likely to meet in such a context. There are only two differences. First, the whole range of problems is going to appear in one meeting and, second, it's just pretend. If you are a competent professional and react to the situations you face in a professional manner, you will do just fine.

Your assessors may set up a leaderless group discussion and watch what happens. These groups may include an assortment of applicants, existing employees and selection centre staff, some of them 'planted' there to cause disruption or otherwise throw you off-balance. Just knowing who is who and why they're there can be a big help. This is a test of your assertiveness skills.

Anything you face in one of these situations will mirror the challenges you face in the real work world. If your appraisal of the job is that 'taking control' and 'demonstrating leadership' are likely to be the goals of the mock meeting, *how* you take control and demonstrate leadership will be crucial to your success. You need to set a standard of democratic leadership; you have to become the parent who sets firm limits, but gives support. Be sure to give everyone 'air time' while keeping the group on-target and on-schedule.

Sometimes taking charge can be dangerous, however. If you come across as too tough, bossy or autocratic, forget it! You can't just say, 'OK, this is a test of my decision-making and leadership skills, so move over, and let *me* take over.' You should encourage a more team-oriented approach: 'Let's take a moment to gather our thoughts, then each, in turn, address the issues from our unique perspective.' You must keep the meeting moving if someone tries to dominate the discussion or move it away from the agenda. You can then demonstrate your leadership by thanking everyone for their contributions.

If someone else beats you to it and assumes the leadership role, don't try to show everyone how tough you are by fighting to regain control. Instead, act like the archetypal active team member. Use the time you have while the leader is busy managing the meeting to plan your strategy and develop your contributions to the idea or plan the group is working on. Position yourself as a team player and consensus builder, but show you can take the initiative, too.

From this position, you can be ready to scoop the opposition at the end of the meeting. While the 'leader' is busy making sure that every voice is heard, you can prepare to help the group summarize its common ground and establish possible next steps.

For more information on what the testers will be looking for in terms of teamwork and leadership, see the related questions on pages 177–180.

In-tray: a test of organized action

You're staring at a huge stack of reports, memos and phone messages on your desk. The red light on the phone is flashing to let you know you've got voice mail messages. The computer screen glares at you with a dozen as yet unread e-mail messages. Confronting applicants with a virtual day at the office is yet another technique companies use to screen out the wheat from the chaff. In this example, you're facing an in-tray test and it is being used primarily to examine your time management and organization skills.

The in-tray test confronts the job candidate with overwhelming amounts of information and often conflicting priorities. Then the observers sit back, put their feet up and watch you wither or shine before their eyes. There are many ways to tackle this kind of test, but the main thing is to make sure that you come prepared with a system to prioritize and organize the work.

Alan Lakein, the godfather of time management, introduced me to a wildly effective and widely accepted approach to time management. Take everything out of the in-tray and place each document in one of three piles:

▍ the A pile is *urgent* and you will act on it 'today' – in other words, during the test;

▍ the B pile is *important* and needs attention – you'll start on it when and if you get through your A pile; if not, much of it will move into your A pile, as you plan for 'tomorrow' at the end of 'today';

▍ the C pile is to file or just put in a drawer – it is still important work, but not as urgent as your A and B work, and if someone makes it urgent for you, via a telephone call or an urgent e-mail message, you'll know where to find it.

Working out these priorities is the first step to winning in an in-tray test. Once established, you'll be able to prioritize those pesky interruptions that are always programmed into this partic-ular type of test. When the calls come in, as they will, you must have a system in place that can help you decide how to respond. For example, you need to find out:

▍ who's calling and what that person does – you want to estab-lish his or her name, department and reporting relationship so that, if your 'boss' of the day calls, you instantly know he or she has the power to move something from your C pile directly to your A pile;

▍ what the person is calling about – you can put him or her on hold while you find the appropriate paperwork, consider the relative importance of the call and decide how to handle it with efficiency and professionalism.

It is important, at the end of the test, to make sure that the assessor understands that you have been using an effective and logical system.

For more information on what assessors are looking for in this kind of test, see the question about scheduling on pages 180–81 and the question on working methods on page 189.

Role playing

You may be asked to handle a sticky staff problem, an employee calling in sick from the golf course, a malfunctioning team, an inventory problem, a broken machine or cold calls to a series of prospective 'clients'.' The goal of role playing is invariably to see how you handle the people and situations that are likely to crop up in the day-to-day execution of your duties.

Are you a hard-nosed so-and-so or do you cave in under the slightest pressure? Do you want the world to love and admire you or are you out to settle a score? How do you handle a belligerent customer or salvage a tough sale when it turns sour at the last moment?

What's the best way to handle these situations? Consider the role you are playing – is it to land a job as a customer service representative, sales training specialist, finance director or union lawyer? In handling role-playing tests, you need to be clear about the job you're facing and the challenges it typically generates. You will then understand exactly what the testers are looking for and the role you should choose to play in their scenarios.

In each of these stressful interviewing situations the key is to determine which professional hat you should be wearing and the behaviour the testers will expect from someone wearing that hat.

Interviewers may pull all kinds of tricks on you, but you will come through with flying colours once you realize that they're trying to discover something extremely simple – whether or not you can take the heat. After all, those interviewers are only trying to sort out the good corporate warriors from the walking wounded. If you successfully handle these trick and negatively phrased questions, the interviewer will end up looking at you favourably. Stay calm, give as good as you get and take it all in your stride. Remember that no one can intimidate you without your permission.

19 **Strange venues**

Learn the tips that will help you master interviews in noisy, distracting hotel lobbies, restaurants, poolsides and other unusual settings.

Why are some interviews conducted in strange places? Are meetings in noisy, distracting hotel lobbies designed as a form of torture? What are the real reasons for an interviewer inviting you to eat at a fancy restaurant?

For the most part, these tough-on-the-nerves situations happen because the interviewer is a busy person, fitting you into a crowded schedule. Take the case of a woman I know. She had heard stories about tough interview situations but never expected to face one herself. It happened at a retail convention. She had been asked to meet for a final interview by the pool. The interviewer was there, taking a short break between meetings, in his bathing suit, and the first thing the interviewer did was suggest that my friend 'slip into something comfortable'!

That scenario may not lurk in your future, but the chances are that you will face many tough interview situations in your career. They call for a clear head and a little gamesmanship to put you ahead of the competition. The interviewee at the pool used both. She removed her jacket, folded it over the arm of the chair and seated herself, saying pleasantly, 'That's much better. Where shall we begin?'

It isn't easy to remain calm at such times. On top of interview nerves, you're worried about being overheard in a public place or, worse, surprised by the appearance of your current boss. That last nightmare isn't too far-fetched. It actually happened to a reader who was being interviewed in the departure lounge at the airport when his boss walked through the arrivals door. Oops – he had asked for the day off 'to go to the doctor'.

Could he have avoided this situation? Certainly, if he had asked for privacy when the meeting was arranged. That would have reminded the interviewer of the need for discretion. The point is to do all you can in advance to make such a meeting as private as possible. Once that's done, you can ignore the rest of the world and concentrate on the interviewer's questions.

Hotel lobbies and other strange places

Strange interview situations provide other wonderful opportunities to embarrass yourself. You come to a hotel lobby in full corporate battle dress – coat, briefcase, perhaps an umbrella. You sit down to wait for the interviewer. 'Aha,' you think to yourself, opening your briefcase, 'I'll show him my excellent work habits by delving into this computer printout.'

That's not such a great idea. Have you ever tried rising with your lap covered with business papers, then juggling the briefcase from right hand to left to accommodate the ritual handshake? It's quite difficult. Besides, while you are sitting in nervous anticipation, pre-interview tension has no way of dissipating. Your mouth will become dry and your 'Good morning, I'm pleased to meet you' will come out sounding like a cat is being strangled.

To avoid such catastrophes in places like hotel lobbies, first, remove your coat on arrival. Then, instead of sitting, walk around a little while you wait. Even in a small lobby, a few steps back and forth will help you reduce tension to a manageable level. Keep your briefcase in your left hand at all times – it makes you look purposeful and, an added bonus, you won't trip over it when you meet the interviewer.

If, for any reason, you must sit down, make a conscious effort to breathe deeply and slowly. This will help control the adrenaline that makes you feel jumpy.

A strange setting can actually put you on an equal footing with the interviewer. Neither of you is on home ground, so, in many cases, the interviewer will feel just as awkward as you do. A little gamesmanship can turn the occasion to your advantage.

To gain the upper hand, get to the meeting place early to scout the territory. By knowing your surroundings, you will feel more relaxed. Early arrival also allows you to control the outcome of the meeting in other subtle ways. You will have time to stake out the most private spot in an otherwise public place. Corners are best. They tend to be quieter and you can choose the seat that puts your back to the wall (in a practical sense, that is). In this position, you have a clear view of your surroundings and will feel more secure. The fear of being overheard will evaporate.

The situation is now somewhat in your favour. You know the locale and the meeting place is as much yours as the interviewer's. You will have a clear view of your surroundings and the odds are that you will be more relaxed than the interviewer. When he or she arrives, say, 'I arrived a little early to make sure we had some privacy. I think over here is the best spot.' With that positive demonstration of your organizational abilities, you give yourself a head start over the competition.

The meal meeting

Breakfast, lunch and dinner are the prime choices for interviewers who want to catch the seasoned professional off-guard. In fact, the meal is arguably the toughest of all tough interview situations. The setting offers the interviewer the chance to see you in a non-office (and therefore more natural) setting, observe your social graces and consider you as a whole person. Here, topics that would be impossible to address in the traditional office setting will naturally surface, often with virtually no effort on the part of the interviewer. The slightest slip in front of the interviewer could affect your candidacy.

Usually you will not be invited to an 'eating meeting' until you have already demonstrated that you are capable of doing the job. It's a good sign, actually, as an invitation to a meal means that you are under strong consideration and, by extension, intense scrutiny.

The meeting is often the final hurdle and could lead directly to a job offer – assuming, of course, that you handle the occasional surprises that arise properly. The interviewer's concern is not if you can do the job, but if you have the growth potential that will allow you to fill more senior slots as they become available.

However, be careful. Many have fallen at the final hurdle in a close-run race. Being interviewed in front of others is bad enough; eating and drinking in front of them at the same time only makes it worse. If you knock over a glass or dribble spaghetti sauce down your chin, the interviewer will be so busy smirking that he or she won't hear what you have to say.

To be sure that the interviewer remains as attentive to the positive points of your candidacy as possible, let's discuss table manners.

Your social graces and general demeanour at the table can tell as much about you as your answer to a question. For instance, overordering food or drink can signal poor self-discipline. At the very least, it will call into question your judgement and maturity. High-handed behaviour towards waiters and waitresses could reflect negatively on your ability to get along with subordinates and your leadership skills. These concerns are amplified when you return food or complain about the service – actions that, at the very least, find fault with the interviewer's choice of restaurant.

By the same token, you will want to observe how your potential employer behaves. After all, you are likely to become an employee and the interviewer's behaviour to servers in a restaurant can tell you a lot about what it will be like on the job.

Alcohol

Soon after being seated, you will be offered a drink – if not by your host, then by the waiter or waitress. There are many reasons to avoid alcohol at interview meals. The most important reason is that alcohol fuzzes your mind and research proves that stress increases the intoxicating effect of alcohol. So, if you order something to drink, try to stick with something non-alcoholic, such as a coke or simply a glass of water.

If you do have a low-alcohol drink, never have more than one. If there is a bottle of wine on the table and the waiter or waitress offers you another glass, simply place your hand over the top of your glass. It is a polite way of signifying no.

You may be offered alcohol at the end of the meal. The rule still holds true – turn it down. You need your wits about you, even if the interview seems to be drawing to a close. Some interviewers will try to use such moments, when your defences are at their lowest, to throw in a couple of zingers.

Smoking

Don't do it. If both the interviewer and you are smokers and he or she encourages you to smoke, still follow a simple rule: never smoke between courses, only at the end of a meal. Even most confirmed nicotine addicts, like the rest of the population, hate smoke while they are eating.

Utensils

Keep all your cups and glasses at the top of your place setting and well away from you. Most glasses are knocked over at a cluttered table when one stretches for the condiments or gesticulates to make a point. Of course, your manners will prevent you from reaching rudely for the pepper.

When you are faced with an array of knives, forks and spoons, it is always safe to start at the outside and work your way in as the courses come. Keep your elbows at your sides and don't slouch in the chair. When pausing between mouthfuls (which, if you are promoting yourself properly, should be frequently), rest your knife and fork on the plate.

The time to start eating, of course, is when the interviewer does; the time to stop is when he or she does. At the end of a course or the meal, rest your knife and fork together on the plate.

Here are some other helpful hints.

▌ Never speak with your mouth full.

▌ To be on the safe side, eat the same thing as the interviewer, or close to it. Of course, while this rule makes sense in theory, the fact is that you probably will be asked to order first. Solve the problem before you order by complimenting the restaurant during your small talk and then, when the menus arrive, ask, 'What do you think you will have today?'

▌ Do not change your order once it is made and never send the food back.

▌ Be polite to your waiters or waitresses, even when they spill soup in your lap.

▌ Don't order expensive food. Naturally, in our heart of hearts, we all like to eat well, especially when someone else is paying, but don't be tempted. When you come right down to it, you are there to talk and be seen at your best, not to eat.

▌ Eat what you know. Stay away from awkward, messy or exotic foods, such as artichokes, long pasta and escargot. Do not choose finger foods, such as lobster or spare ribs. In fact, you should avoid eating with your fingers altogether, unless you are in a sandwich bar, in which case you should make a point of avoiding the leaky, overstuffed options.

▌ Don't order salad – the dressing can often get messy. If a salad comes with the meal, request that the dressing be on the side. Then, before pouring it on, cut up the lettuce.

▌ Don't order anything with bones. Stick with filets as there are few simple, gracious ways to deal with any type of bone.

The bill and goodbyes

I know an interviewer whose favourite test of composure is to have the waiter or waitress, by prior arrangement, put the bill on the interviewee's side of the table. She then chats on, waiting for something interesting to happen. If you ever find yourself in a similar situation, never pick up the bill, however long it is left by your plate. When ready, your host will pick it up, because that's the simple protocol of the occasion. By the same token, you should never offer to share payment.

When parting company, always thank the host for his or her hospitality and the wonderful meal. Of course, you should be sure to leave on a positive note by asking good-naturedly what you have to do to get the job.

Strange interview situations can arise at any time during the interview cycle and in any public place. Wherever you are asked to go, keep your guard up. Your table manners, listening skills and overall social graces are being judged. The question on the interviewer's mind is 'Can this person be trusted to represent the company graciously?'

20 The graceful exit

Is parting such sweet sorrow? The end of an interview will more likely mean relief, but here are some dos and don'ts to bear in mind as your meeting comes to a close.

To paraphrase Shakespeare, all the employment world's a stage, and all the people on it merely players making their entrances and exits. Curtains rise and fall and your powerful performance must be capped with a professional and memorable exit. To ensure you leave the right impression, this chapter will review the dos and don'ts of leaving an interview.

A signal that the interview is drawing to a close comes when you are asked if you have any questions. Ask questions and, by doing so, highlight your strengths and show your enthusiasm. Your goal at the interview is to generate a job offer, so you should find it easy to avoid the crimes that damage your case.

Dos

Ask appropriate job-related questions

When the opportunity comes to ask any final questions, review your notes. Bring up any relevant strengths that haven't been addressed.

Show decisiveness

If you are offered the job, react with enthusiasm. Then sleep on it. If it's possible to do so without making a formal acceptance, lock the job up now and put yourself in control; you can always change your mind later. However, before you make any commitment with regard to pay, see Chapter 23, Negotiating the offer.

233

When you are interviewed by more than one person, be sure you have the correct spellings of their names

'I enjoyed meeting your colleagues, Ms Smith. Could you give me the correct spellings of their names, please?' This question will give you the names you forgot in the heat of battle and will demonstrate your consideration.

Review the job's requirements with the interviewer

Match them point by point with your skills and attributes.

Find out if this is the only interview

If so, you must ask for the job in a positive and enthusiastic manner. Find out the time frame for a decision and finish with, 'I am very enthusiastic about the job and the contributions I can make. If your decision will be made by the fifteenth, what must I do in the meantime to assure I get the job?'

Ask for the next interview

When there are subsequent interviews, ask for the next interview in the same honest and forthright manner. 'Is now a good time to schedule our next meeting?' If you do not ask, you do not get.

Keep yourself in contention

A good leading question to ask is, 'Until I hear from you again, what particular aspects of the job and this interview should I be considering?'

Always depart in the same polite and assured manner in which you entered

Look the interviewer in the eye, put on a smile (there's no need to grin), give a firm handshake and say, 'This has been an exciting meeting for me. This is a job I can do and I feel I can contribute to your goals, because the atmosphere here seems conducive to doing my very best work. When will we speak again?'

Don'ts

Don't discuss salary, holidays or benefits

It is not that the questions are invalid, just that the timing is wrong. Bringing such topics up before you have been offered the job is asking what the company can do for you – instead, you should be saying what you can do for the company. These topics are part of the negotiation (handled in Chapter 23, Negotiating the offer) and, without an offer, you have nothing to negotiate.

Don't press for an early decision

Of course you should ask, 'When will I know your decision?' but don't press it. Also, don't try to use the 'there are other opportunities I have to consider too' gambit as leverage when no such offers exist – that annoys the interviewer, makes you look foolish and may even force you to negotiate from a position of weakness. Timing is everything; the issue of how to handle other opportunities as leverage is explored in detail later.

Don't show discouragement

Sometimes you can be offered a job on the spot. Usually, though, you won't, so don't show discouragement if you are not offered the job at the interview, because discouragement shows a lack of self-esteem and determination. Avoiding making a bad impression is merely laying the foundations for leaving a good one, and the right image to leave is one of enthusiasm, guts and openness – just the traits you have been projecting throughout the interview.

Don't ask for an evaluation of your interview performance

To do so forces the issue and puts the interviewer in an awkward position. You *can*, though, say that you want the job and ask what you have to do to get it.

Part IV

Finishing Touches

Statistics show that the last person to interview usually gets the job. Here are some steps you can take that will keep your impression strong.

The successful completion of every interview is a big stride towards getting job offers, yet it is not the end of your job hunt.

A company rarely takes on the first competent person they see. A hiring manager will sometimes interview as many as 15 people for a particular job, but the strain and pace of conducting interviews naturally dim the memory of each applicant. Unless you are the last person to be interviewed, the impression you make will fade with each subsequent interview the interviewer undertakes. If you are not remembered, you will not be offered the job. You must develop a strategy to keep your name and skills constantly in the forefront of the interviewer's mind. These finishing touches often make all the difference.

Some of the suggestions here may not seem earth-shattering, just simple, sensible demonstrations of your manners, enthusiasm and determination, but remember that today all employers are looking for people with that extra little something. You can avoid the negative or merely indifferent impression and be certain of creating a positive one by following these guidelines.

21 *Out of sight, out of mind?*

Don't let the interviewer forget you! The follow-up is simple and here are seven steps that guarantee the continuation of your candidacy.

The first thing you do on leaving the interview is breathe a sigh of relief. The second is to make sure that 'out of sight, out of mind' will not apply to you. You do this by starting a follow-up procedure immediately after the interview.

Sitting in your car, on the bus, train or plane, do a written recap of the interview while its still fresh in your mind. Answer the following questions.

▌ Who did you meet? (Write down their names and titles.)

▌ What does the job entail?

▌ What are the first projects, the biggest challenges?

▌ Why can you do the job?

▌ What aspects of the interview went poorly? Why?

▌ What is the agreed-on next step?

▌ What was said during the last few minutes of the interview?

Probably the most difficult – and most important – thing to do is analyse what aspects of the interview went poorly. A person is not offered a job based solely on strength. On the contrary, many people get new jobs based on their relative lack of negatives as compared with the other applicants. So, it is mandatory that you look for and recognize any negatives from your performance. That is the only way you will have an opportunity to package and overcome those negatives in your follow-up procedure and during subsequent interviews.

The next step is to write the follow-up letter or e-mail to the interviewer to acknowledge the meeting and keep you fresh in his or her mind. Sending a follow-up letter also shows that you are both appreciative and organized and it refreshes the urgency of your candidacy at the expense of other candidates. However, remember that a standard follow-up letter could hurt your candidacy. Outlined below are the steps to take to get it right.

Compose the letter

It exhibits greater professionalism. Write a follow-up letter to be sent as an e-mail or as a traditional letter. The follow-up should make four points clear to the interviewer:

▌ you paid attention to what was being said;

▌ you understood the importance of the interviewer's comments;

▌ you are excited about the job, can do it, and want it;

▌ you can contribute to those first major projects.

Use the right words and phrases in your letter

Here are some you might want to include:

▌ 'On reflection' or 'Having thought about our meeting…';

▌ recognize – 'I recognize the importance of…';

▌ listen – 'Listening to the points you made…';

▌ enthusiasm – let the interviewer catch your enthusiasm as it is very effective, especially when your letter will arrive while other applicants are nervously sweating their way through the interview;

▌ impressed – let the interviewer know you were impressed with the people/product/service/facility/market/position, but do not overdo it;

▌ challenge – show that you feel you would be challenged to do your best work in this environment;

▌ confidence – there is a job to be done and a challenge to be met, so let the interviewer know you are confident of doing both well;

▌ interest – if you want the job (or next interview), say so as, at this stage, the company is buying and you are selling – ask for the job in a positive and enthusiastic manner;

▌ appreciation – as a courtesy and mark of professional manners, you must express appreciation for the time the interviewer took out of his or her busy schedule.

Mention the names of the people you met at the interview

Do this whenever it is possible and appropriate to do so. Draw attention to one of the topics that was of general interest to the interviewers.

Address the follow-up letter to the main interviewer

Send a copy to HR with a note of thanks as a courtesy.

Don't write too much

Keep it short – less than one page – and don't make any wild claims that might not withstand close scrutiny.

Send the letter within 24 hours of the interview

If the decision is going to be made in the next couple of days, e-mail the letter or hand deliver it. The follow-up letter will help to set you apart from other applicants and will return your image to the mind of the interviewer just when it would normally be starting to dim.

Perhaps call the interviewer

If you do not hear anything after five days, which is quite normal, you could phone the interviewer. Reiterate the points made in the letter, saying that you want the job (or next interview), and finish your statements with a question: 'Mr Smith, I feel confident about my ability to contribute to your departments efforts and I really want the job. Could you tell me what I have to do to get it?' Then be quiet and wait for the answer.

Of course, you may be told you are no longer in the running. The next chapter will show you that this is a great opportunity to snatch victory from the jaws of defeat.

22 Snatching victory from the jaws of defeat

Rejection? Impossible! Then again, you won't be right for every job. Here are some techniques that help you to create opportunity even in the face of rejection.

During the interviewing process, there are bound to be interviewers who erroneously come to the conclusion that you are not the right person for the job they need to fill. When that happens, you will be turned down. Such an absurd travesty of justice can occur in different ways:

▌ at the interview;

▌ in a letter of rejection;

▌ during your follow-up telephone call.

I have stressed the wisdom of having at least a few interviews in process at the same time – being rejected when you have no others in the pipeline can be devastating to your ego. But it needn't be, so long as you are emotionally and intellectually prepared to take advantage of the opportunity being offered to you.

You will get turned down. No one can be right for every job. The right person for a job doesn't always get it, however – the best-prepared and most determined often does. While you may be responsible in part for the initial rejection, you still have the power to correct the situation and get the job in the end. What you do with the claimed victory is a different matter – you will then be in a seller's market with choice and control of your situation.

To turn around a rejection often requires only willpower and determination. Almost every job you desire is obtainable once you understand the process from the interviewer's side of the desk. Your initial – and temporary – rejection is attributable to one of these reasons:

▌ the interviewer does not feel you can do the job;

▌ the interviewer feels you lack a successful profile;

▌ the interviewer did not feel your personality would contribute to the smooth functioning of the department – perhaps you didn't portray yourself as either a team player or as someone willing to take the extra step.

With belief in yourself, you can still succeed. Repeat to yourself constantly through the interview cycle, 'I will get this job because no one else can give as much to this company as I can!' Do that and implement the following plan immediately when you hear of rejection, whether in person, via a letter or over the telephone.

Step 1

Thank the interviewer for his or her time and consideration. Then ask politely, 'To help my future job search, why wasn't I chosen for the position?' Assure the interviewer that you would truly appreciate an honest, objective analysis. Listen to the reply and do not interrupt regardless of the comments. Use your time constructively and take notes furiously. When the interviewer finishes speaking, show you understood the comments. (Remember, understanding and agreeing are different animals.)

'Thank you, Mr Smith – now I can understand the way you feel. Because I am not a professional interviewer, I'm afraid my interview nerves got in the way. I'm very interested in working for your company [use an enthusiastic tone] and am determined to get the job. Let me meet with you once again. This time, when I'm not so nervous, I am confident you will see I really do have the skills you require' [then provide an example of a skill you have in the questionable area]. 'You name the time and the place and I will be there. What's best for you, Mr Smith?'

End with a question, of course. An enthusiastic request like that is very difficult to refuse and will usually get you another interview. An interview, of course, at which you must shine.

Step 2

Check your notes and accept the interviewer's concerns. Their validity is irrelevant; the important point is that the negative points represent the problem areas in the interviewer's perception of you. List the negative perceptions and, using the techniques, exercises and value keys discussed throughout the book, develop different ways to overcome or compensate for every negative perception.

Step 3

Reread Part III of this book.

Step 4

Practise aloud the statements and responses you will use at the interview. If you can practise with someone who plays the part of the interviewer, so much the better. That will create a real interview atmosphere and be helpful to your success. Lacking a role-play partner, you can create that live answer by putting the anticipated objections and questions on a tape and responding to them.

Step 5

Study all available information on the company.

Step 6

Congratulate yourself continually for getting another interview after initial rejection. This is proof of your self-worth, ability and tenacity. You have nothing to lose and everything to gain, having already risen phoenix-like from the ashes of temporary defeat.

Step 7

During the interview, ask for the job in a positive and enthusiastic manner. Your drive and staying power will impress the interviewer. All you must do to win the job is overcome the perceived negatives and you have been given the time to prepare. Go for it.

Step 8

Even when all has failed at the subsequent interview, do not leave without a final request for the job. Play your trump card: 'Mr Smith, I respect the fact that you allowed me the opportunity to prove myself here today. I am convinced I am the best person for the job. I want you to give me a trial and I will prove on the job that I am the best decision you have made this year. Will you give us both the opportunity?'

A reader once wrote to me as I was revising this book. The letter read, in part, 'I read the chapter entitled Snatching victory from the jaws of defeat, and did everything you said to salvage what appeared to be a losing interview. My efforts did make a very good impression on the interviewer, but, as it was finally explained to me, I really did not have equal qualifications for the job and finally came in a close second. I really want to work for this growing company and they say they have another position coming up in six months. What should I do?'

I know of someone in the airline business who wanted a job working on Concorde. He had been recently laid off and had high hopes for a successful interview. As it happened, he came in second for the Concorde position. He was told that the firm would speak to him again in the near future. So he waited – for eight months. Finally, he realized that waiting for the job could only leave him unemployed. The moral of the story is that you must be brutally objective when you come out second-best and, whatever the interviewer says, you must sometimes assume that you are getting a polite brush-off.

With that in mind, let's see what can be done on the positive side. First of all, send a thank you note to the interviewer, acknowledging your understanding of the state of affairs and reaffirming your desire to work for the company. Conclude with a polite request that he or she bear you in mind for the future.

Then, keep an eye out for any news item about the company in the press. Whenever you see something, cut it out and post it to the interviewer with a very brief note that says something like, 'I came across this in *The Financial Times* and thought you might find it interesting. I am still determined to be your next account manager, so please keep me in mind when the next opening occurs.'

You can also call the interviewer once every couple of months, just to check in. Remember, of course, to keep the phone call brief and polite – you simply want to keep your name at the top of the interviewer's mind.

Maybe something will come of it. Ultimately, however, your only choice is to move on. There is no gain to be had from waiting on an interviewer's word. Go out and keep looking because chances are that you will come up with an even better job. Then, if you still want to work for the company that gave you the brush-off, you will have some leverage.

Most people fail in their endeavours by quitting just before the dawn of success. Follow these directions and you can win the job. You have proven yourself to be a fighter and that is universally admired. The interviewer will want you to succeed because you are made of stuff that is rarely seen today. You are a person with guts, drive and endurance – the hallmarks of a winner. Being turned down for a job is an opportunity to exercise and build on your strengths and, by persisting, you may well add to your growing number of job offers, now and in the future.

23 *Negotiating the offer*

They want you! Before you sign on the dotted line, however, you should be well schooled in the essentials of good salary and benefits negotiations. After all, you're never going to have this much leverage again unless you start over from square one.

The crucial period after you have received a formal offer and before you accept it is probably the one point in your relationship with an employer at which you can say with any accuracy that you have the whip hand. The advantage, for now, is yours. They want you but don't have you and their wanting something they don't have gives you a negotiating edge. An employer is also more inclined to respect and honour a person who has a clear understanding of his or her worth in the marketplace – they want a savvy and businesslike person.

You don't have to accept or reject the first offer, whatever it is. In most instances you can improve the initial offer in a number of ways, but you have to know something about the existing market conditions for those employed in your area of endeavour.

There is no guarantee that you are being paid what you are worth at the moment. The simple facts are these: if you don't get it while they want you and don't have you, you sure can't count on getting it once they do have you. Remember, too, that if you start at a reduced figure, every subsequent pay rise will come from a proportionately lower base, so the real amount of money lost over an entire career span could actually be substantial.

To get what you have coming at the negotiating table, you must take the time to understand what you have achieved, what you have to offer and what you are worth to the employer. You should be able to get a better handle on that final item by doing good research, but remember that regional influences can affect pay levels, as can current business conditions.

Everything in this book has been written with the aim of maximizing your professional worth and salary negotiation is certainly no exception. Please bear in mind that there are no shortcuts. The ideas presented in this chapter will be helpful to you if they represent the culmination of your successful campaign to set yourself apart from the competition, but you cannot negotiate a terrific salary package if an employer is not convinced that you are in the top tier of applicants.

Follow this three-step procedure when planning your salary discussions with employers.

Step 1

Before getting into negotiations with any employer, work out your minimum cash requirements for any job – you must know what it is going to take to keep a roof over your head and bread on the table. It's necessary to know this figure, but you need never discuss it with anyone – knowing it is the foundation of getting both what you need and what you are worth.

Step 2

Get a grip on what your skills are worth in the current market. There are several ways to do that. Consider the resources and methods outlined below:

▊ you can find salary surveys at online employment sites;

▊ you may be able to find out the salary range for the level above you and the level beneath you at the company in question;

▊ ask headhunters – they know better than anyone what the market will bear and you should, as a matter of career prudence, establish an ongoing relationship with a reputable headhunter because you never know when his or her services will come in handy;

▊ many professional journals publish annual salary surveys

that you can consult and look in recent newspapers and compare salaries offered to people with your skills.

Step 3

This is the fun part. Come up with the figure that would make you smile, drop dead and go to heaven on the spot (but try to keep it somewhere within the bounds of reality – multimillion-pound offers with stock options and other benefits being in relatively short supply for most of us).

You now have three figures: a minimum, a realistic middle of the road desired salary and a dream salary.

Your minimum is, you will recall, what you need to cover personal consumption – never discuss it with anyone. Put it aside and what do you have left? A salary range, just like the one every employer has for every interview you attend. Yours extends from your midpoint to your dream salary. Yes, that range represents the 'top half' of what you want or, more accurately, could conceivably accept, but there's a reason for that. In the event, you will find that it is far easier to negotiate down than it is to negotiate up and you must find a starting point that gives you every possible advantage.

Negotiate while you can

I have said throughout this book that your sole aim at the interview is to get the job offer, because without it you have nothing to negotiate. Once the offer is extended to you, the time to negotiate has arrived and there will never be a more opportune time. Your relationship with the potential employer has gone through a number of distinct changes – from 'Perhaps we should speak to this one' to 'Yes, he/she might be able to do the job' until finally 'This is the top candidate, we really like him/her and want to have him/her on board.' However, now is the only point in the relationship when you will have the upper hand. Enjoy it while you can.

Although questions of salary are usually brought up after you are under serious consideration, you must be careful to avoid painting yourself into a corner when you fill out the initial company application form that contains a request for required salary. Usually you can get away with 'open' as a response; sometimes the form will instruct you not to write 'open', in which case you can write 'negotiable' or 'competitive'.

So much for basic considerations. Let's move on to the money questions that are likely to be flying around the room.

The salary/job negotiations begin in earnest in two ways. The interviewer can bring up the topic with statements like the following.

▌ 'How do you think you would like working here?'

▌ 'People with your background always fit in well with us.'

▌ 'You could make a real contribution here.'

▌ 'Well, you certainly seem to have what it takes.'

Alternatively, if it is clearly appropriate to do so, you can bring on the negotiating stage. In that case, you can make mirror images of the above, which make the interviewer face the fact that you certainly are able to do the job and that the time has therefore come to talk turkey.

▌ 'How do you think I would fit in with the group?'

▌ 'I feel my background and experience would definitely complement the work group, don't you?'

▌ 'I think I could make a real contribution here. What do you think?'

▌ 'I know I have what it takes to do this job. What questions are lingering in your mind?'

Now then. What do you do when the question of money is brought up before you have enough details about the job to negotiate from a position of knowledge and strength? Postpone money talk until you have the facts at hand. Do that by asking something like, 'I still have one or two questions about my responsibilities and it will be easier for me to talk about money when I have cleared them up. Could I first ask you a few questions about…?'

Then proceed to clarify duties and responsibilities, being careful to weigh the relative importance of the position and the individual duties to the success of the department you may join.

The employer is duty-bound to get your services as reasonably as possible, while you have an equal responsibility to do the best you can for yourself. Your goal is not to settle for less than will enable you to be happy in the job – unhappiness at work can taint all the other areas of your life. As noted earlier, it is far easier to negotiate down than it is to negotiate up. The value of the offer you accept depends on your performance throughout the interviewing process and, especially, the finesse you display in the final negotiations. The rest of this chapter is going to address the many questions that might be asked or that you might ask to bring matters to a successful conclusion.

'What is an adequate reward for your efforts?'

A glaring manageability question and money probe all in one. The interviewer probably already has a typist on staff who expects a Nobel Prize each time he or she gets out a faultless letter. Your answer should be honest and cover all angles. 'My primary satisfaction and reward comes from a job well done and completed on time. The occasional good word from my boss is always welcome. Last but not least, I think everyone looks forward to a salary review.'

'What is your salary history?' or 'How did your salary progress in your last job?'

The interviewer is looking for a couple of things here. First, for the frequency, percentage and monetary value of your pay rises, which, in turn, tell him or her about your performance and the relative value of the offer that is about to be made. What you want to avoid is tying the potential offer to your salary history – the offer you negotiate should be based solely on the value of the job in hand.

Your answer needs to be specifically vague. Perhaps, 'My salary history has followed a steady upwards path and I have never failed to receive merit increases. I would be glad to give you the specific numbers if needed, but I shall have to sit down and give it some thought with a pencil and paper.' The odds are that the interviewer will not ask you to do that; if he or she does, nod in agreement and say that you'll get right to it when you get home. Don't begin the task until you are requested a second time, which is unlikely.

If for any reason you find yourself with your back against the wall with this one, be sure to include in the specifics of your answer that 'one of the reasons I am leaving my current job is that pay rises were standard for all levels of employees, so, despite my superior contributions, I got the same percentage rise as the tardy or poor output employee. I want to work in an environment where I will be recognized and rewarded for my contributions.' Then end with a question: 'Is this the sort of company where I can expect that?'

'What were you earning at your last job?'

A similar but different question. It could also be phrased, 'What are you earning now?' or 'What is your current salary?'

While I have said that your current earnings should bear no relation to your starting salary on the new job, it can be difficult to make that statement clear to the interviewer without appearing objectionable. Although the question asks you to be specific, you needn't get too specific. Instead, you should try to draw attention to the fact that the two jobs are different. A short answer might be, 'I am earning £X, although I'm not sure how that will help you in your evaluation of my worth for this job, because the two jobs are somewhat different.'

It is important to understand the areas of allowable fudge. For instance, if you are considerably underpaid, you may want to include the monetary value of such perks as medical and other health plans, pay in lieu of holidays, profit-sharing and pension plans, bonuses, stock options and other incentives. For many people, these can add between 20 and 35 per cent to their basic salary, so you might honestly be able to mention a higher figure than you at first thought possible. Also, if you are due for a pay rise imminently, you are justified in adding it in.

It isn't common for current or previous salaries to be verified by employers, although certain industries, because of legal requirements, check more than others do. Before your 'current salary' figure disappears through the roof, however, it is safest to remain within credible bounds. After all, once you have been given the job and are starting work at the company, you will have to hand over your P45 and your present salary could be extrapolated from that.

'Have you ever been refused a salary increase?'

This implies that you asked. An example of your justifiable request might parallel the following true story. An accountant for a tyre distributorship made changes to an accounting system that saved thousands of pounds a year, plus 30 staff hours a week. Six months after the methods were obviously working smoothly, he requested a salary review, was refused, but was told he would receive a year-end bonus. He did: £75. If you can tell a story like that, by all means tell how you were turned down for a pay rise. If not, it is best to play it safe and explain that your work and salary history showed a steady and marked continual improvement over the years.

'How much do you need to earn to support your family?'

As we have seen, your best advice is to find some way to sidestep this by discussing your midpoint desired salary.

This question is sometimes asked of people who will be working in a sales job, where remuneration is based on a draw against forthcoming commissions. If this scenario describes your income patterns, be sure you have a firm handle on your basic needs before you accept the position.

For salaried positions, this question is of little relevance. It implies the employer will try to get you at a subsistence salary, which is not why you are there. In this instance, give a range from your desired high-end salary down to your desired midpoint salary.

'How much will it take to get you?' 'How much are you looking for?' 'What are your salary expectations?' 'What are your salary requirements?'

You are being asked to name a figure here. Give the wrong answer and you can find you're eliminated. It is always tempting to ask for the moon, knowing you can come down later, but there are better approaches. It is wise to confirm your understanding of the job and its importance before you start throwing numbers around, because you will have to live with the consequences. You need to ensure the best possible offer without pricing yourself out of the market, so it's time to dance with one of the following responses.

'Well, let's see if I understand the responsibilities fully…' You then proceed to itemize exactly what you will be doing on a daily basis and the parameters of your responsibilities and authority. Once that is done you will seek agreement: 'Is this the job as you see it or have I missed anything?' Remember to describe the job in its most flattering and challenging light, paying special attention to the way you see it fitting into the overall picture and contributing to the success of the department, work group and company. You can then finish your response with a question of your own: 'What figure did you have in mind for someone with my track record?' or 'What range has been authorized for this position?' Your answer will include, in part, something along the lines of, 'I believe my skills and experience will warrant a starting salary between _____ and _____.'

You also could ask, 'What would be the salary range for someone with my experience and skills?' or 'I naturally want to make as much as my background and skills will allow. If I am right for the job, and I think my credentials demonstrate that I am, I am sure you will make me a fair offer. What figure do you have in mind?'

Another good response is, 'I would expect a salary appropriate to my experience and ability to do the job successfully. What range do you have in mind?'

Such questions will get the interviewer to reveal the salary range and concentrate his or her attention on the challenges of the job and your ability to accept and work with those challenges.

When you are given a range, you can adjust your money requirements appropriately, latching on to the upper part of the range. For example, if the range is £30,000–£35,000 a year, you can come back with a range of £34,000–£37,000.

Consequently, your response will include: 'That certainly means we have something to talk about. While your range is £30,000–£35,000, I am looking for a minimum of £34,000 with an ideal of £37,000. Tell me, what flexibility is there at the top of your salary range?' You need to know this to put yourself in the strongest negotiating position and this is the perfect time and opportunity to gain the information and the advantage.

All this fencing is aimed at getting the interviewer to show his or her hand first. Ask for too much and it's 'Oh dear, I'm afraid you're overqualified', to which you can reply, 'So, overpay me.' (Actually, that works when you can carry it off with an ingratiating smile.) If your request is too low, you are likely to be ruled out as lacking the appropriate experience.

When you have tried to get the interviewer to name a range and failed, you must come up with a specific figure. At this point, the key is to understand that all jobs have salary ranges attached to them. Consequently, the last thing you will ever do is come back with a specific figure – that traps you. Instead, you will mention your own range, which will not be from your minimum to your maximum, but, rather, from your midpoint to your maximum. Remember, as before, you can always negotiate down, but rarely negotiate up.

'What kind of salary are you worth?'

This is a 'How much do you want?' question with a slight twist. It is asking you to name a desired figure, but the twist is that it also asks you to justify that figure. It requires that you demonstrate careful analysis of your worth, industry norms and job requirements. You are recommended to try for a higher figure rather than a lower one. 'Having compared my background and experience with industry norms and salary surveys, I feel my general worth is in the region of £X to £Y. My general background and credentials fit your needs and my first-hand knowledge of the specific challenges and projects I would face in this job are an exact match, so I feel worthy of justifying an offer towards the top of this range. Don't you agree?'

After your response to a salary question, you can expect to hear, 'That's too much' or 'Oh, that is more than we were hoping to pay' or 'That would be stretching the budget to the breaking point.' When this happens, accept it as no more than a negotiating gambit and come back with your own calm rebuttal: 'What did you have in mind?'

'What do you hope to be earning two to five years from now?'

A difficult question. The interviewer is probing your desired career and earning path and is trying to see if you have your sights set high enough – or too high. Perhaps a jocular tone doesn't hurt here: 'I'd like to be earning just about as much as my boss and I can work out!' Then, throw the ball back with your own question: 'How much is it possible to make here?'

If you give a specific figure, the interviewer is going to want justification. If you come up with a salary range, you are advised also to have a justified career path to go along with it.

You could also say, 'In two years, I will have finished my exams, so with that plus my additional experience, industry norms say I should be earning between £X and £Y. I would hope to be earning at least within that range, but hopefully, with a proven track record of contributions, I would be making above the norm.' The trick is to use industry statistics as the backbone of your argument, express confidence in doing better than the norm and, whenever possible, stay away from specific job titles unless pressed.

'Do you think people in your occupation should be paid more?'

This one can be used prior to serious salary negotiation to probe your awareness of how your job really contributes to the bottom line. Otherwise, it can occur in the middle of salary negotiations to throw you off-balance. The safe and correct answer is to straddle the fence. 'Most jobs have salary ranges that reflect the job's relative importance and contribution to a company. Those salary ranges reflect the norm for the great majority of people within that profession. That does not mean, however, that the extraordinary people in such a group are not recognized for their extra performance and skills. There are always exceptions to the rule.'

Good offers, poor offers

After a period of bantering back and forth like this, the interviewer names a figure, hopefully meant as a legitimate offer. If you aren't sure, qualify it: 'Let me see if I understand you correctly: Are you formally offering me the position at £X a year?'

The formal offer can fall into one of two categories.

It sounds fair and equitable

In that case, you still want to negotiate for a little more – employers almost expect it of you, so don't disappoint them. Mention a salary range again, the low end of which comes at about the level of their offer and the high end somewhat above it. You can say, 'Well, it certainly seems that we are close. I was hoping for something more in the range of £X to £Y. How much room do we have for negotiation here?'

No one will withdraw an offer because you say you feel you are worth more. After all, the interviewer thinks you are the best person for the job and has extended a formal offer – the last thing he or she needs now is to start from square one again. The employer has a vested interest in bringing the negotiation to a satisfactory conclusion. In a worst case scenario, the interviewer can stick to the original offer.

It isn't quite what you expected

Even if the offer isn't what you thought it would be, you still have options other than accepting or rejecting it as it stands. However, your strategy for now is to run the money topic as far as you can in a calm and businesslike way. Then, once you have gone that far, you can back off and examine the other potential benefits of the job. That way you will leave yourself with an opening, if you need it, to hit the money topic once more at the close of negotiations.

If you feel the salary could do with a boost, say so: 'I like the job and I know I have what it takes to be successful in it. I would also be prepared to give you a start date of 1 March, to show my sincerity, but, quite honestly, I couldn't justify it with your initial salary offer. I just hope that we have some room for negotiation here.'

Alternatively, you can say, 'I could start on 1 March and I do feel I could make a contribution here and become an integral part of the team. The only thing standing in the way is my inability to make ends meet based on your initial offer. I am sincerely interested in the opportunity and flattered by your interest in me. If we could just solve this money problem, I'm sure we could come to terms. What do you think can be done about it?'

The interviewer will probably come back with a question asking how much you want: 'What is the minimum you would be prepared to work for?' Respond with your range again – with your minimum really your midpoint – and the interviewer may well then come back with a higher offer and ask for your concurrence. This is the time to be non-committal but encouraged and move on to the benefits included with the position: 'Well, yes, that is a little better. Perhaps we should talk about the benefits.'

Alternatively, the interviewer may come back with another question: 'That's beyond our salary range for this job title. How far can you reduce your salary needs to fit our range?'

That question shows good faith and a desire to close the deal, but don't give in too easily – the interviewer is never going to want you as much as he or she does now. Your first response might be: 'I appreciate that, but if it is the job title and its accompanying range that is causing the problem, couldn't we upgrade the title, thereby putting me near the bottom of the next range?' Try it – it often works. If it doesn't, it is probably time to move to other negotiable aspects of the job offer, but not before one last try. You can take that final stab by asking, 'Is that the best you can do?' With this question, you must look the interviewer directly in the eye, ask the question and maintain eye contact. It works surprisingly well. You should also remember to try it as a closing gambit at the very end of negotiations when you have received everything you can hope for. You may get a pleasant surprise.

Negotiating your future salary

At this point, you have probably ridden present salary as hard as you reasonably can (for a while, anyway), so the time has come to shift the conversation to future remuneration.

'Even though the offer isn't quite what I'd hoped for to start the job, I am still interested. Can we talk about the future for a while?' Then you move the conversation to an on-the-job focus. Here are a few arrangements corporate headhunters frequently negotiate for their recruits.

A single lump sum signing bonus

Known as a 'golden hello', it is nice to have, though it is money that is here today and gone tomorrow. Don't make the mistake of adding it on to the basic salary figure. If you get a £2,500 signing bonus, that money won't be included when it comes to your year-end review – your pay rise will be based on your actual salary – so the bonus is a little less meaningful than it appears.

A performance review with pay rise attached

You can frequently negotiate a minimum percentage increase here, if you have confidence in your abilities.

Promotion

You might be able to negotiate a review after a certain period of time.

Influencing and evaluating the offer

No two negotiations are going to be alike, so there is no absolute model you can follow. Nevertheless, when you have addressed present and future remuneration, this might be the time to get some more information about the company and the job itself.

Even if you haven't agreed on money, you are probably beginning to get a feeling as to whether or not you can put the deal together – you know the employer wants to. Many of the following questions will be appropriate here; some might even be appropriate at other times during the interview cycle.

Full knowledge of all the relevant facts is critical to your successful final negotiation of money and benefits. Your prudent selection of questions from this list will help you negotiate the best offers and choose the right job for you. (At this point, asking some pertinent questions from the following list also serves as a decompression device of sorts for both parties.)

The questions come in these categories:

▐ nuts-and-bolts job clarification;

▐ job and department growth;

▐ corporate culture;

▐ company growth and direction.

The following section is also worth reading between first and second interviews.

Nuts and bolts

First, if you have career aspirations, you want to land a job in an outfit that believes in promoting from within. To find out, ask a few of these questions: 'How long has the job been open?' 'Why is it open?' 'Who held the job last?' 'What is he/she doing now?' 'Promoted, fired, quit?' 'How long was he/she in that job?' 'How many people have held this job in the last three years?' 'Where are they now?' 'How often and how many people have been promoted from this position and to where?'

You could also ask, 'What is the timetable for filling the position?' The longer the job has been open and the tighter the time frame for filling it, the better your leverage. That can also be determined by asking, 'When do you need me to start? Why on that date particularly?'

Here are some more good questions.

▐ 'What are the first projects to be addressed?' or 'What are the major problems to be tackled and conquered?'

▌ 'What do you consider the five most important day-to-day responsibilities of this job? Why?'

▌ 'What personality traits do you consider critical to success in this job?'

▌ 'How do you see me complementing the existing group?'

▌ 'Will I be working with a team or on my own? What will be my responsibilities as a team member? What will be my leadership responsibilities?'

▌ 'How much overtime is involved?'

▌ 'How much travel is involved?' and 'How much overnight travel?' With overnight travel you need to find out the number of days per week and month and, more importantly, whether or not you will be paid for weekend days or given time off in lieu. I have known companies that expect you to get home from a long weekend trip at 1 o'clock in the morning and be at work at 8.30 am on Monday – all without extra pay or time off.

▌ 'How frequent are performance and salary reviews? What are they based on – standard pay rises for all or are they weighted towards merit and performance?'

▌ 'How does the performance appraisal and reward system work? Exactly how are outstanding employees recognized, judged and rewarded?'

▌ 'What is the complete financial package for someone at my level?'

Job and department growth

Gauging the potential for professional growth in a job is very important for some; for others, it comes slightly lower down the list. Even if you aren't striving to head up the company in the next few years, you will still want to know what the promotional and growth expectations are so that you don't end up with a company expecting you to scale the heights. Here are some questions you will find useful for finding these things out.

■ 'To what extent are the functions of the department recognized as important and worthy of review by upper management?' If upper management takes an interest in the doings of your work group, rest assured you are in a visible position for recognition and reward.

■ 'Where and how does my department fit into the company pecking order?'

■ 'What does the department hope to achieve in the next two to three years? How will that help the company? How will it be recognized by the company?'

■ 'What do you see as the strengths of the department? What do you see as weaknesses that you are looking to turn into strengths?'

■ 'What role would you hope I would play in these goals?'

■ 'What informal/formal benchmarks will you use to measure my effectiveness and contributions?'

■ 'Based on my effectiveness, how long would you anticipate me holding this position? When my position and responsibilities change, what are the possible titles and responsibilities I might grow into?'

■ 'What is the official corporate policy on internal promotion? How many people in this department have been promoted from their original positions since joining the company?'

■ 'How do you determine when a person is ready for promotion?'

■ 'What training and professional development assistance is available to help me grow professionally?'

▌ 'Does the company encourage outside professional development training? Does the company sponsor all or part of any costs?'

▌ 'What are my potential career paths within the company?'

▌ 'To what jobs have people with my title risen in the company?'

▌ 'Who in the company was in this position the shortest length of time? Why? Who has remained in this position the longest? Why?'

Corporate culture

All companies have their own way of doing things – that's corporate culture. Not every corporate culture is you. To find out more, try asking the following questions.

▌ 'What is the company's mission? What are the company's goals?'

▌ 'What approach does this company take to its marketplace?'

▌ 'What is unique about the way this company operates?'

▌ 'What is the best thing you know about this company? What is the worst thing you know about this company?'

▌ 'How does the reporting structure work? What are the accepted channels of communication and how do they work?'

▌ 'What kinds of checks and balances, reports or other work-measurement tools are used in the department and company?'

▌ 'What do you and the company consider important in my fitting into the corporate culture – the way of doing things round here?'

▌ 'Will I be encouraged or discouraged from learning about the company beyond my own department?'

Company growth and direction

For those concerned about career growth, a healthy company is mandatory; for those concerned about stability of employment, the same applies. See how things are by asking the following questions.

▌ 'What expansion is planned for this department, division or organization?'

▌ 'What markets does the company anticipate developing?'

▌ 'Does the company have plans for mergers or acquisitions?'

▌ 'Currently, what new endeavours is the company actively pursuing?'

▌ 'How do market trends affect company growth and progress? What is being done about them?'

▌ 'What production and employee layoffs and cutbacks have you experienced in the last three years?'

▌ 'What production and employee layoffs and cutbacks do you anticipate? How are they likely to affect this department, division or organization?'

▌ 'When was the last corporate reorganization? How did it affect this department? When will the next corporate reorganization occur? How will it affect this department?'

The package

Take-home pay is, naturally, the most important part of your package. (You'll probably feel that the only thing wrong with your pay is that it gets taxed before you get to take it home!) That means you must carefully negotiate any possible benefits accruing to the job that have a monetary value, but are tax deductible and/or add to your physical and mental happiness. The list is almost endless, but below you will find those most commonly available. Although many of these benefits are available to all employees at some companies, you should know that, as a rule of thumb, the higher up the ladder you climb, the more benefits you can expect. Because the corporate world and its concepts of creating a motivated and committed workforce are constantly in flux, you should never assume that a particular benefit will not be available to you.

The basic rule is to ask – if you don't ask, there is no way you will get. A few years ago, it would have been unthinkable for anyone but an executive to expect something as glamorous as a leisure club membership in a benefits package. Today, however, more companies have a membership as a standard benefit; an increasing number are even building their own health club facilities. What's this benefit worth in your area? Call a club and find out.

Benefits to your package may include some of the following:

▌ investment opportunities

▌ insurance plans

▌ car allowance

▌ car insurance or an allowance

▌ car servicing and petrol or an allowance

▌ car

▌ time off in lieu – as recompense for unpaid overtime/business travel time

▌ country club or health club membership

▌ accidental death insurance

▌ deferred compensation

▌ dental insurance – note deductibles and the percentage that is employer-paid

▌ employment contract and/or termination contract

▌ expense account

▌ financial planning help and tax assistance

▌ life assurance

▌ medical insurance – note deductibles and percentage that is employer-paid

▌ pension plans

▌ personal days off

▌ profit sharing

▌ short- or long-term disability compensation plans

▌ shares

▌ more holidays.

Evaluating the offer

Once the offer has been negotiated to the best of your ability, you need to evaluate it – which doesn't have to be done on the spot. Some of your requests and questions will take time to be answered and, very often, the final parts of negotiation – 'Yes, Mr Jones, we can give you the extra £2,000 and six months of holiday you requested' – will take place over the telephone. Regardless of where the final negotiations are completed, never accept or reject the offer on the spot.

Be positive, say how excited you are about the prospect and that you would like a little time (overnight, a day, two days) to think it over, discuss it with your spouse, whatever. Not only is this delay standard practice, but it will also give you the opportunity to influence other offers, as discussed in the next chapter.

Use the time you gain to speak to your mentors or advisers. However, a word of caution: when asking advice from those close to you, be sure you know exactly where that advice is coming from – you need clear-headed objectivity at this time.

Once the advice is in, and not before, weigh it up along with your own observations – no one knows your needs and aspirations better than you do. While there are many ways of doing that, a simple line down the middle of a sheet of paper, with the reasons to take the job written on one side and the reasons to turn it down on the other, is about as straightforward and objective as you can get.

You will weigh salary, future earnings and career prospects, benefits, journey time, lifestyle, and stability of the company, along with all those intangibles that are summed up in that technical term 'gut feelings'. Make sure you answer these next questions for yourself.

∎ Do you like the work?

∎ Can you be trained in a reasonable period of time, thus having a realistic chance of success on the job?

∎ Are the title and responsibilities likely to provide you with a challenge?

∎ Is the opportunity for growth in the job compatible with your needs and desires?

∎ Are the company's location, stability and reputation in line with your needs?

∎ Is the atmosphere/culture of the company conducive to your enjoying working at the company?

▌ Can you get along with your new manager and immediate work group?

▌ Is the money offer and total compensation package the best you can get?

Notice that money is but one aspect of the evaluation process. There are many other factors to take into account as well. Even a high-paying job can be less advantageous than you think. For instance, you should be careful not to be foxed by the gross figure. It really is important that you get a firm handle on that actual, spendable, after-tax money – the money that pays the rent or mortgage and puts food on the table, and all those other necessities. Always look at an offer in the light of how much spendable money a week it will put in your pocket.

Evaluating the new boss

When all that is done, you must make a final, but immensely important, decision – whether or not you will be happy with your future manager. Remember, you are going to spend the majority of your waking hours at work and the new job can only be as good as your relationship with your new boss. If you felt uncomfortable with the person after an interview or two, you need to evaluate carefully the kind of discomfort and unhappiness it could generate over the coming months and years.

You'll want to know about the manager's personal style. Is he or she confrontational, authoritarian, democratic, hands-off? How would reprimands or differing viewpoints be handled? Does he or she share information on a need to know basis, the old military-management style of keep 'em in the dark? When a group member makes a significant contribution, who gets the credit as far as senior management is concerned – the person, manager or group? You can find out some of that information from the manager; other aspects you'll need to review when you meet team members or the people from HR.

Accepting new jobs, resigning from others

Once your decision has been made, you should accept the job verbally. Spell out exactly what you are accepting: 'Mr Smith, I'd like to accept the position of engineer at a starting salary of £X. I will be able to start work on 1 March. I understand my package will include life, health, and dental insurance and a company car.' Then, you finish with: 'I will be glad to start on the above date pending a written offer received in time to give my present employer adequate notice of my departure. I hope that's acceptable to you.'

Until you have the offer in writing, you have nothing. A verbal offer can be withdrawn – it happens all the time. That's not because the employer suddenly doesn't like you, but because of reasons that affect, but bear no real relationship to, your candidacy. I have known of countless careers that have stalled through reneged verbal offers – they lead to unemployment, bitterness and even lawsuits. So, avoid the headaches and play it by the numbers.

Once you have the offer in writing, notify your current employer in the same fashion. Resigning is difficult for almost everyone, so you can write a pleasant letter, walk into your boss's office, hand it to him or her, then discuss things calmly and pleasantly once he or she has read it.

You will also want to notify any other companies who have been in negotiation with you that you are no longer on the market, but that you were most impressed with meeting them and would like to keep communications open for the future. (Again, see the next chapter for details on how to handle – and encourage – multiple job offers.)

24 *Multiple interviews, multiple offers*

Relying on one interview at a time can only lead to anxiety, so you must create and foster an ever-growing network of interviews and, consequently, job offers.

False optimism and laziness lead many job hunters to be content with only one interview in process at any given time. That severely reduces the odds of landing the best job in town within your chosen time frame. Complacency guarantees that you will continue to operate in a buyer's market.

The recommended approach is to generate as many interviews as possible in a two- to three-week period. Interviewing skills are learnt and consequently improve with practice. With the improved skills comes a greater confidence and those natural interview nerves disperse. Your confidence shows through to potential employers and you are perceived in a positive light. Also, because other companies are interested in you, everyone will move more quickly to secure your services. That is especially important if you are unfortunate enough to be unemployed. Being out of work is when you need money the most and is the time when the salary you can command on the open market is substantially reduced. The interview activity you generate will help offset this.

By generating multiple interviews, you bring the time of the first job offer closer and closer. That one job offer can be quickly multiplied into a number of others. With a single job offer, your unemployed status has, to all intents and purposes, passed.

Immediately, you can call every company with whom you've met and explain the situation. 'Mr Johnson, I'm calling because, while still under consideration by your company, I have received a job offer from one of your competitors. I would hate to make a decision without the chance of speaking with you again. I was very impressed by my meeting with you. Can we get together in the next couple of days?' End, of course, with a question that carries the conversation forward.

If you were in the running at all, your call will usually generate another interview – Mr Johnson does not want to miss out on a suddenly prized commodity. Remember, it is human nature to want the very things one is about to lose. So, you see, your simple offer can be multiplied almost by the number of interviews you have in process at the time.

A single job offer can also be used to generate interviews with new firms. It is as simple as making your usual telephone networking presentation, but you end it differently. You would be very interested in meeting with them because of your knowledge of the company/product/service, but also because you have just received a job offer – would it be possible to get together in the next couple of days?

Relying on one interview at a time can only lead to prolonged anxiety, disappointment and, possibly, unemployment. That reliance is due to the combination of false optimism, laziness and fear of rejection. These are traits that cannot be tolerated, except by confirmed defeatists, for defeat is the inevitable result of these traits. As Heraclitus said, 'Character is destiny.' Headhunters say, 'The job offer that cannot fail will.'

Self-esteem, on the other hand, is vital to your success and happiness is found with it. Also, with it you will begin to awake each day with a vitality previously unknown. Vigour will increase, your enthusiasm will rise and desire to achieve will burn within. The more you do today, the better you will feel tomorrow.

Even when you follow this plan to the letter, not every interview will result in an offer. However, with many irons in the fire, an occasional firm 'no' should not affect your morale. It won't be the first or last time you face rejection. Be persistent and, above all, close your mind to all negative and discouraging influences. The success you experience from implementing this plan will increase your store of willpower and determination, affect the successful outcome of your job hunt and enrich your whole life. Start today.

The key to your success is preparation. Remember, it is necessary to plan and organize in order to succeed. Failing is easy – it requires no effort. It is the achievement of success that requires effort, which means effort today, not tomorrow, for tomorrow never comes. So, start building that well-stocked briefcase today.

25 Conclusion: the glittering prizes

All victories have their foundation in careful preparation and, having read this book, you're ready to win.

Your attitude is positive and active – dream jobs don't come to those who sit and wait – and you realize that success depends on getting out and generating interviews for yourself. At those interviews, you will maintain the interviewer's interest and attention by carrying your half of the conversation. What you ask will show your interest, demonstrate your analytical abilities and carry the conversation forward. If in doubt about the meaning of a question, you will ask one of your own to clarify it.

The corporate body recognizes that its most valuable resource is those employees who understand and contribute towards its goals. These people have something in common: they all recognize their differing jobs as a series of challenges and problems, each to be anticipated, met and solved. It's that attitude that lands jobs and enhances careers.

People with such an attitude advance their careers faster than others because they possess a critical awareness of universally admired business practices and value systems. They then advance their careers by projecting the personality traits that most closely complement those practices and values.

As I said at the beginning of this book, your job search can be seen as a ritualized mating dance. The name of that dance is 'attitude'. Now that you know the steps, you are ready to whirl away with the glittering prizes. There is no more to say except go to your next interview and knock 'em dead.

Index to the questions

Are you looking for a permanent or temporary job? 139
Are you married? 221
Are you willing to go where the company sends you? 152
Are you willing to take calculated risks when necessary? 205
Can we check your references? 161
Can you give me an example that didn't work out so well? 190
Can you take instructions without feeling upset or hurt? 142
Can you work under pressure? 158
Define cooperation. 182
Describe a difficult problem you've had to deal with. 160
Describe a situation where your work or an idea was criticized. 171
Describe how your job relates to the overall goals of your department and company. 152
Do you consider yourself a natural leader or a born follower? 179
Do you have a degree? 74
Do you have any questions? 168
Do you like routine tasks/regular hours? 141
Do you make your opinions known when you disagree with the views of your supervisor? 178
Do you pay attention to detail? 194–95
Do you plan to have children? 221
Do you prefer working with others or alone? 177
Do you think your exam results should be considered by first employers? 144
Do you think people in your occupation should be paid more? 257
Explain your role as a group/team member. 177
Give me an example of a method of working you have used. How did you feel about it? 189
Have you done the best work you are capable of doing? 154
Have you ever been asked to resign? 165
Have you ever been fired? 164
Have you ever been refused a salary increase? 254
Have you ever had any financial difficulties? 208
Have you ever had difficulties getting along with others? 142
Have you successfully worked with a difficult person? 215
How did you get your last job? 216
How did you get your summer jobs? 137
How did you pay for university? 140
How did your boss get the best out of you? 176
How did your salary progress in your last job? 252

How do you feel about your progress to date?   154
How do you get along with different kinds of people?   173
How do you handle rejection?   209
How do you handle tension?   163
How do you interact with people at different levels?   187
How do you manage to interview while still employed?   181
How do you organize and plan for major projects?   157
How do you take direction?   170
How does this job compare with others you have applied for?   167
How have you benefited from your disappointments?   190
How have you successfully worked with this difficult type of person?   215
How interested are you in sports?   177
How long have you been looking for another position?   163
How long would it take you to make a contribution to our company?   155
How long would you stay with the company?   155
How many hours a week do you find it necessary to work to get your job done?   157
How many other jobs have you applied for?   167
How much are you looking for/making/do you want?   73, 255
How much do you need to earn to support your family?   254
How much experience do you have?   75
How much will it take to get you?   255
How old are you?   220
How well do you feel your boss rated your job performance?   176
How will you be able to cope with a change in environment after [say] five years with your current company?   206
How would you define a conducive work atmosphere?   178
How would you define your profession?   207
How would you evaluate me as an interviewer?   216
I'd be interested to hear about a time when you experienced pressure in your job.   199
I'd be interested to hear about some things you learnt at university that could be used on the job.   140
I don't have time to see you.   79
I don't need anyone like you now.   81
Illegal interview questions.   219–22
I'm not sure you're suitable for the job.   216
In hindsight, what have you done that was a little harebrained?   183
In what areas do you feel your supervisor could have done a better job?   175
In what ways has your job changed since you originally joined the company?   167
In what ways has your job prepared you to take on greater responsibility?   166
In your last job, how did you plan for the interview?   190
In your last job, what were some of the things you spent most of your time on and why?   166

I really wanted someone with a degree.   81

Jobs have pluses and minuses. What were some of the minuses on your last job?   214

Rate yourself on a scale of 1 to 10.   173

See this pen I'm holding? Sell it to me.   205

Tell me about a time when you put your foot in your mouth.   210

Tell me about an event that really challenged you. How did you meet the challenge? In what way was your approach different from others?   188

Tell me about something you are not very proud of.   191

Tell me about the last time you felt anger on the job.   174

Tell me about the problems you have living within your means.   203

Tell me about yourself.   172

Tell me a story.   182

Tell me how you've moved up through the organization.   157

Tell me why you have been with one company so long without any appreciable increase in rank or salary.   204

That is an excellent answer. Now to give me a balanced view, can you give me an example that didn't work out so well?   191

We have tried to hire people from your university before and they never seem to work out. What makes you different?   140

We only promote from within.   79

Were you ever dismissed from your job for a reason that seemed unjustified?   166

What are some of the problems you encounter in doing your job and what do you do about them?   213

What are some of the things about which you and your supervisor disagreed?   175

What are some of the things that bother you?   174

What are some of the things you find difficult to do? Why do you feel that way?   214

What are some of the things your supervisor did that you disliked?   175

What are the broad responsibilities of a ...?   151

What are the reasons for your success in this profession?   149

What are you looking for in your next job?   159

What are you making now?   73

What are your biggest accomplishments?   156

What are your future vocational plans?   138

What are your outstanding qualities?   158

What are your pet hates?   174

What are your qualifications?   156

What are your salary expectations?   255

What are your salary requirements?   255

What area of your skills/professional development do you want to improve at this time?   204

What aspects of your job do you consider most crucial?   152

What can you do for us that someone else cannot?   160
What did you like/dislike about your last job?   152
What difficulties do you have tolerating people with different backgrounds and interests from yours?   183
What do you feel is a satisfactory attendance record?   212
What do you hope to be earning two to five years from now?   257
What do you know about our company?   143
What do you think determines progress in a good company?   144
What do you think of your current/last boss?   171
What have you done that shows initiative and willingness to work?   141
What have you done that shows initiative?   174
What have you learnt from jobs you have held?   154
What have your other jobs taught you?   182
What interests you least about this job?   211
What interests you most about this job?   159
What is an adequate reward for your efforts?   252
What is the least relevant job you have held?   153
What is the most difficult situation you have faced?   174
What is the worst thing you have heard about our company?   207
What is your current salary?   253
What is your energy level like? Describe a typical day.   150
What is your general impression of your last company?   213
What is your greatest strength?   158
What is your greatest weakness?   201
What is your salary history?   252
What kind of experience do you have for this job?   150
What kind of salary are you worth?   256
What kinds of decisions are most difficult for you?   203
What kinds of people do you find it difficult to work with?   215
What kinds of people do you like to work with?   215
What kinds of things do you worry about?   173
What levels are you most comfortable with?   187
What makes this job different from your current/last one?   167
What personal characteristics are necessary for success in your field?   177
What problems do you have getting along with others?   142, 215
What qualifications do you have that will make you successful in this field?   142
What religion do you practice?   219
What types of decisions did you make in your last job?   162
What type of position are you interested in?   142
What university did you attend and why did you choose it?   139
What was the last book you read/film you saw? How did it affect you?   162
What was there about your last company that you didn't particularly like or agree with?   212
What was your salary progress on your last job?   252

What were some of the minuses on your last job?   152–53, 214

What were you earning at your last job?   253

What would you do when you have a decision to make and no procedure exists?   190

What would you like to be doing five years from now?   155

What would you say about a supervisor who was unfair or difficult to work with?   178

What would you say if I told you your presentation this afternoon was pretty bad?   218

What would your references say?   161

What's your idea of how industry works?   143

When do you expect a promotion?   181

When you joined your last company and met the group for the first time, how did you feel? How did you get on with them?   189

Which of the jobs you have held have you liked least?   138

Who else have you applied to?   167

Why aren't you earning more at your age?   206

Why did you leave your last job?   211

Why don't you send me a CV?   78

Why do you feel you are a better [for example] assistant than some of your colleagues?   180

Why do you think you would like this type of work?   143

Why do you want to leave your current job?   211

Why do you want to work here?   150

Why have you changed jobs so frequently?   210

Why should I take on an outsider when I could fill the job with someone inside the company?   207

Why should I give you the job?   160

Why were you fired?   164

Why were you out of work for so long?   209

With hindsight, how could you have improved your progress?   202

Would you like to have your boss's job?   171

Wouldn't you feel better off in another firm?   218

You are earning too much.   79

You have a doctor's appointment arranged for noon. You've waited two weeks to get in. An urgent meeting is scheduled at the last moment, though. What do you do?   180

You have been given a project that requires you to interact with different levels within the company. How do you do this? What levels are you most comfortable with?   187

Your application shows you have been with one company a long time without any appreciable increase in rank or salary. Tell me about this.   204

You'll have to talk to HR.   80